# ANGELS ON THE EDGE OF THE WORLD

# ANGELS ON THE EDGE OF THE WORLD

## GEOGRAPHY, LITERATURE, AND ENGLISH COMMUNITY, 1000–1534

### KATHY LAVEZZO

Cornell University Press
Ithaca and London

First published 2006 by Cornell University Press
First printing, Cornell Paperbacks, 2006

Printed in the United States of America

Library of Congress Cataloging-in-Publication Data

Lavezzo, Kathy.
    Angels on the edge of the world : geography, literature, and
English community, 1000–1534 / Kathy Lavezzo.
        p. cm.
    Includes bibliographical references and index.
    ISBN-13: 978-0-8014-4429-6 (cloth : alk. paper)
    ISBN-10: 0-8014-4429-2 (cloth : alk. paper)
    ISBN-13: 978-0-8014-7309-8 (pbk. : alk. paper)
    ISBN-10: 0-8014-7309-8 (pbk. : alk. paper)
    1. English literature—Middle English, 1100–1500—History
and criticism.   2. Geography, Medieval, in literature.   3. Geography, Medieval—England.   4. Nationalism and literature—
England—History—To 1500.   I. Title.
    PR275.G46L38   2006
    820.9′32—dc22                                    2005037249

Cornell University Press strives to use environmentally responsible suppliers and materials to the fullest extent possible in the publishing of its books. Such materials include vegetable-based, low-VOC inks and acid-free papers that are recycled, totally chlorine-free, or partly composed of nonwood fibers. For further information, visit our website at www.cornellpress.cornell.edu.

Cloth printing           10 9 8 7 6 5 4 3 2 1
Paperback printing       10 9 8 7 6 5 4 3 2 1

TO JOHN LAVEZZO, MARY LAVEZZO, HARRY STECOPOULOS, NINA,

AND IN MEMORY OF MARIE LAVEZZO (1902–1992)

*SEMPRE AVANTI*

# CONTENTS

# ILLUSTRATIONS

Plates    *following page 80*

# ACKNOWLEDGMENTS

It is a long-anticipated pleasure to acknowledge the many forms of support I have received while writing this book.

At UCLA, the example and support of Jennifer Bradley, John Clark, and, above all, Seth Weiner, fostered a desire to devote myself to literary study. At the University of Virginia, Tony Spearing gave me the courage to become a medievalist. At the University of California, Santa Barbara, I was privileged to inhabit a stimulating and compassionate community of graduate students, faculty, and staff. I owe special thanks to fellow grads Jon Connolly, for his tactful input, girl rocker and fellow medievalist Jennifer Hellwarth, and cool Early Modernists Julia Garrett and Roze Hentschell for all sorts of support, both intellectual and emotional. Other friends whose support I wish to acknowledge are: Jon Hegglund, Claire Busse, Laura Holliday, Jeanne Scheper, Rachel Adams, Rachel Borup, Parker Douglas, Johanna Blakley, and Eileen Fung. I learned much about methodology and rigor from an independent study and seminar taken with Steven Justice at UC Berkeley. I owe a special debt to my mentors at UC Santa Barbara. Jody Enders taught me professionalism, as well as how to root out what is at stake in my project. Adviser extraordinaire Carol Braun Pasternack introduced me to Anglo-Saxon culture and was an unstintingly conscientious and smart reader. Richard Helgerson, groundbreaking scholar of early forms of nationhood, provided countless kinds of support and first alerted me to the issue of England's place in the world. My debt to him is immense. Louise Aranye Fradenburg, goddess among medievalists, was and remains a source of inspiration to me. Her example, through both her pedagogy and her scholarship, reveals just how high the stakes of medieval scholarship can be.

During the year I was privileged to spend at the University of Wisconsin, Madison, many scholars provided support, in particular David Loewenstein, who read a version of my final chapter, and the greatly missed David Woodward (1942–2004), who provided expert feedback on most of the manuscript.

At my home institution, the University of Iowa, my sincerest gratitude for responding to various parts of the book belongs to: "metallurgists" David Wittenberg and Melissa Deem; fellow medievalist Susie Phillips; the ever savvy Alvin Snider; the fab foursome of Laura Rigal, Claire Fox, Priya Kumar, and Doris Witt, who helped me keep the faith early on; superwoman Judith Pascoe, who provided crucial commentary; and expert readers Jon Wilcox, Claire Sponsler, Huston Diehl, and Garrett Stewart. I also am grateful for the research assistance provided by Iowa graduate students Scott Nowka, Stacy Erickson, Kurt Rahmlow, and Rufo Quintavalle, as well as the feedback I received from the graduate students who took my 2004 spring seminar on medieval cultural geographies: Nate Mitchell, Mike Chasar, Mark Bresnan, Katie Gubbels, Jeff Doty, Jeff Butler, and Matthew Purdy.

For other astute commentary, I am particularly thankful to: Christopher Cannon; Andy Galloway; renaissance man Chris Gaggero; Nicholas Howe; H. Marshal Leicester; Larry Scanlon; Lynn Staley; the members of the 2002 and 2003 Medievalists' Writing Workshops, particularly Lianna Farber and Cathy Sanok; and audience members who responded to talks based on chapter 5, in particular, Antony Hasler, David Wallace, Glenn Burger, and Lynn Staley. I would also like to thank the two anonymous readers for Cornell University Press for their thorough and thoughtful readings of the manuscript. Finally, many thanks belong to my ideal editors at Cornell, Bernhard Kendler and the director of the Press, John Ackerman, as well as my astounding manuscript editors, Kay Scheuer and Karen Hwa, and designer, Scott E. Levine.

My dedication only begins to acknowledge the debt I owe my parents; they provided invaluable financial, intellectual, and emotional support over the years. I owe most to my best friend, life partner, and "commando twin," Harry Stecopoulos. Harry's faith in me and his brilliance have sustained me through graduate school and its attending crises as well as the writing of this first book. My unacknowledged collaborator, Harry has shaped my thinking so much that the line between his ideas and mine is always confused. This book is his as much as it is mine.

This project received generous financial support. Full-time work on the project was made possible by a Friends of English Fellowship, a Graduate Humanities Research Associateship, and other grants from the University of California, Santa Barbara, as well as a Mayers Fellowship from the Huntington Library. A Solmsen Postdoctoral Fellowship from the University of Wisconsin Institute for Research in the Humanities sponsored a year of full-time work on the book. The University of Iowa gave support through an Old Gold summer fellowship, a CIFRE award for archival research, and a semester developmental leave. Iowa also generously defrayed photo and permissions fees.

Sections of chapter 1 appeared as essays in *New Medieval Literatures* 3 (2000) and *Sex and Sexuality in Anglo-Saxon England,* ed. Carol Braun Pasternack and Lisa Weston (Tempe: MRTS, 2005), and sections of chapter 4 appeared in *Studies in the Age of Chaucer* 23 (2002). The editors of these volumes kindly have granted permission to use this material.

# ABBREVIATIONS

EETS    Early English Text Society

*EH*    Bede. *The Ecclesiastical History of the English People.* Ed. Bertram Colgrave and R. A. B. Mynors. Oxford: Clarendon Press, 1969.

*EN*    Thorlac Turville-Petre. *England the Nation: Language, Literature, and Identity, 1290–1340.* Oxford: Clarendon Press, 1996.

*ER*    M. T. Clanchy. *England and Its Rulers: 1066–1272.* 2nd ed. Oxford: Blackwell, 1998.

*GCO*    *Giraldi Cambrensis Opera.* Ed. J. S. Brewer, J. F. Dimock, and G. F. Warner. 8 vols. RS 21. London: Longman's, 1861–91.

*HC*    David Woodward and J. B. Harley, eds. *The History of Cartography, Volume One: Cartography in Prehistoric, Ancient, and Medieval Europe and the Mediterranean.* Chicago: University of Chicago Press, 1987.

*HKB*    Geoffrey of Monmouth. *The History of the Kings of Britain.* Ed. and trans. Lewis Thorpe. New York: Penguin, 1966.

*HRB*    Geoffrey of Monmouth. *Historia regum Brittanniae.* Ed. Acton Griscom. New York: Longman's, 1929.

*IC*    Benedict Anderson. *Imagined Communities: Reflections on the Origin and Spread of Nationalism.* 2nd ed. London: Verso, 1991.

*JMEMS*    *Journal of Medieval and Early Modern Studies*

*MI*    Jacques Le Goff. *The Medieval Imagination.* Trans. Arthur Goldhammer. Chicago: University of Chicago Press, 1988.

*MR*    John Block Friedman. *The Monstrous Races in Medieval Art and Thought.* Cambridge: Harvard University Press, 1981.

MTS     Evelyn Edson. *Mapping Time and Space: How Medieval Mapmakers Viewed Their World.* London: British Library, 1997.

RS     Rolls Series

SAC     *Studies in the Age of Chaucer*

ANGELS ON THE EDGE OF THE WORLD

# INTRODUCTION

## Modern Motherland and Ancient Otherworld

"Sovereignty," Henri Lefebvre tells us, "implies space."[1] Power territorializes; it permeates, controls, and fashions space. Space, in turn, wields a kind of power, insofar as it visualizes authority, allowing us to behold a kingdom, a nation, or an empire. Thus it is no accident that, at the apex of their imperial history, the English most famously celebrated themselves in geographic terms. As the masters of "an empire on which the sun never sets," the English transcend quotidian temporality but also inexorably inhabit space.[2] The sun always shines somewhere in the British Empire. That famous phrase evokes an image of global geographic expansion that was reiterated in British imperial cartography via maps of the world.[3] Whether published independently as wall maps or as the nearly ubiquitous featured illustration in both popular histories and primary-school textbooks, these world maps visualize, legitimate, and promote the empire in terms that are as hegemonic as they are spatial.[4] Take the world map made by process engravers Emery Walker and Walter Boutall for the frontispiece of *The Growth of the British Empire* (1911), a primer written by British statesman Philip Kerr and his wife Cecil (plate 1).[5] Like virtually all documents of its kind, the Walker-Boutall map separates the world into empire and non-empire through the color red. The crimson splashes signifying English holdings draw initial commentary from the Kerrs, who instruct the young reader to "look at the map at the beginning of the book and you will see that a large part of it is painted red; that is the British Empire. There is huge Canada; there is South Africa; there is Australia, a continent in herself, and close beside her New Zealand; there is India, and there are many other countries, and islands more than you can count."[6] In the Kerrs' imperial geography, the spaces "painted red" constitute either innumerable islands or immense landmasses: "huge Canada" and "Australia, a continent in herself." The British Empire seems vast, sublime, difficult to comprehend in its multiplicity ("more than you can count") and its sheer enormity. What one can discern clearly, however, is the centrality of England. As the Kerrs put it, "in the middle is tiny England, which is the Mother-country of them all. They are all one big family. England is the Mother-land and they are the children."[7] While England may be as small as the other islands of the empire, she is as pivotal, natural, and irreplaceable a force throughout the globe as a mother is within the family.

Reflecting how, as David Harvey points out, "space . . . gets treated as a fact of nature," the centrality of England appears to be part of a natural or divinely ordered plan.[8] Yet the image of the world offered by the Walker-Boutall map misleads the reader. Thanks to the "positional enhancing" geometry of the Mercator projection, the map constructs a Eurocentric image of the world.[9] Furthermore, by using Greenwich as Prime Meridian (following the 1884 ruling at Washington, D.C.) the map renders England the focal point of the globe.[10] Such cultural factors reveal how the Walker-Boutall map does not simply reflect but also contributes to English territorial sovereignty. Through a variety of geographic fictions and distortions, the England of the Walker-Boutall map enjoys an intrinsic place at the heart of the world that makes the nation seem to be destined to become its imperial capital and motherland.

Yet England did not always enjoy such perceived centrality.[11] If we turn from twentieth-century mapmaking to medieval cartography, we find England occupying a very different global position. Based upon classical and biblical literary sources as well as contemporary travel information, medieval world maps or *mappae mundi* were the most common kind of map drawn in the Middle Ages and emerged in a variety of guises: fashioned upon stained glass windows, molded into sculptures, carved into benches, shaped on floor mosaics, displayed upon wall-hangings and (most commonly) illustrating manuscript books.[12] The structure of mappae mundi varied, but the majority of them constituted versions of what is known as the Noachid, wheel, tripartite, or T-O form. In the first printed map in Europe, for example (illustrating a 1472 edition of Isidore's *Etymologies*), an "O"-shaped ocean defines a circular earth (called by the Romans the *orbis terrarum*), that is divided by a "T" representing the trio of waterways (the Don, Nile, and Mediterranean) believed to divide the three continents of the earth (Asia, Africa, and Europe) (fig. 1).[13] Typically oriented toward the East, these maps situate Britain in the northwestern edge of the *oikoumené* or known world.[14] Hence in the eleventh-century map illustrating a copy of Beatus of Liebana's *Commentary on the Apocalypse of St. John,* an oblong Britannia hugs the lower left-hand corner of an equally oblong world (fig. 2).[15] And in one of the maps illustrating Ranulf Higden's *Polychronicon* (1327–ca. 1360) a mandorla or almond-shaped *Anglia* occupies the northwestern margin of an oval world (figs. 3–4).

As the Beatus map, Higden map, and other medieval mappae mundi make clear, England's geographic positioning in the medieval world was the furthest thing from central. In the Beatus map, that privileged positioning is enjoyed not by the English imperial seat of modernity but by its ancient counterpart, Rome, which appears as a large multicolored symbol near the middle of the map. In the case of the Higden map, Rome shares territorial centrality with two key sites in Greek mythology and Christian

europa & affrica

**De. Asia & eius partibus Ca·iii·**

Sia ex noie
cuiusdā mu/
lieris est ap/
pellata· que apud anti/
quos imperiū orientis
tenuit· Hec in tercia or
bis parte disposita· ab
oriente ortu solis·a me
ridie·oceāo·ab occiduo
nostro mari finitur· a
septentrione meothide
lacu & tanai fluuio ter
minatur·Habet autem
prouincias multas et re
giones·quarū breuiter nomina et situs expediam·sumpto initio
a paradiso **Paradisus est locus in orientis partibus constitu/
tus·cuius vocabulum ex greco in latinum vertitur ortus·Porro
hebraice eden dicitur·quod in nostra lingua delicie interpretat̄·

**Fig. 1.** First printed map in Europe. From Isidore of Seville, *Etymologiarum sive Originum libri XX* (Augsburg: Günther Zainer, 1472). London, British Library IB.5441. By permission of the British Library.

history, Mount Olympus and Jerusalem.[16] In contrast to these classical and biblical centers, Britain occupies the border of the world, reflecting the ancient perception of the Britons as living, to cite the thirty-fifth ode of Horace, in the ends of the earth or *in ultimo orbis.* Indeed, due to its location not in the *orbis terrarum* but in its oceanic border, premodern Britain was perceived from the ancients onward as not simply marginal but also other to the world. Virgil describes Britain as wholly sundered from the entire world or *penitus toto divisos orbe* (*Eclogues* 1). Even more evocatively, the great compiler Gaius Julius Solinus writes in his late classical *Collections of Memorable Matters* that Britain deserves "the name almost of another world [*nomen paene orbis alterius*]."[17] Far from the modern "mother" of a world empire, medieval England was a global other.

If the medieval English were physically remote from world centers, they were not so distant as to be ignorant of their border identity. The immense popularity of Solinus's compendium, as well as Isidore's citation of Virgil in his well-known *Etymologies* (622–33), guaranteed that the educated medieval Englishman knew of the marginal nature of his homeland.[18] And the occasional presence of detailed wall maps (such as the spectacular thirteenth-century example still hanging in Hereford Cathedral) made it possi-

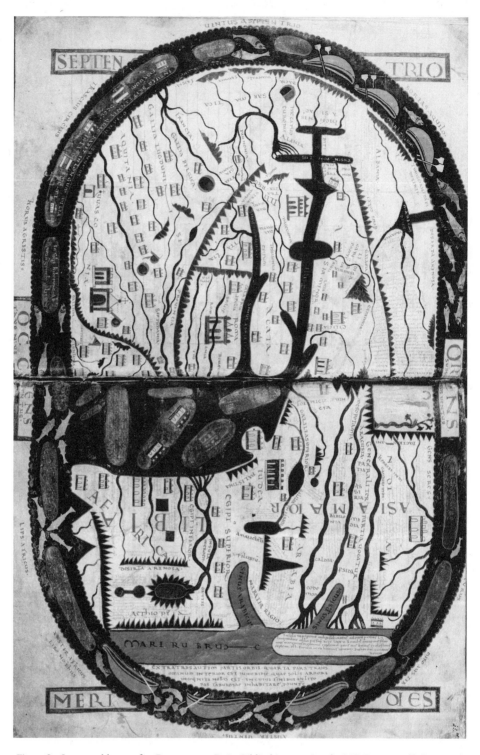

**Fig. 2.** St. Sever world map after Beatus, 1050. Paris, Bibliothèque nationale, MS. Lat. 8878 (S. Lat. 1075), fol. 45. By permission of the Bibliothèque nationale de France.

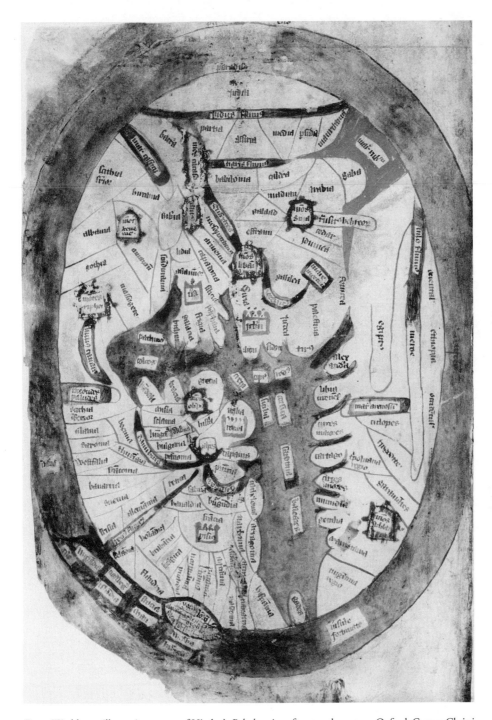

**Fig. 3.** World map illustrating a copy of Higden's *Polychronicon,* fourteenth century. Oxford, Corpus Christi College, MS. 89, fol. 13v. By permission of the President and Fellows of Corpus Christi College, Oxford.

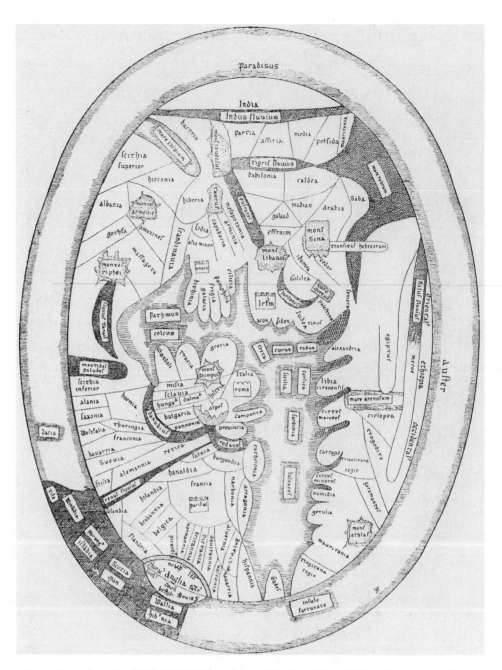

**Fig. 4.** Drawn facsimile of Oxford CCC MS. 89, fol. 13v. Taken from Konrad Miller, *Mappaemundi: Die ältesten Weltkarten,* vol. 3 (Stuttgart: J. Roth, 1895–98), 98.

ble for any English churchgoer to be conscious of her geographic isolation.[19] That geographic consciousness was, moreover, not something that the English rejected. We might presume that, in the same way that non-western peoples have criticized the Mercator projection for its Eurocentrism and even constructed alternative world maps,[20] the medieval English must have renounced or, at the very least, shied away from creating what they termed a "mappemounde." If the modern English made maps highlighting their global centrality, surely the medieval English opposed the production of a world from which England was disjoined. Yet in fact the situation was precisely the opposite. The English actually *led* the cartographic production of an English otherworld during the Middle Ages. The "group of world maps that mark the culmination of the early medieval tradition" either were produced in England or have English associations, as P. D. A. Harvey notes.[21] And the late medieval tradition of mappae mundi is dominated by the group of maps that illustrated many manuscript copies of Higden's hugely popular chronicle.[22] We can cite literary examples of this trend as well, from the time of Bede, who describes Britain as "an island sundered so far from the rest of mankind" in his *Ecclesiastical History of the English People* (721), to the time of the Gawain-poet, who locates Britain "fer ouer þe French flod" in *Sir Gawain and the Green Knight* (ca. 1375–ca. 1400).[23] The English were not simply self-conscious of their marginality during the Middle Ages; English writers and cartographers actively participated in the construction of England as a global borderland.

But to what end? If, in the symbolic geometry of world cartography, the center is a charged site of social power, why this English attraction to the edge? Cognizant of how geography and literature worked together to produce an image of English isolation, *Angels on the Edge of the World* answers this question by looking at English writers' and cartographers' engagements with the perceived geographic marginality of their homeland in an array of texts and maps produced from the tenth century through the Reformation.[24] These include: the interrelated grouping of English maps such as the Cotton "Anglo-Saxon" map, the Ebstorf map, and the Hereford map; the Irish books of Gerald de Barri (a.k.a. Gerald of Wales); the chorographic beginning of and geographic illustrations to the *Polychronicon;* the world travels of the Roman pseudo-saint Constance in Chaucer's *Man of Law's Tale* (ca. 1394); and the global journeys of an exotic bird in John Skelton's *Speke Parott* (1520). Through close analysis of these and other texts, I argue that, in the case of English culture up to the early decades of the sixteenth century, not only geographic centers but also geographic margins had a certain social authority. As we shall see, the power of medieval English marginality paradoxically resembles the might of modern English centrality, as it is generated by the Kerrs in their reading of the Walker-Boutall world map. We can gather as much from a comment made by Lancastrian ally Thomas Arundel before Parliament in 1400, shortly after Henry IV's accession to the throne. Punning on his homeland's name and geographic marginalization, Arundel extols England as the "most fertile *Angle* of riches in the entire world [cest honorable Roialme d'Engleterre, q'est la plus habundant *Angle* de Richesse parmy tout le monde]" (my emphasis).[25] Like the Kerrs, Arundel acknowledges a certain geographic insufficiency on the part of England. The global *angle* of medieval *Anglia* looks toward the "tiny England" of modernity. Yet in the case of both "Englands," that apparent territorial deficiency is paired with a remarkable fecundity.[26] Despite her miniscule size, the English "mother" of modernity manages to beget a prodigious empire. And, notwithstanding its marginalization, medieval England is superlatively abundant. In effect, Arundel evokes the plenitude and exceptionalism that we associate with idealizations of national identity past and present. For Arundel as well as many English cultural producers during the Middle Ages, geographic remoteness provided the means to articulate English national fantasy.[27] Geographical otherness premised both the exaltation and the marginalization of England during the Middle Ages.

## A Medieval English Nation?

Of late, the question of medieval English "national identity" and "national fantasy" has attracted much scholarly attention. While, as Geraldine Heng has observed, "the arguments are multifarious, occasionally contradictory, and undeniably en procès," scholars in medieval studies have gone far in querying the traditional notion that the medieval West was incapable of national discourse.[28] According to that older perspective, the overwhelming "imperialism" of Christianity—itself indebted to the imperialism of ancient Rome—transformed Europeans into a single religious siblinghood in which all persons are equated as children of god or brothers in Christ.[29] That Christian universalism presumably rendered inconsequential more particular bonds to tribe, kingdom, biological family, and nation. Thanks in large part to Benedict Anderson's adherence to such a notion of medieval western civilization in his hugely influential *Imagined Communities* (1983), many scholarly discussions of national identity still presume its modernity. But at least within medieval academic circles (and, to a considerable degree, early modern circles as well), scholars are increasingly challenging the chestnut of a medieval universal Christian monolith.

Some of these scholars point to indications of a medieval nation-state. In the case of England, evidence appears as early as the Anglo-Saxon period. As such historians as M. T. Clanchy, Alfred Smyth, and Adrian Hastings have demonstrated, by 1066 a confluence of factors effected the political unification of what the *Anglo-Saxon Chronicle* terms the *Angelcynn* and what Bede terms *nostra natio*.[30] By disrupting the regional political structures outside of Wessex, the Vikings set the groundwork during the reign of Alfred the Great (ca. 848–99) for a possible political unification of England through reconquest.[31] Aided by the Romans' and Carolingians' examples of strong centralized governments,[32] and the ecclesiastical unification of England under a church headed at Canterbury,[33] Alfred and his successors had taken, by the end of the tenth century, full advantage of the opportunity created by the Vikings. Clanchy describes the potential political, economic, linguistic, and juridical forces moving England toward unity during this time, writing that, at "its best, a sacrosanct king headed a well-defined structure of authority (consisting of shires, hundreds and boroughs), which used a uniform system of taxation and coinage and a common written language in the Anglo-Saxon of writs and charters."[34] As the Middle Ages drew on, other elements also pushed England toward statehood. By the mid-thirteenth century, there "stretched," as Thorlac Turville-Petre points out in his pioneering book on medieval nationhood, "from Westminster throughout the land" a "web of bureaucracy" that administered the law, levied taxes, regulated currency, licensed markets, and raised troops.[35] Even as such phenomena attest to the establishment of a late medieval state whose secular authority came from the crown, other phenomena suggest the beginnings of the more participatory government championed by contemporary liberal scholars of the nation-state.[36] Minor rural nobility gained a voice in political affairs when Edward I included them in the holding of parliament from 1297 on.[37] And, while members of the squirearchy hardly lived up to their designation as the "Commons" in any real sense of the word, the peasant majority did engage in an unprecedented assertion of their rights during the period, as the status of the *nativi* rose after 1350–51 and came to a head in 1381.

Such intimations of bureaucratic formation certainly provide an important corrective to the view that all political distinctions between peoples in the medieval Occident were erased under Christianity. Yet we need not prove the existence of a state to locate notions of national identity during a particular time and in a particular place.[38] In the case of contemporary nationhood, the variety and multiplicity of governmental institutions within some nations can seem to render definition futile. Conversely, there also exist stateless nations such as the Kurds who, despite their long-standing occupation of a particular territory, have never established a sovereign state.[39] Above all, the impulse to cite evidence of a state (whether medieval or modern) often emerges from a desire to ascertain historical "realities," when the nation is fundamentally an imagined community. The idea of an imagined community, of course, returns us to the work of Benedict Anderson and demonstrates how *Imagined Communities* paradoxically offers, as Patricia Ingham puts it, "an account of nation that medievalists love to hate," which nevertheless "has also been useful for medievalists."[40] However various and contradictory, the recent literary critical scholarship on the medieval English nation avers that, as is the case with more contemporary forms of national identity, the medieval nation emanates as much from structures of fantasy as it does from "objective" political realities.[41] National fantasies can help inspire responses to sociohistorical crises such as civil uprisings and economic troubles. And those sources of inspiration, in turn, can have historical agency, as the modern state's utilization of cultural nationalisms attests.[42] National fantasies can perform such social and historical work because they approximate a communal ideal, an ideal that speaks to impossible and sometimes contradictory psychic desires: the wish for communal wholeness, homogeneity, and independence; the urge for territorial coherence; the yearning for loving camaraderie; and the aspiration for sovereign power. National discourse addresses such longings by invoking an ever-shifting bundle of collective quasi-mythic national traits. While these phenomena can include a shared state apparatus (whose mythic nature emerges from the fact that no government ever fully succeeds in creating the unified and sovereign social community that is the national ideal), they also can consist of a common history, "race," ethnicity, religion, language, and territory.

It is of course the last, geographic, item from that list of imagined national charac-teristics that this book stresses.[43] And geography certainly merits such emphasis, as the book-length studies of Heng, Ingham, Turville-Petre, and Michelle Warren all make clear.[44] We can cite innumerable examples of the workings of territory in national fan-tasy, from the erection of national monuments such as the Lincoln Memorial, to the territorializations involved in national hobbies such as the English garden and interna-tional sporting competitions such as World Cup football. Fundamentally, however, space works to circumscribe the nation, providing a crucial indicator of its distinctive-ness. As Anderson puts it, "no nation imagines itself as coterminous with mankind."[45] All nations, no matter how large, define themselves in terms of their boundaries, be-yond which lie other, separate peoples.

How are those national boundaries imagined? Typically, scholars point to verbal and graphic representations of the space of the nation itself. Hence Turville-Petre initiates *England the Nation* with a look at Matthew Paris's maps of England, which for the first time enabled the visualization of the territorial limits of the English, their spatial sepa-ration from other places and peoples. As Turville-Petre is quick to point out, however, thanks to the presence of Scotland and Wales, whose "status and constitutional posi-tions . . . were a cause of constant dispute and eventually open warfare," the borders of England are themselves at issue in Paris's maps.[46] The unstable boundaries of the British have figured prominently in major work on English national identity. In particular, both Warren and Ingham have analyzed how tales of King Arthur straddle the line between the communal formations of England and its neighbors (namely the Welsh). My book complicates such work by considering not only the borders of Britain but also Britain *as border.* To do so, I turn from documents such as the Paris maps that focus upon En-gland and its surrounding territories to artifacts that represent England as it relates to the rest of the world. As we shall see, in both their cartography and their geographically informed literature, the medieval English reveal how they found their status as world border paradoxically worth privileging. Writers from Ælfric to Chaucer do not merely deride but also celebrate England as an island on the edge of the world. And they do so because it was precisely through their marginality that such writers could resist the re-ligious universalism that, according to Hans Kohn and others, supposedly dominated the medieval West.

We can gain a sense of how that English geographic opposition to Christian univer-salism functioned by turning to a legend that serves as the focus of chapter 1 and as a kind of touchstone for the rest of the book: the story of how Pope Gregory the Great's admiration for some pagan English slave boys at the Roman Forum led him to convert the English to Christianity. An Anglo-Saxon myth told and retold by the English for English audiences throughout the Middle Ages, the tale emphasizes the status of the En-glish as exoticized ethnic others, a people, indeed, of whose very existence Gregory was unaware until that fortuitous day at the Forum. And of course, why would Gregory know about the English, given the radical geographic alterity of their homeland? De-picting the English as mute, enslaved, and heathen foreigners, the tale renders England a wilderness governed by the devil and inhabited by the disenfranchised and the subhuman. Yet Gregory's response to the strangers before him also suggests the magnificence of the English otherworld. Upon learning the name of the boys' homeland, Gregory playfully remarks, "rightly are they called *English* [*angli*], for they have the beauty of *angels* [*angeli*]." By having Gregory praise the boys as angels, a category of identity that suggests a kind of exceptional strangeness, the legend renders the English otherworld sublime. The oft-recounted tale of Gregory's pun encapsulates how English writers turned to imperial authorities such as Gregory the Great as a means of legitimating their "savage" world frontier, but resisted reducing the English to members of the Roman Christian brotherhood. While the pun does authorize the translation of the strange English into the Christian family, it also imagines the English as an elect and blessed people, whose geographic detachment is of a piece with their religious elevation above the ordinary members of the universal religious siblinghood. Setting the slave boys and their people apart from ordinary Christians—including, indeed, even Pope Gregory the Great himself—the legend extols the English as angels on the edge of the world.

## The New Cultural Geography and the Medieval English Otherworld

As my earlier citation of Lefebvre suggests, my approach to medieval English uses of geographic otherworldliness engages with recent theories of space, namely scholarly work on what is often called the new cultural geography. The new cultural geography refers to both a recent cultural bent in geography and a recent spatial bent in the humanities. In the case of geographers, this movement—whose prominent proponents include David Harvey, Doreen Massey, Edward Soja, and Peter Jackson—rethinks the interest in geography and culture first put forth by Carl Sauer's Berkeley School.[47] That reconceptualization has been notably diffuse, primarily because of its engagement with a field that is itself hard to pin down, cultural studies.[48] Cultural geographers' unstable identity, however, is rather deceptive, insofar as it also emerges from the very goal that unites them: the querying of space itself as an analytical category. If traditional geography conceives of space as a static entity possessed of universal and essential attributes, the new geography stresses the dynamic and fragmentary nature of spaces as well as, to cite Harvey, "the role of human practices in their construction."[49] Far from an objective context for social action, space is itself, for these scholars, socially produced.

While this insight has rendered cultural geography "a privileged field of inquiry into the present," that is, into postmodernity, an understanding of the constructedness of space is equally useful as a strategy for analyzing the past.[50] In fact, among the theorists of postmodernity, the new cultural geographers stand out for their tendency to compare modern and postmodern artifacts with their medieval counterparts.[51] Most striking for our purposes are the links new geographers draw between medieval and contemporary mapmaking. Historians of cartography once bemoaned the ideological elements in medieval geography that differentiated it from the supposedly scientific and objective geography of modernity. Pointing out how the location of particular peoples and places on mappae mundi has much more to do with mythology, theology, morality, politics, anthropology, and history than with matters of practical geography, scholars sharply opposed premodern and modern world maps.[52] Thus W. L. Bevan and H. W. Phillott point to a "'chaos of error and confusion' which characterizes mediaeval maps"; John Kirkland Wright describes the Middle Ages as a time of "scientific stagnation," when "new information acquired by exploration and travel was ignored" in lieu of "a host of legends, fancies, and false theories"; and W. W. Jervis writes of mappae mundi that "to us, accustomed as we are to have the images of the continental outlines stamped upon our minds, these world maps give a glimpse of a mentality wholly different from our own."[53] Now, however, scholars increasingly acknowledge how the objectivity of the modern map is merely a cover for elements just as ideological as those found at the surface of medieval cartography.[54] As J. B. Harley writes, "Representation is never neutral, and science is still a humanly constructed reality." Hence Harley links "modern" projections like the Mercator to medieval world maps as comparable examples of ethnocentricity.[55] By demonstrating the shared socially constructed nature of modern world maps and mappae mundi, he and like-minded critics remind us that the forms of contemporary life are not always as different from their historical predecessors as we moderns believe them to be.[56]

In this spirit, cultural geographers since the late 1980s have turned from assessing the accuracy of maps to analyzing their politics and unmasking the contradictory circumstances of their production. Recognizing that, as Harvey puts it, "beneath the veneer of common-sense and seemingly 'natural' ideas about space and time, there lie hidden terrains of ambiguity, contradiction, and struggle," cultural geography endeavors to unearth those buried sites of conflict.[57] The problem of the nature of the social struggle encrypted in space—like the question of power generally in contemporary theory—is ongoing in cultural geography. Some geographers emphasize the capacity of spatial discourse to control society. Those interested in emergent and subaltern social groups, by contrast, stress how the social effects of space are subject to transformation and reinterpretation. Yet, regardless of the social groups they examine, all new geographers acknowledge that the spatiality of power and the power of spatiality make geography hardly as straightforward as we once perceived it to be. Structured by a host of social forces, space is porous, layered, and ever variable.

Prominent among the many advantages of the new geographers' insistence on the complexity of space is its capacity, as Patricia Yaeger points out, to take us beyond "some of the dead-end binarisms within cultural studies."[58] She singles out discussions of otherness as offering a particularly intransigent binary opposition. Those dichotomies of "self" and "other" are of course virtually omnipresent in theoretical work on nationalism, which often takes as its premise the idea that nations construct themselves against what they perceive to be strange and different.[59] A field of critical inquiry in which the discourse of alterity plays a crucial role, nationalism can benefit greatly from the "unlimited multiplicity" of space hailed by Yaeger. By analyzing England's vexed place in medieval world cartography, *the present book* offers one means of furthering our thinking on alterity and national identity.

To be sure, recent work on social identity already has taken us far in complicating the binary of "self" and "other" in national fantasy. For one thing, as those who describe the relationality of the nation note, the "othering" entailed by national fantasy is far from a neutral process. In the same way that men and women understand themselves reciprocally but not as equals, the production of the nation and its others is one-sided, whereby the foreign connotes any number of offensive characteristics.[60] *We* are not, so the national story goes, evil, savage, idolatrous, contentious, etc. Slavoj Žižek provides a particularly subtle analysis of the operation of national relationality. Žižek contends that the nation defines itself as possessing some "thing," the "real, non-discursive kernel of enjoyment" analyzed by the psychoanalytic theorist Jacques Lacan. It is this "nation-thing"—which the members of a nation locate in the various ceremonies (weddings, festivals, and so on) through which they organize their enjoyment—that gives the nation "ontological consistency."[61] For Žižek, the national other is thus primarily constructed in terms of her improper relation to "enjoyment." Strangers, that is, are denigrated as lazy, dirty, depraved, thieving, or any other pejorative connoting a menacing excess of enjoyment.

Further complicating the asymmetry of national processes of othering is the fact that nations are themselves intimately connected to strangeness: "strangely," Julia Kristeva writes, "the foreigner lives within us."[62] Like Freud's uncanny, the foreigner "leads back to what is known of old and long familiar" to the nation.[63] A broad continuum of interrelated forms of internal difference troubles the nation. At one end of this spectrum, we can cite Anderson's insight that, given the impossibility of their face-to-face contact, the members of a nation are destined logistically to experience a certain estrangement.[64] Beyond that logistical brand of otherness are more disturbing alienations, such the presence of ethnic, racial, gendered, religious, and economic others within the borders of national space. Finally, we can consider the alienation that troubles the nation at the very moment of its symbolic creation. That foundational lack emerges, for example, in the manner in which the "real, non-discursive kernel of enjoyment" analyzed by Žižek paradoxically "constitutes itself as 'stolen,'" and "only comes to be through being left behind" by the national symbolic order.[65] In other words, the exclusions and repressions entailed by national discourse encompass ironically what the nation most cherishes as its own.

Such internal forms of estrangement deeply threaten the national ideal of unity and homogeneity. Seeking to disavow and conceal the threat of domestic difference, the nation attempts to project its own dangerous otherness onto others located outside itself. No actual menacing form of enjoyment on the part of another people inspires a nation to hate those others and define itself against them. Rather, a threatening alterity inside the nation itself mobilizes such aggression. That strategy of repression and displacement, however, is doomed to failure. As Homi Bhabha has taught us, for all the nation's attempts to deny it, difference nevertheless haunts the language of national belonging.[66]

As this brief overview suggests, scholarship on difference and national fantasy has gone far in complicating the binary of "self" and "other," by revealing their intricate overlapping and enfolding. Over the last two decades, medieval studies as well has contributed to our understanding of alterity, by exploring thoughtfully how the West constructed an oriental other, how the East constructed an occidental other, and how modernity generally has constructed a medieval other.[67] Yet a more nuanced engagement with space and place as it is understood within the new geography can take us still further in our analysis of self and other.[68] In particular, the example of medieval English texts and maps suggests how one portion of the West officially addressed its own geographic otherness, as well as the role such considerations played in the development of a national consciousness. For medieval English writers and mapmakers, the extent to which the nation is "other to itself" doesn't only haunt and endanger the official narrative of national unity. Instead, the image of their geographic otherworldliness contributes to the production of national identity. In the hands of Chaucer, Higden, and others, alterity becomes a component of not only—to use Bhabha's terms—the performative but also the pedagogic aspect of the narration of the English nation. If, for the modern nation alterity is something to shun, in the case of medieval England otherness is something to embrace.[69]

This isn't to say that problematic forms of alterity didn't exist within medieval England. On the contrary, a multitude of dangerous brands of difference circulated on the island. Everyone from social outcasts to aristocrats undermined the image of a harmonious and homogeneous England. On the one hand, living on the island were various disenfranchised others—the peasantry, Jews, women, and so on—who had no place in the elite fraternal collective of the medieval English nation.[70] On the other hand, the nobility had their divisions as well. Barons and other rivaling members of the aristocracy, for example, vied for power throughout the period. Even the very terminology of the nation figured during the Middle Ages as a problematic type of diversity, as it still does today. In both medieval texts and mappae mundi, the name of both the entire island and the space bounded by its Celtic fringe slips unsteadily between "Britaine" and "Engelonde."[71] Medieval England was hardly immune from the alienations from which the nation seeks to disassociate itself.

Providing geographic support for such problematic national differences were the ignominious rationales for England's habitation of a world border. One could be set apart from the world for different reasons, and some of those reasons were hardly worth celebrating. The positing of places and peoples on the borders of a mappa mundi often signified their lack of the power, centrality, and prestige attributed to those persons inhabiting the center of the civilized world. The farther away a people lay from the center, the greater their perceived disenfranchisement from the Christian *oikoumené:* beyond the Christian nations at the heart of mappae mundi lay the Jews and Moslems; beyond the Jews and Moslems lay the barbaric tribes; and beyond them, at the very edges of the world, lay the Plinian or monstrous races.[72] For example, at the southernmost border of the world, on a band of land between the upper Nile and the world ocean, the Hereford map depicts ten monstrous races, including the Blemyae, whose eyes and mouth appear between their breasts, and the four-eyed Maritimi (figs. 5–6). And just inland of the band, to the north of the upper Nile, the Hereford mapmaker alerts the reader to the location of the barbarian tribes of the Garamantes, Nothabres, and Gaetuli.

**Fig. 5.** Hereford world map, ca. 1290. Hereford Cathedral. By permission of The Dean and Chapter of Hereford and the Hereford Mappa Mundi Trust.

The Judeo-Christian and classical sources for mappae mundi similarly disparage geographic borders, though typically not global but *local* frontiers of the civilized world (notably the desert and forest) receive such criticism. As a "realm of desiccation" that threatened to encroach upon the cultivated lands of a Hebrew people living on its edges, the desert in the Old Testament was a site of moral temptation and a place infested with beasts and demons.[73] And the desert is, in the *vitae* of the Christian monks of Egypt

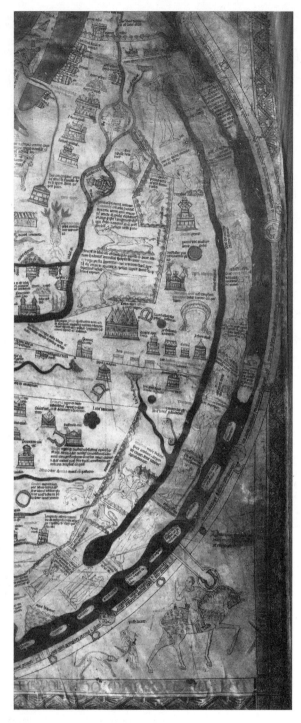

**Fig. 6.** Africa in the Hereford world map, ca. 1290. Hereford Cathedral. By permission of The Dean and Chapter of Hereford and the Hereford Mappa Mundi Trust.

(which began to circulate in the West from the early fifth century on), "the region of tombs, domain of death" described by Antoine Guillamont.[74] The lethal, sinful, and wild desert-wilderness of the Judeo-Christian tradition finds a counterpart in the brutal forest-wilderness of classical antiquity. As Robert Pogue Harrison has demonstrated, the ancient goddess of the forest, the Greeks' Artemis and the Romans' Diana, inspires terror. A deity whose remoteness and virginity refer partly "to the virgin forests beyond the bounds of the *polis* and cultivated fields," but also to her status as an outsider among the gods, Artemis in her cruelty mirrors the ferocity of her wild home.[75]

But crucially, classical society viewed local geographic borders as not only fearsome but also wonderful. Diana and her "virgin forests beyond the bounds of the *polis* and cultivated fields" fascinate through their capacity to inspire not simply terror but a nexus of emotions, among them awe and adulation.[76] The Roman deity's paradoxical identity as chaste goddess and as the great womb of the world, above all, reflects the status of the forest for the ancient Greeks and Romans as a cultural matrix: the primordial origin of civilization itself. In somewhat the same way that, as James Romm has demonstrated, the ancients perceived Ocean (the world's watery boundary) as at once evil and holy, both the origin of the gods and a site of primordial chaos, the Greeks and Romans simultaneously revered and feared their forested frontiers and the goddess of those wild and remote spaces.[77] The classical world's ambiguous stance toward the wilderness was shared by Judeo-Christian culture. Largely due to the "formative" function of the Sinai desert for the Israelites, the Old Testament wilderness was a place not only of moral and physical danger but also of purgation, refuge, spiritual redemption, and covenantal bliss.[78] And, for the desert saints, the very primitivism and wildness that might, from one perspective, subordinate the desert to the *polis,* in fact elevated the wilderness above the city.[79] Viewing the city as a site of tumult and corruption, the monks rejected civic life in favor of a "holy wilderness" existence. A kind of earthly paradise, the desert was a region of spiritual birth and renewal, a place where monks miraculously lived in harmony with animals and consorted with angels, as Adam and Eve did in Eden.

Influenced by the ambivalence toward local frontiers registered by classical and Judeo-Christian cultures, medieval mappae mundi both decry and exalt the global frontier. The alien races of the uttermost reaches of the earth such as the Scythians and Ethiopians, for example, were viewed along ethnocentric lines as savages worth deriding and along utopian lines as moral superiors worth imitating.[80] Hence the Hereford cartographer locates on a promontory in the northern world ocean the Hyperboreans, whom an inscription identifies via Solinus as "the happiest of human races [Yperborei ut dicit Solinus gens est beatissima]."[81] And the Hereford mapmaker's band of monstrous races along the Nile ends at its northern tip with the monk Zosimas, just above whom are the monasteries of Saint Anthony the Great. Beyond, at the very eastern margins of the world, at the top of the Hereford map, the terrestrial paradise appears, while beyond the western and northern borders of the world there also appear the blessed and wondrous islands of classical mythology, such as the fortunate isles and the Hesperides (figs. 7–8).

As the evidence of mappae mundi, Judeo-Christian ideas of the desert, and classical

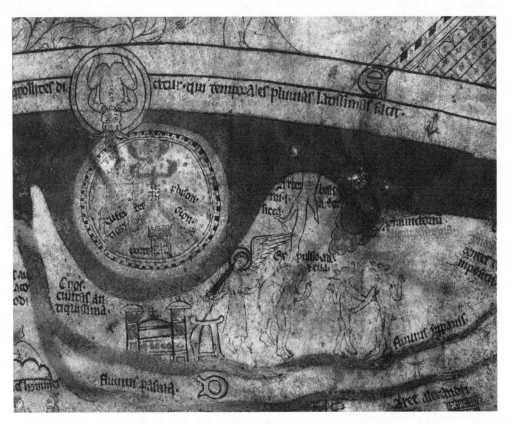

Fig. 7. The terrestrial paradise on the Hereford world map, ca. 1290. Hereford Cathedral. By permission of The Dean and Chapter of Hereford and the Hereford Mappa Mundi Trust.

notions of the forest attest, geographic borders—whether macrocosmic or microcosmic—were objects of idealization and derision, hope and dread; lairs of monsters and devils, angels and saints. Always somehow other to civilization, the margins of the world were spaces possessed of contradictory meanings within medieval western culture. Indeed, those contradictory meanings adhered not simply to territorial otherness, but alterity generally. Consider the word "straunge" in Middle English.[82] If "straunge" could refer to a lack of civility or knowledge (a barbarian, an adulteress, ignorance), it also could mean the epitome of cultural sophistication. Fancy food prepared for a medieval feast, intricately designed armor worn for battle, and recondite texts all are termed "straunge." And while "straunge" could indicate the disaffected, the unfriendly, and the hostile, it also signified extraordinary and wonderful events (an earthquake), entities (a star in the heavens), or experiences (love).

When representing their own insular world frontier, the English could draw upon such polyvalent notions of difference. The various and contradictory signs of English otherworldliness offered medieval writers a remarkably elastic medium with which to construct national identity. In particular, those wondrous aspects of alterity—and,

**Fig. 8.** The fortunate isles on the Hereford world map, ca. 1290. Hereford Cathedral. By permission of The Dean and Chapter of Hereford and the Hereford Mappa Mundi Trust.

above all, the wonderful aspects of geographic otherness—made it possible for English writers to see their homeland as not only barbarously divided but also blessed and united. Even as they acknowledged England as a barbarous wasteland (akin to the rugged home of the Plinian races) or as a site of brutal disorder (like the primordially turgid world ocean), the English also imagined England as a holy wilderness (comparable to the early Christian monks' arid retreats) or as a blessed isle (reminiscent of the Hesperides). Seizing upon this flexible notion of difference, the English absorbed and reconfigured the many others alien to English national fantasy. In other words, the rhetoric of sublime geographic alterity served such writers as a means of imaginatively transforming problematic forms of national difference into signs of national magnificence. Taking the doubleness of English isolation as their cue, English writers resignified internal others by aligning them with the geographic otherness of England itself. Such dangerous forms of domestic difference thus could be imaginatively captured and rewritten in the same way that English otherworldliness was variously interpreted. Differences ranging from civil conflict to the instability of the nation's very name might challenge English welfare, but the eternal geographic marginality of the land overcame such obstacles by suggesting how difference could also benefit England. If English geographic alterity could make England a sublime nation, so too could other forms of domestic strangeness serve less as liabilities than as assets. Hence the paradoxical idealization of slaves in the myth of Gregory's puns and the ironic elevation of woman in the *Man of Law's Tale.*

Those fantasies of sovereign English otherworldliness tended to emerge during the medieval period precisely when the idea of England was historically at risk. Like other forms of self-flattery, the celebration of the nation typically compensates for certain anxieties. The literary chapters that comprise this book suggest the range of purposes English geographic isolation served for writers during certain flash points of historical crisis. As the historical span of the texts I analyze suggests, those junctures extend from the tenth century up to the English Reformation. At the time that the first writer analyzed in the book, the monk, scholar, and reformer Ælfric of Eynsham, began composing his homilies, Æthelræd II "the unready" (ca. 969–1016) had assumed the throne. The civil turmoil that marked the rule of this notoriously weak king, as well as the recurrence of Viking invasions, threatened the religious and political unity of England in a manner that the reformers under King Edgar (943–75) had the luck to avoid. The book then turns to the cartography and historical writing of Gerald de Barri, a Welsh writer, archdeacon, scholar, and royal servant working during the late twelfth century, when relations between the English and the Irish were at issue as never before; that period witnessed England's initial invasion, occupation, and colonization of an island located even further on the world's western border. An act legitimized by King Henry II's supposed ability to foster Christian practice among a barbarously remote Irish people, the English conquest of Ireland was threatened by Henry's notoriety as the man responsible for Archbishop Thomas Becket's murder.

If Gerald faced certain challenges in his attempt to authorize England's conquest of Ireland, matters were even worse for the featured writer of chapter 3, the Cheshire monk and chronicler Ranulf Higden. When Higden wrote, during the early decades of the 1300s, England witnessed perhaps the most volatile moment of its political history, as the coincidence of Edward II's deposition in 1327 with the completion of the first version of the *Polychronicon* makes clear. Famine, poor harvests, and livestock murrains compounded matters, leading to disease, starvation, and cannibalism on the island. Internal upheavals continued to mark the closing decades of the fourteenth century, the period of the poet, parliamentary representative, diplomat, courtier, justice of the peace, and civil servant Geoffrey Chaucer. Most pertinent to Chaucer's *Man of Law's Tale* were the infamous shortcomings of English lawyers. Through bribery and other corrupt practices, English justices notoriously undermined the law, so much so that they constituted a principal object of aggression during the 1381 peasant rebellion. Finally, in the England of the poet, priest, tutor, and courtier John Skelton, the exploits of Cardinal and Lord Chancellor Thomas Wolsey compromised national welfare. A man who notoriously ruled as a second king, Wolsey was perceived by Skelton and others as possessing a personal ambition whose fulfillment entailed the decline of their nation.

Writing during times when these and other forms of social strife threatened to substantiate the barbaric implications of England's otherworldly status, Skelton, Chaucer, Higden, and others imagine how, if the English at times seemed wild dwellers of a world frontier, they also could appear as the blessed inhabitants of a sublime otherworld. Using the concept of their far-off homeland to think of themselves as not only inferior but also superior to other men, English writers engage imaginatively with the problems and potentials of English identity. Jeremiah-like figures, these medieval writers deploy the ambivalent discourse of English isolation to criticize metaphorically the ills of their culture, while at the same time affirming England's select status under God. Mediating between national crises and national desires, they constitute what we might loosely and anachronistically call medieval "intellectuals": educated men who, while not direct participants in the management of their society, engage with the weaknesses and strengths of the English through written and oral communication.[83] Whether addressing their texts, as in the case of Chaucer's *Canterbury Tales,* to a coterie of fellow intellectuals or, as in the case of Higden's immensely popular *Polychronicon,* to a wider, national public, these writers blend geographic with juridical, monastic, historiographic, and other discourses to fashion a national fantasy of a sovereign English community.

## The *Regnum Anglorum* and *Roma Aeterna*

Built into that myth of a sublime English frontier was a related, imperial dream. If their otherworldliness made the English exceptional, their exceptionalism might also suggest how the English should be the rightful masters of the earth itself. The exaltation of the English world margin, in other words, could authorize the expansion of England beyond its borders, into the world. This despite the fact that such a territorial extension opposes the national delimitation of England as a marginalized island and thus denudes England of the very geographical basis for its exceptionalist claims. Such a paradoxical movement between national boundedness and imperial expansion, however, should seem familiar to us. The question of the "modern" English nation, after all, has always been entangled with that of the English empire. We know England as both the "sceptred isle" of *Richard II,* 2.1.40, and an expansive Victorian empire. Or, to return to the Kerr volume, imperial England is both a "tiny" island and a global motherland. In a somewhat similar vein, medieval English writers suggest how the elevation of the marginal English could ironically explain how global dominion was their manifest destiny. Take an emblematic moment from Geoffrey of Monmouth's *History of the Kings of Britain.* Appearing before Britain's mythic founder in a dream, Diana foresees that Brutus will occupy an island located "beyond the setting of the sun . . . in the world ocean."[84] Diana's words link the wilderness deity with her Trojan worshipper, making him the settler of a global frontier that starkly contrasts with the future British Empire of modernity. If England would famously become an empire so vast that somewhere upon it the sun still sheds light, ancient Britain was, in Diana's words, an isle of everlasting dusk. However, Diana turns English otherworldliness on its head through her link with fertility. While the isle Brutus will occupy is presently *deserta* or empty, it will eventually give birth to a "race of kings" who, Diana proclaims, will rule "the round circle of the whole earth." The Britons may be remote, but their sovereignty will ultimately spread throughout the globe.

The newly discovered Evesham map (1390–1400; fig. 9) provides a cartographic counterpart to the imperialism evident in Geoffrey's *History.*[85] Due to the enormous space it allots *Anglia,* as well as its positing of England as a counterweight to the unusually large image of Paradise in the east, the Evesham map visually suggests how important places occupy the margins of the world. The key role of territorial expansion in that elevation of England emerges in the manner that the *Anglia* of the Evesham map *hugs* the earth, as if to merge with and imperialistically engulf the world. And engulf much of the world England does, thanks to the mapmaker's propagandistic rendering of European geography. Reflecting the imperial tenor of the Hundred Years War, the map distorts Europe so as to give pride of place to the recent English acquisition of Calais (called *Callia*). Indicated by a huge tower icon, Calais, along with St. Denis (termed *Deinsia,* with a like symbol), looms like a giant over the lower portion of the entire map, suggesting how the late medieval English had inherited a version of the British global sway prophesied by Diana.

In Geoffrey's *History,* becoming the imperial capital of the world specifically means seizing the global might bound up with the imperial center often highlighted in mappae mundi: Rome. Conquering Rome, becoming its emperor, always serves in the *History of the Kings of Britain* as the ultimate imperial aim of Brutus's descendants from Belinus and Brennius to King Arthur himself. This proto-imperial genealogy exemplifies a trend analyzed throughout *this book:* how English identification with a bounded and marginal otherworld stood in tension with a desire to burst beyond the limits of the distant isle and make a claim on the classical empire highlighted in the Beatus, Higden, and other medieval world maps.[86] If the English privileged their remoteness as a

**Fig. 9.** Evesham world map, ca. 1390. London, College of Arms, Muniment Room 18/19. Courtesy of the College of Arms.

means of setting themselves apart from Rome, they also—like so many medieval Europeans—saw themselves as the rightful inheritors of Rome's global prominence.

And how could it have been otherwise? While the history of the English, of course, roughly coincided with the fall of the Roman Empire, classical Rome was indisputably an immense historical, cultural, religious, political, and geographic presence throughout the medieval period in England. Memorialized both textually in late classical literature and materially in the ancient roads and ruins left on the island, the many achievements of Rome made it the epitome in medieval England of the cultural sophistication and political power attached to civilized world centers. That power was perpetuated in England (and elsewhere in medieval Europe) through two interconnected phenomena. The identification of imperial conquest with Rome persisted in the medieval Occident partly through the espousal by the Carolingian, Hohenstaufen, and other medieval "empires" of the notion of *translatio imperii* or the "westering" of empire, which refers to the idea that Rome was the last of the four historical empires described in Daniel and that the rule of a united Roman Empire was transferred in 800 from the Greeks to the Franks and then later to the Germans.[87]

The English were not members of these "Roman" empires. Yet, as we have seen, they were members of another Roman "empire," one related at times to those of the Franks and Germans: the Roman Christian church. Thanks largely to the imperial theology of Eusebius of Caesarea (and despite the claims of Augustine) Christianity came to be linked closely with the Roman Empire in the west. In particular, the universal spread of Christian monotheism was identified with the imperial sway of the Romans, whereby, as Eusebius wrote, the preaching of the "kingdom of God . . . to all men, . . . and to those who resided in the extremities of the earth" closely mirrored the union by the "Roman empire . . . [of] the whole race of man into one state of accordance and agreement."[88] The powers accorded the church all carried distinctly Roman valences and had tangible political effects, among them: the universal dominance of Latin, the jurisdictional supremacy of canon law and church officials over their secular counterparts, and the heading of the papacy in Rome.

To be sure, by the end of the Middle Ages, the holy Roman "mother" of the medieval west was tarnished by, among other things, schism.[89] Yet despite such problems, the idea of Rome—in both her classical and her Christian incarnations—persisted with considerable force. Most relevant to our purposes, perhaps, is the fact that, throughout the period, Rome's geographic centrality continued to be experienced viscerally by the throngs of visitors who traveled there—from as far as England—with the intent of worshipping sacred sites and touring ancient ruins.[90] In the case of the latter brand of traveler, we can get a sense of such tourism from Englishman "Master Gregory." In his thirteenth-century account of the classical sights of Rome, Gregory declares that "although Rome lies in ruins, nothing intact can be compared to this."[91] However long dead, the "ghost" of Rome effectively served as a standard against which the isolated English measured their accomplishments. For even the earliest writers on English identity, celebrating the English edge of the world inevitably meant comparing England to Rome, with its ancient secular glory and contemporary religious power.

Given Rome's intimidating authority, such comparisons often resulted in English national anxiety: the fear that, far from surpassing Rome, England desperately needed the aid of Rome to achieve communal legitimacy. Hence, in the slave-boy story, it is none other than Gregory the Great who raises the distant English to angelic status. And, in the *Man of Law's Tale,* it is the holy Roman woman Custance who signifies the status of the Anglo-Saxons as God's chosen people. Such symbolic appropriations of Roman authority should be considered in tandem with the role things Roman played in generating things English during the medieval period. However inadvertently, Rome helped produce English identity in diverse yet related social arenas. As early as the Anglo-Saxon period, as Nicholas Brooks has recently demonstrated, a "campaign of *imitatio Romae* was an essential element in the process of English ethnogenesis, that is in a programme of constructing a single *gens Anglorum*" on the part of the Canterbury See.[92] And in the years following 1066, the canon law fostered the system of common law that is a hallmark of English juridical identity. During the High Middle Ages, as Johan Huizinga points out, the Crusades promulgated by Roman Christendom encouraged national feeling on the part of the English and other European peoples, insofar as they brought the members of Latin Christendom "together again and again in martial equipment, battle array and a more or less sanctified rivalry."[93] As these and other examples make clear, contrary to the arguments of Hans Kohn and other scholars, the Roman church did not always hinder but at times actually contributed to medieval national feeling.

However, the very achievements that made Rome a kind of benefactor for the English also made Rome England's rival. The Rome whose aid England sought was also the Rome whose centralized place in the world a remote England desired to assume. In the *Polychronicon,* Higden thus styles history as a story in which first the Romans and then the British emerge as the prime historical figures among world peoples, a temporal juxtaposition that implies that the British are somehow successors to the Romans. Portraying a kind of *translatio imperii* at work in English history, Higden suggests that the glory of the Roman center of the world is being carried on by its English edge. The examples of Higden and the other writers analyzed in this book all reveal how the notion of English territorial alterity, if properly celebrated, could lead to the idea that the English merit the very sovereignty and imperial sway attached to Rome.

The foremost example of such English aggression toward Rome is the Protestant Reformation. By bringing the analysis of representations of English geographic marginality up to 1534, I aim in this book to demonstrate how the English's sense of themselves as a people on the edge of the world played a previously unexamined role in this watershed event. By the time of the Reformation, an event had occurred that should have demolished the notion of English geographic isolation: the "discovery" of the New World. Columbus's voyage to the American continent brought to Europe new geographic knowledge that pushed the old western boundaries of the Earth far beyond the English Channel. Elsewhere in Europe such developments led to an outpouring of "modern" cartographic treatises, but such was not the case in England, where traditional historiographic and cartographic texts such as the *Polychronicon* continued to be produced. *Angels on the Edge of the World* concludes by examining this lasting English investment in otherworldliness in Skelton's *Speke Parott,* the writings and ritual perfor-mances of Cardinal Wolsey, and other texts produced during the fifteenth and early six-teenth centuries. As this final chapter demonstrates, the English continued to embrace an outmoded view of world geography because of that model's long-standing utility for national thinking. To reimagine a world including the Americas was to forsake England's claim on sublime geographic alterity. And assertions of territorial remoteness would in-deed prove key to political assertions of English sovereignty in the years preceding 1534. Indeed, two central documents of the Reformation, the *Collectanea satis copiosa* of Thomas Cranmer and Edward Foxe (1530), and Thomas Cromwell's *Act in Restraint of Appeals* (1533), invoke England's unusual geographic distance from Rome as grounds for its independence from the papacy.

Ultimately, this book suggests how a reciprocal ambivalence on the part of the En-glish toward both their homeland and Rome continued throughout the period under analysis. With the same vigor with which they embraced their isolation during certain moments in their medieval history, the English, at other times, wished for centrality. Modeling themselves along Roman lines—and in so doing transgressing the boundaries that defined their geographically marginalized homeland—figured for the medieval En-glish as a prospect as fascinating as it was terrifying, as exhilarating as it was monstrous. Thus before Henry VIII asserted England's sovereign independence from the church, he (outrageously) pondered sacking Rome. Due to the long and fraught history of En-glish engagements with English geographic isolation and centralized Roman authority, the agents of the Reformation had a rich and nuanced tradition of national geographic thought from which to draw. That tradition may not have caused the break with Rome, but it did help the English imagine its possibility. Such ambivalent responses to English otherworldliness foreshadow as well the ironies that mark the modern geographic pro-duction of English imperial identity. Well before the Kerrs in their imperialist school-book ironically extolled their home as at once "tiny England" and prodigious motherland, Higden, Chaucer, Wolsey, and other intellectuals celebrated the English as a people both set apart from and destined to rule the medieval Christian *mundus.*

# CHAPTER ONE

# ANOTHER COUNTRY

Ælfric and the Production of English Identity

According to an English legend first recorded in Bede's *Ecclesiastical History* (731), the future pope Gregory the Great (540–604), while browsing through the Forum one day, happened upon some attractive English slave boys. Upon learning that the beautiful youths were pagan, Gregory lamented their subjection to Satan. Then, after discovering the name of their people, tribal kingdom, and king, Gregory foretold the Anglo-Saxons' conversion to Christianity through a series of puns. "Rightly are they called Angles (*angli*)," he first remarked, "since they have the beauty of angels (*angeli*)." Gregory then proclaimed in praise of their kingdom, Deira, "De *ira*! Saved from the wrath of Christ and called to his mercy." And finally, punning on the name of their king, Ælle, Gregory exclaimed "Alleluia! The praise of God the Creator must be sung in those parts!"[1] Bringing together issues of ethnic fantasy, spirituality, and Roman authority, the tale of Gregory's puns and the boys' beauty fascinated generations of English writers during the Middle Ages and is still well known to both medievalists and most readers of early English history. Since the late nineteen-eighties, moreover, the legend has received a considerable amount of critical attention. Through the work of such scholars as Jonathan Culler, Nicholas Howe, Ruth Karras, Patrick Wormald, and, above all, Allen Frantzen, we have come to appreciate how the story of Gregory and his "boys" interestingly comments on a variety of issues in medieval culture, ranging from religious conversion, to wordplay, slavery, and sodomy.[2] In this chapter, I focus upon another key element of the slave-boy story, an aspect of the legend that reflects a crucial obsession of the medieval English: their own strangeness. For Gregory's encounter with the youths is a moment of discovery; the boys' appearance, language, and homeland are unknown to him. Because "West meets West" in this legend through Gregory's Roman eyes, the tale allows the English to imagine themselves as others, a people whose particular "racial" and ethnic affiliations mark them as foreigners before the pope-to-be. As we shall see, the alterity of the youths in the legend goes far in accounting for its enduring popularity in medieval England, for it is precisely through that strangeness that the tale responds to and imaginatively fulfills a bundle of complex and contradictory English desires.

Over the following pages, I analyze one of the earliest versions of the legend, that offered by Ælfric the abbot of Eynsham (ca. 950–ca. 1010) in his vernacular sermon on Gregory (ca. 994).[3] While not as acclaimed as Bede's version, Ælfric's account nevertheless offers us an excellent place to start examining the legend critically, as his rendering of the narrative is unprecedented for its exploitation of otherness for specifically English purposes. That Ælfric would be the first writer to tease out the national uses of the Gregory tale, as we shall see, reflects the unique conditions of the historical moment in which he wrote. In Ælfric's England the *fantasy* (if not the reality) of a united Christian *þeod* or people existed, though the realization of such an ideal was threatened from both within and without the island.[4] The strange boys at the Forum provide Ælfric with the means of addressing and imaginatively overcoming such challenges. Through the invention of Gregory the Great's authoritative gaze, Ælfric depicts the English slaves as what we might call religio-national icons—figures, that is, who render a sovereign spiritual identity the birthright of a divided English people.

Ælfric's production of English election hinges upon an ethnic alterity possessed by the boys that intimately relates to the problem of English geographic isolation. By representing a group of Anglo-Saxons as foreigners in Rome, the slave-boy legend cannot help but point to the radical geographic differences between England and Rome. At the very heart of the Christian West was Rome. That privileged status was impressed upon the Anglo-Saxons in spiritual terms by the status of Rome as a prime pilgrimage destination, the seat of the papacy, the home of the missionaries who ministered to the English, and the authorizer of the liturgical calendar that the English (since the Whitby Synod) followed. In classical terms, the Anglo-Saxons knew Rome as the center of the empire whose past conquest of Britain was evident through an abundance of physical remains, and whose geographic and historical prominence was memorialized in an Old English translation of Orosius's *The Seven Books of History against the Pagans*.[5] We can gain a graphic sense of the centrality of Rome for the Anglo-Saxons in what P. D. A. Harvey rightly has described as an "extraordinarily important" artifact, the so-called Cotton map of the world (fig. 10).[6] Produced during or shortly after the time of Ælfric, the Anglo-Saxon map situates Rome at the very center of the western world, a positioning that reflects the standing of the city as the erstwhile seat of a western empire and the contemporary capital of western Christendom. In contrast, the stereotypical navel of the Christian world, Jerusalem, appears, as C. Raymond Beazley pointed out long ago, "well away from the central part of this square design," south of the Cotton map's middle.[7] The manuscript in which the Cotton map appears, Cotton MS. Tiberius B.V., further underscores Rome's central importance.[8] From its inclusion of *computus* tables for figuring the Roman liturgical year (fols. 11r–18r), to its inclusion of an Anglo-Saxon itinerary to Rome (fols. 23v ff.), and a classical description of Rome (fols. 57r–73r), the manuscript combines issues of time and space to stress the singular importance of the eternal city.[9]

**Fig. 10.** Anglo-Saxon or Cotton world map, tenth century. London, British Library, Cotton MS. Tiberius B.V., fol. 56v. By permission of the British Library.

At the same time that the Cotton map attests to the centrality of Rome on earth, that map also makes clear how England lay at that world's very edge. On the lower left-hand corner of the document, in the northwestern edge of the world, appears *Britannia,* which is by far the largest island of the world ocean. Our earliest evidence that the inhabitants of Britain were conscious of their isolation appears in the *The Ruin of Britain* by the British historian Gildas (d. 570), who writes that "the island of Britain lies virtually at the end of the world, towards the west and north-west."[10] Thanks not only to Gildas but moreover to the tremendous popularity and influence of Isidore's *Etymologies* (which repeats Virgil's claim that Britain is an island sundered from the entire world), early English intellectuals from Bede to Ælfric, the maker of the Cotton map, and still later, the monk Eadmer (ca. 1064–ca. 1124) were well aware of their homeland's extreme isolation.[11] In particular, the Anglo-Saxons were attuned to their great distance from Rome. Thus Bede records from Cædwalla's tomb how the West Saxon king traveled "From earth's remotest end, from Britain's isle, / to Romulus's town."[12] And as Howe has pointed out, when Ælfric writes in passing to his fellow monks that during the summer they may modify their psalm recitals because nights at that time of year are shorter in Britain than in Italy, he testifies to just how profoundly was rooted in the Anglo-Saxons a sense "of the earth's shape and Eynsham's place toward its northern edge," and of Rome's more southeastern (and more central) placement.[13]

The implications of their island's marginal relation to the rest of the world (and Rome in particular) were manifold and contradictory for the Anglo-Saxons. Somewhat like the geographic isolation of the *anhaga* or solitary man, which is conceived of within the Old English literature of exile in terms of a series of problematic losses (kin, treasure, and homeland), English geographic isolation is tied to a troubling lack of the goods (religion, culture, and the like) associated with Rome and other Christian world centers.[14] As Ælfric puts it in a sermon from his *Lives of Saints* on Moses' prayer against Amalac in Exodus, living "on the outer edge of the earth's surface" exerts such a detrimental effect upon the English that they cannot be as rigorous in their piety as those who live in *to-middes* or the center of the world.[15] Yet geographic isolation does not always have negative consequences in Anglo-Saxon culture. For example, even as the cannibalistic Mermedonians in the Old English *Andreas* demonstrate the link between barbarity and strange lands, the multiple representations of angels throughout that text intertwine a sublime spirituality with the members of an "other" world.[16] Similarly, the very geographic isolation that suggests the barbarity or religious deficiencies of the English in Anglo-Saxon culture also suggests their specialness—the singularity, that is, of the English as an insular people set apart from other believers.

To return to the Cotton world map, the precision and intricacy of the mapmaker's portrayal of Britannia, as well as the inordinately large size of the island, set it apart from all other territories. Only much later in the medieval period, during the time of Portolan cartography, would England and the British Isles again receive such a simultaneously accurate and detailed rendering.[17] That stress on England also emerges elsewhere in the manuscript, which contains lists of English bishops and English kings. Thus, at the same time that the contents of Cotton Tiberius B.V. testify to the importance of

Rome, they also represent England as a place worth visually highlighting and as a site whose ecclesiastical and political leaders are worth recording. Other Anglo-Saxon artifacts go further, suggesting the Christian election of the English edge of the world. In the account of the monastic revival on BM Cotton Faustina A.X., for example, God's decision to extend the Word beyond the Roman world "wondrously illumined and glorified that almost extremest island of the whole earth [ytemerte iȝlond ealler middanȝearder]," and displayed the majesty of a people "so glorious and so well worth winning to God."[18] While from a Roman perspective, then, England's location on the margins of the Christian world could suggest its tenuous relation to Christian civilization, taken differently, the link between England and Christian civilization appears remarkable. In Ælfric's Moses sermon, the monk describes the geographically marginalized English as both problematically weak *and* as figures of God's chosen people, the Israelites.[19]

Ælfric's take on the slave-boy legend well exemplifies the utility of the ambivalent valences of geographic alterity for a national literary project. As we shall see, owing to their enslavement and paganism, the Anglo-Saxon youths register the religious and political disenfranchisement of an isolated English people during both the historical moment to which the myth refers and Ælfric's own time. However, over the course of the anecdote, the "racial" and vernacular signs of the slave boys' location on the "wild" English global border also emerge as symbols of the Anglo-Saxon's privileged positioning in the world as a chosen Christian people. In part, the slave-boy story looks toward the incorporation of an isolated pagan people into the Roman Christian world.[20] Yet as Ælfric's account most clearly demonstrates, Gregory's puns do not simply prophesy the English's eventual Christian conversion but also distinguish the English from the universal Christian siblinghood. Specifically, by having Gregory identify a whiteness on the slaves' bodies that opposes their allegiance to a "black devil," and by having him claim universal Christian meanings for key English words, Ælfric fashions these boyish signs of barbaric strangeness into emblems of Christian election.

## Saving Souls, Making Nations

Before we turn directly to Ælfric's text, some discussion of his sources and the historical context in which he wrote is necessary for our apprehension of the exceptionally nationalistic quality of his version of the slave-boy myth. The legend appears first in two early eighth-century texts: the anonymous Whitby writer's life of Gregory (ca. 704–14) and Bede's *Ecclesiastical History*.[21] It is found later in Paul the Deacon's late eighth-century life of Gregory and the Old English translation of Bede (ca. 871–99). Ælfric's sermon on Gregory, which forms part of the monk's two-volume series of *Catholic Homilies*, draws upon Bede, Paul, and the Old English Bede.[22] Several important factors make Ælfric's version unique. For one thing, more than any of these writers, Ælfric intends for his homiletic series an audience drawn not from the Latin-literate religious elite, but from the English laity. Our chief indicator of that intended English audience consists in the fact that, unlike the Whitby writer, Bede, and Paul, Ælfric incorporates the legend into a homiletic project written in his native language. The Old Enigsh Bede also appears in the vernacular as a translation of the *Ecclesiastical History;* however, Ælfric wrote his two-volume sermon series (which provided priests with homilies for specific days in the church year) primarily for a wider, national distribution by priests to the laity during the mass in monastic and secular churches.[23] In the Gregory homily itself, Ælfric makes explicit his assumption that his sermons will reach a broader audience than that enjoyed by the Old English Bede, telling his intended lay readership that while the "history of the English which King Alfred translated from Latin into English speaks clearly enough of this holy man," the speaker will relate details of Gregory's life "because the aforesaid book is not known to all of you, although it is translated into English."[24]

In the Latin preface to the first volume of the series, Ælfric defends his writing in "plain English [simplicem Anglicam]" on grounds of spiritual instruction—so that the reformers' Christian message "might the more readily reach the hearts of those who read or hear, to the profit of the souls of those who cannot be taught in any other tongue, than that to which they are born."[25] Yet even as Ælfric's use of the vernacular reflects his evangelism, it also suggests the monk's investment in English identity. As Thorlac Turville-Petre notes, the "very act of writing in English is a statement about belonging."[26] To be sure, Ælfric did not solely concern himself with the vernacular, as his Latin grammar and *Colloquy* demonstrate.[27] Yet in the case of his vernacular sermons, by writing in English Ælfric posits a community defined not along universal Latin lines, but along particular English lines. Moreover, in a move that reflects "the Grammarian's" interest in standardizing English, the monk's turn to the vernacular legitimates the "native" language of the English as a medium worthy of his theological project.[28]

The national audience that Ælfric had in mind for his sermons influenced his subject matter as well his choice of language. As he asserts in the preface to his second homiliary, his sermons "are not all taken from the gospels, but are very many of them gathered from the life or passion of God's saints, of those only whom the English nation [angelcynn] honours with feast-days."[29] Alluding to saints who are special to the English (such as the beloved monk Cuthbert), Ælfric complicates the traditionally universal scope of Christian discourse. We typically ascribe a drive toward similitude to Christianity, as it renders all believers—regardless of their particular secular affiliations—brothers in Christ. But by centering some of his homilies upon saints such as Gregory and Cuthbert, holy men whose popularity spanned the whole of England, Ælfric caters to what he imagines as a distinctly English audience, possessed of a particular language and unique tastes.

What might have led Ælfric to conceive of his homiletic series—and, as we shall see, his Gregory sermon—in such national terms? One immediate answer to the question of the monk's investment in English identity is suggested by the growing certainty among scholars that the tenth century witnessed the unification of the several tribal kingdoms on the island under one *Rex Anglorum*.[30] While not all historians agree on the degree to which a uniform administrative system had been achieved, most do concur that the concept of both *Engla Londe* as one kingdom and a single *gens Anglorum* was firmly established by the end of the tenth century.[31] Largely due to the successful efforts of King Edgar (943–75) in uniting Wessex, Mercia, and Northumbria, by Ælfric's time the idea of a united English community certainly had become more conceivable than it had ever been before.[32] Moreover, the character of the monastic reform movement that was occurring in England made it likely that monks such as Ælfric concerned themselves not only with the salvation of the English, but also with the political well-being of England. To a great extent, the mingling of religious and secular interests resulted from the fact that, unlike their continental counterparts, the reformers found crucial support from the West Saxon royal line. Edgar, in particular, by funding the work of the three prime movers of the revival (Æthelwold, Dunstan, and Oswald), enabled monastic life to resume in the many areas of the country united under his rule. The essential role played by the West Saxon dynasty in the revival obtains in the single most important document of the movement, the *Regularis Concordia*. In the preface to this version of the Benedictine Rule, the monks claim the royal family as their sole protectors; continental reformers, conversely, tended to cultivate ties with the papacy rather than local rulers.[33] As the reform grew successful, monks found themselves participating in secular affairs, mainly as a result of the appointment of monks to the episcopate. During the time Ælfric was writing his homilies, for example, thirteen of England's eighteen bishoprics were occupied by monks.[34]

As a member of the second wave of the movement, Ælfric inherited a sense that reformist monks such as himself had an interest in the political welfare of the realm.[35] But the confluence of the secular and the spiritual during the reform only partially explains Ælfric's English interests. While the idea of a united England had become increasingly important during the reform, by Ælfric's time a number of problems in England threatened its political identity. When Ælfric began writing his homilies, Æthelræd II, "the unready," had assumed Edgar's place upon the throne. The civil turmoil that marked the rule of this notoriously weak king, in addition to the recurrence of Viking invasions, threatened the religious and political unity of England in a manner that Edgar's reign had the luck to avoid. Civil attacks upon church property took place immediately after Edgar's death; and the resumption of invasions recalled the Viking attacks that had preceded the revival, invasions that had all but annihilated the church as an institutional authority in England.[36] The unsettling events of Æthelred's reign would have been perceived by monks like Ælfric as genuine threats to England's religious and political unity. As many scholars of nationalism have observed, it is precisely during those periods when a communal identity is at risk that images of a cohesive nation tend to emerge. The dangers posed to England by weak rule and Scandinavian invaders called for resolution.[37]

In the face of these problems, Ælfric did not assume an explicitly public role. Unlike those monks who moved into the worldly episcopal arena, he chose to remain out of the immediate gaze of the English people. Yet through his writings—works that he often wrote for the use of public authorities such as the Archbishop of Canterbury Sigeric and the nobleman Æthelmær—Ælfric did serve as an Anglo-Saxon intellectual. In an effort to demonstrate Ælfric's interest in the state of his nation, several scholars have noted instances in his texts when he alludes to political problems within England. M. R. Godden, for example, observes that certain moments in Ælfric's *Lives of Saints*— such as the monk's reference in his legend of Saint Alban to Absalon and Achitophel as examples of how "lord betrayers [hlaford-swican]" ultimately die—suggest how the monk used Old Testament history and hagiography as "parallels and precedents for the lay nobility and the clergy in the face of the troubles of his own time."[38] And Mary Clayton contends that Ælfric invokes the theme of divine retribution in his second homily for the Feast of a Confessor in order to address upheavals at Æthelred's court in 1005 and 1006.[39] While, as Godden notes, the *Catholic Homilies* "are remarkably free of reference to the current troubles," I would argue that the extent to which the *Homilies* constitutes a national "English" fantasy nevertheless offers us another important example of how the monk responded to his troubled times.[40] That is, such aspects of the homilies as their intended English audience and stress on "English" saints function as symbolic analogues to the allusions to the political and ethical state of the island offered in the sermons. During a period in which the English identity that had seemed close to realization only a generation before now appeared in jeopardy, Ælfric helped articulate the ideal of a coherent English people.

We can hardly ascertain the degree to which Ælfric's *Catholic Homilies* succeeded in instilling national feeling among a people troubled by dangers from within and without the region. The manuscript evidence, however, is compelling. Manuscript copies of the series circulated throughout England, from Canterbury to Exeter to Worcester and as far north as Durham.[41] That "widespread geographical dissemination" of Ælfric's sermons offers us provocative grounds for conjecture on whether the monk may have enabled, during this time of national insecurity, English feeling to circulate among the readers and auditors of his homilies.[42] At the very least, we can speculate that on some Sundays and holidays throughout the country the English laity heard in their native tongue the same sermon, one geared toward their English tastes. This scenario suggests how, in the public space of the minster, the English laity who heard Ælfric's *Catholic Homilies* may have experienced the kind of synchronic homogeneity we associate with a national consciousness—the sense of a solid community that, even as it partakes in a universal family of believers, is also distinguished from them by its vernacular language and its unique relationship to Christianity.[43]

## Strangers to Themselves

More than any other sermon in his homiletic series, Ælfric's Gregory homily could have developed in parishioners a national sensibility. Given his responsibility for the Canterbury mission, Gregory—whom Ælfric identifies as "the apostle to the English people [Engliscre þeode apostol]" and whom the *Old English Martyrology* calls nothing less than "our father [ure fæder]"—figured as one of the most beloved saints in Anglo-Saxon England.[44] Indeed, as Mechtild Gretsch puts it, at the time Ælfric wrote his homily on Gregory, "he was recording the vita of the saint who, apart from Christ's apostles, had enjoyed the longest and most universal veneration in Anglo-Saxon England."[45] Ælfric highlights Gregory's relationship to England in his sermon, which takes as its subject less Gregory's life than the story of his role in the English mission.[46] And within this homily on the origins of English Christianity, the slave-boy story performs a pivotal role. Rather than simply telling the story of a future pope's conversion of the English into a Christian brotherhood and the Anglo-Saxons' concomitant incorporation into a Christian empire, the homily produces the English as privileged missionary objects, whom Gregory fervently desires to convert. By offering the Anglo-Saxon auditors of the sermon an opportunity to gaze, with Gregory, upon their angelic and beautiful ancestors, the Gregory homily encourages the Anglo-Saxons to blend faith and love, and imagine themselves as belonging to a chosen people, whose worthiness for conversion inspires a long religious expedition.

That generation of English election hinges on the idea of English strangeness, a notion that emerges early—and in multifarious forms—in Ælfric's homily, which relates how Gregory saw (*geseah*) at the Forum

> between the wares slaves exposed (for sale); they were men white of body and beautiful of visage, and with noble hair. Gregory then beheld the beauty of the youths and asked from what country they were brought; then it was said to him that they were from England and that the people of that nation were as beautiful. Gregory then again asked whether the people of that country were Christians or heathens. They said to him that they were heathens.[47]

With his focus upon the unique aspects of the young men's bodies—their white skin, their noble hair, and their beautiful faces—Ælfric produces a specifically English corporeality, but within a Roman context. Displaced from their home—as Gregory himself puts it in a letter to the bishop of Alexandria—in a "corner of the world" to Rome, the boys figure in this story as "racial" others, whose strange yet beautiful white bodies attract Gregory.[48] As a land isolated from the *orbis terrarum,* England is a world frontier populated by an exotic people with whom a Roman such as Gregory understandably would be unfamiliar.

That foregrounding of English geographic isolation in the figure of the slave boys at Rome results in a highly complex national fantasy. Thanks to the double-edged nature of English otherworldliness, the strange English slave boys enable Ælfric not only to promote the notion of a chosen English people but also to engage with the challenges to that national ideal. The *hæðen* or pagan identity of the boys as well as their status as *cypecnihtas* or slaves suggests the barbarous distance of England from Christian civilization during the late sixth-century past to which the boys literally refer. The boys' heathenness would remind the Anglo-Saxons that for some one hundred and fifty years the Anglo-Saxons in England lay outside the boundaries of the Roman Christian world.[49] Geographic isolation is here of a piece with temporal disruption. By alerting the Anglo-Saxon auditors of the Gregory homily to the fact that they were not always Christian, the pagan boys acknowledge the uneven nature of Anglo-Saxon religious history.

That the boys are slaves in a sense underscores the Anglo-Saxons' pagan roots, insofar as the boys' literal enslavement refers to their spiritual "bondage" to Satan (as Gregory himself suggests later in the story), particularly given Ælfric's use of slavery as a metaphor for sin throughout his work.[50] Yet on a literal level as well, the boys' servitude points to a problematic discontinuity between present and past. During the time of the Augustinian mission to England, slavery typically resulted, as David Pelteret has shown, from the strife between the "congeries of chiefdoms and tribes" that defined early Anglo-Saxon life in England.[51] Insofar as the pagan slaves at the Forum suggest this common source of slavery in the past, then, they would recall for Ælfric's audience how they not only were once pagan but also lacked the political cohesiveness and social order achieved by the tenth century. The warring Anglo-Saxon kingdoms of the island during the sixth century rendered it a truly wild and violent world frontier.

Just as the heathen slave boys recall the unruly and impious beginnings of Anglo-Saxon history, they also point to contemporary problems that threatened to *return* late Anglo-Saxon England to its barbaric and war-torn origins. That is, even as Anglo-Saxon England had come far from its divided and heathen beginnings, the very image of an unstable and divided English margin of the world conjured by the slave boys still applied somewhat to Ælfric's period. For one thing, as the very need for a monastic revival suggests, paganism never lurked that far away for Christians in England. And the renewal of Viking attacks two years after Æthelred's accession only intensified the sense that it was still possible for England to constitute a disorderly world border. The murder of Archbishop Ælfeah of Canterbury at Greenwich in 1012 by a band of drunken pagan Danes offers just one example of the threats posed to Christianity by the Vikings during Ælfric's lifetime.[52]

At the same time that the youths symbolized the still tenuous status of Christianity on the island, so too did they figure the lingering problem of Anglo-Saxon slavery, which persisted throughout the eleventh century. The nature of slavery in the late Saxon period, however, had changed somewhat from the days of the Augustine mission. Anglo-Saxons still enslaved their fellows, though by Ælfric's time the practice resulted not from the capture of Anglo-Saxons during intra-tribal warfare but from the punitive enslavement of Anglo-Saxons for crime or debt. In addition, from the ninth century through Ælfric's own time, Anglo-Saxon slaves typically did not serve their fellow countrymen.[53] When Ælfric wrote his Gregory homily around 994, the second wave of Viking attacks had been occurring for over fifteen years, during which time the attackers resumed their practice of capture and enslavement.[54] Through their enslavement, the boys powerfully evoke the fragile state of Ælfric's Anglo-Saxon England, an isle whose coastal borders were vulnerable to infiltration by Scandinavian invaders eager to drain the island of its population.

Most interesting of all, perhaps, the boys' enslavement resonates with the probable fate of some of the Anglo-Saxon slaves captured by the Vikings. For just as the slave boys in the homily find themselves far from their home in England, so too did certain Anglo-Saxon slaves taken by the Danes end up in lands distant from England. The Vikings were notorious for their slave raiding and trading practices, which were incited largely by the demand for slaves in the Muslim east and southwest, where one of the greatest civilizations of the early Middle Ages thrived from the eighth to the eleventh centuries. Prompted by a desire initially for cheap labor for Baghdad and Samarra, and later for enormous quantities of men and women to staff the courts at such sites as Cordoba and Cairo, Islam created a need for slaves that the Vikings in tandem with other merchants actively met.[55] Once captured by the invaders, Anglo-Saxons were sold at international emporia such as Dublin or Hedeby and transported east (via either Gaul and Venice or the eastern rivers of Russia) and southwest (directly from the Atlantic).[56] Upon their arrival in Islam, Anglo-Saxon slaves worked in bondage alongside Turks, Slavs, Africans, and other European peoples.[57]

The enslavement of Anglo-Saxons to Moslems reinforces, on one hand, the power-lessness, vulnerability, and overall disenfranchisement of the English, and on the other hand, the tremendous power and economic influence of Islam. During its two-hun-dred-year heyday between the eighth and tenth centuries, after all, the Muslim empire had become "a gigantic economic unit . . . never before equaled in the history of the old world."[58] If we were to mark out upon the Cotton map that Islamic world, which spread from Asia to Africa and a considerable portion of western Europe, it would cover the vast majority of the *orbis terrarum* the early English map depicts. But just how aware were the Anglo-Saxons of the mighty Islamic civilization of the early Middle Ages and its employment of English slaves? To what extent could the auditors of the Gregory homily have viewed Gregory's Roman gaze as a metaphor for the Islamic gaze that un-doubtedly fell upon Anglo-Saxons caught by the Vikings? The Anglo-Saxons, of course, hardly knew of the extent and power of Islamic civilization with any precision, but they no doubt learned something about Islam through east-west communications resulting from trade and pilgrimage. Moreover, they may well have gained a general sense of the eastern and southwestern Moslem destinations of Viking captives due to such factors as the gradual integration of Danes into the English population from the beginning of the Viking raids, as well as the return of ransomed slaves to England. Through communi-cation with either former slavers or slaves, the Anglo-Saxons would at least have un-derstood that the eastern Islamic center of the world possessed a might that so outshone their western borderland that it assumed nothing less than a master-slave relationship to the English.

To the extent that the Anglo-Saxons were apprised of the slave trade, the image of the slave boys at the Forum would surely have served as a troubling suggestion of the equation between geographic alterity and ethnic disenfranchisement, whereby the Mus-lims viewed England as a distant land populated by exotic white *objects* available for pur-chase and use. In particular, the gorgeous physicality of the slaves—their beautiful hair, faces, and skin—may have suggested to the Anglo-Saxon consumers of the legend the sexual practices of the Muslim world in which enslaved Anglo-Saxons could have found themselves. By the tenth century, slaves no longer worked on building projects in Bagh-dad and other major cities in Islam but labored instead for the pleasure industry (harems, and their like) in such sites as Cordoba and Cairo.[59]

To be sure, the erotics of the slave-boy myth as well pointed to troubling sexual practices closer to home. Namely, the status of the boys as objects of visual pleasure for an older male recalls the sexual uses to which boys were put in the monastic setting in which Ælfric and other tellers of the tale such as Bede resided.[60] As the *Regularis Concordia,* Anglo-Saxon penitentials, and other documents confirm, oblates were sexually abused by monks in Anglo-Saxon England.[61] Monk-oblate love figures as yet another social practice that undermined any attempt to imagine a sovereign, unified, and pious England during Ælfric's lifetime. Indeed, by representing male-male desire in a context that also suggested Islam's pleasure industry, Ælfric's homily only intensified the disturbing national ramifications of monastic sodomy. By engaging in a deviant erotic act, Anglo-Saxon monks not only opposed the aims of the monastic reformers in England, but also rendered themselves tantamount to the Muslim other who put English boys into similar sexual service.

## White Angels on the Edge of the World

The notion of Angle slaves on the market in Rome, then, could have conjured up multiple forms of English disenfranchisement for the eleventh-century auditors of Ælfric's Gregory homily. Of course, the many challenges to English identity raised by the image of the slave boys comprise only one aspect of the legend. For even as Ælfric points to the more disconcerting ramifications of English alterity, he also overcomes them. For one thing, the *æðellice* or royal hairstyles of the boys point to an inherent nobility within the youths that mitigates their enslavement. But more than any other physical attribute of the boys, it is their white skin that enables the transcendence of the anxieties addressed by the legend. After discovering the heathen nature of the English, Gregory bemoans that spiritual affiliation with words that indicate both his attraction to and admiration of the boys' physical appearance: "Gregory then from inside (his) heart drew a long sigh, and said: 'Alas, that men of such a beautiful hue [fægeres híwes] are subjected to the black devil [sweartan deofle].'"[62] While Ælfric's earlier portrayal of the slaves as "men white of body and beautiful of visage, and of noble hair" conflates categories of "race," aesthetics, and social station, the boys' whiteness emerges as their pre-eminent attribute in Gregory's lament. In certain respects, Ælfric's notably racialist characterization of the slave boys provides us with a unique opportunity to analyze whiteness as an ethnic category. As Richard Dyer points out, analyzing whiteness in modern culture is made difficult "partly because white power secures its dominance by seeming not to be anything in particular," but rather what is universal, normal, and ordinary.[63] But while whiteness proves so quotidian as to be invisible in contemporary culture, Ælfric's version of the Anglo-Saxon legend renders whiteness legible by making it a physiognomic characteristic bound up with the boys' identity as barbaric foreigners from the English border of the world. Thus, as Frantzen points out, Gregory's "admiration suggests that he prefers their unfamiliar appearance . . . to that of his own people"; the fair-skinned Englishman becomes visible in this national myth as more aesthetically pleasing than the swarthy Roman.[64] Furthermore, Gregory's dismay at the thought of white Englishmen morally "enslaved" to a black devil suggests a racist distaste for the literal enslavement of pale Anglo-Saxons by darker-skinned Arab masters. The racial form that Gregory's concern for the boys' souls assumes points to Anglo-Saxon anxiety over the reality of disenfranchised white males in the early Middle Ages, when Arabic power dominated.

Yet the very white skin that points to literal and spiritual modes of white English enslavement also proclaims the propriety of the English's membership in the Christian brotherhood. By having the slaves' whiteness inspire Gregory to assert the impropriety of their pagan identity, Ælfric implies that, as a result of their "hiwe" or skin color, these boys are meant to be Christian.[65] Ælfric thus makes a "racial" claim for the transparency of appearances. By having Gregory lament the impropriety of a black devil having white men in his service, Ælfric suggests that the slaves' white complexions must refer to something Christian inside these boys that undercuts their present subjection to a demon whose evil nature is bound up with his dark color. This type of racial discourse circulates throughout the monk's sermon series. His homily on the passion of Bartholomew offers detailed portrayals of both the physical appearance of the apostle, a man "white of body [hwit on lichaman]" and that of the devil Berith, whom he describes as an "immense Ethiopian [ormæte Silhearwa]."[66] And in his Benedict homily, Ælfric portrays the abbot preventing a devil in the form of a "black child [blacan cildes]" from further tormenting a monk.[67] In these moments, the monk makes the issue of one's spiritual status a matter of both one's skin color, and—as the depiction of white Angle slaves and the demonic Ethiopian makes clear—one's ethnic identity.

While an explicit and fully formulated notion of "race" would not emerge in the West until the Enlightenment, Ælfric's rhetoric well demonstrates how prejudices based upon fantasies of physiognomic differences such as skin color extend back into earlier periods.[68] Of course, Ælfric was far from alone in his racial formulation of Christian identity. What makes the naturalization of whiteness especially insidious in western society, as Dyer points out, is its long-term association with extra-ethnic notions such as "the Judeo-Christian use of white and black to symbolize good and evil."[69] The Christian association of blackness and evil emerges clearly in the Old English literary corpus, where, for example, hell is the "blackest of lands [landa sweartost]" in *Genesis B*, *Juliana* alludes to "black sin [sweart syn]," and the life of Saint Margaret represents the devil as a "black and ugly [sweart and unfæger]" man.[70] And along similar lines, as David Pelteret has pointed out, Old English Riddle § 12 contrasts the "black Welsh [swearte Wealas]" with *sellan* or better men who implicitly function in the riddle as (white) Anglo-Saxons.[71]

Yet Ælfric is unique in deploying a racialist denigration of blackness and celebration of whiteness in the context of the Gregory/slave story. While Bede and Paul qualify the value of physical appearances by depicting Gregory acknowledging a discrepancy between the boys' beautiful outer and impoverished inner states, Ælfric never shores up this possibility. In the *Ecclesiastical History*, for example, Gregory regrets that "minds devoid of inward grace should bear so graceful an outward form."[72] Paul's version nearly mirrors that of Bede, diverging only in its description of the difference between outer and inner as a matter of beauty, not grace.[73] Including in their texts Gregory's further lament that the boys' beautiful and graceful bodies do not house beautiful or grace-filled souls, Bede and Paul mitigate the value of external appearances. Ælfric, however, makes no mention of the boys' lack of grace and represents instead the racial fantasy that body color may be trusted. Unlike earlier tellers of the legend, Ælfric implies that due to their appearance, the youths must also possess the inner purity to which their whiteness should refer.[74]

Through this fetishization of whiteness Ælfric overcomes the problem of the slaves' spiritual and "racial" otherness, as well as that of monk-oblate love. By repressing the possibility that white signs may not reflect Christian souls, Ælfric resolves the problem of historical rupture that the legend raises: despite their pagan origins, the Anglo-Saxons possess a holy whiteness that renders them "always already" Christian. Moreover, by making that holy whiteness the primary physical characteristic that attracts Gregory, Ælfric makes the boys safe to love: the beautiful young male bodies that could lead to sin among Anglo-Saxon monks instead do quite the opposite: enable the spiritual election of the English themselves. Poststructuralist thinking on "race" has taught us, of course, that Ælfric's association of an essential, white, and Christian identity with the English is, like all notions of racial identity, a fantasmatic construction. To cite Henry Louis Gates Jr., whiteness, like "blackness[,] exists, but 'only' as a function of its signifiers"; or, as Dyer puts it, "only non-whiteness can give whiteness any substance."[75] The indeterminacy of these white signifying slaves is demonstrated by the fact that the value of the boys' white bodies emerges only in relation to another signifier—the black body of the devil. That Ælfric needs to conjure up the image of blackness in order to claim the transparency of whiteness indicates what Augustine would call the conventional or arbitrary nature of both signs, rather than their participation in a universal system of meanings.[76]

The logic of this "racial" fantasy continues in the next—and most retold—aspect of the legend, quoted here in its entirety:

> Again he asked what was the name of the people from which they came. He was answered that they were named "Angle"; then said he, "rightly are they called 'Angle,' because they have the beauty of angels and it is befitting for such men that they should be companions of angels in heaven." Again then Gregory asked what the name of the shire was from which the youths were taken. He was answered that the shire-men were called "Deira." Gregory answered, "well are they called 'Deira,' because they are saved from the wrath and called to the mildheartedness of Christ." Again he asked, "what is the king of their country called?" He was answered that the king was called "Ælle." Lo, then Gregory played with his words at that name, and said, "it is befitting that 'alleluia' be sung in that land, in praise of the almighty creator."[77]

Before beginning close analysis of Gregory's puns, we should note the boys' synecdochic role. While the slaves are literally Anglians and subjects of Ælle, the first historical king of English Deira, they stand in for the whole of Anglo-Saxon England. For in the Gregory homily, the pope sends Augustine to convert not just the Anglians, but all the people of "Engla lande."[78] Later versions of the legend (such as those found in Layamon's *Brut* and the *South English Legendary*) drop the puns on Deire and Ælle and hence render the boys generically English. Why would Ælfric choose to retain the boys' Northumbrian identity? Unlike the legend's earlier tellers such as Bede or the Whitby writer, Ælfric bore no particular affiliation with Northumbria. Indeed, no participant in the Benedictine revival could have, since the reform failed to reach the north. However we might speculate that Ælfric keeps the boys' Deirian identification precisely because of the problematic positioning of the north in the tenth century. The synecdochic role of Deira as a sign of the whole of England in the slave-boy homily, that is, imaginatively resolves the separation of Northumbria from England during Ælfric's lifetime. By representing both Gregory's Christian interpretation of the Anglian boys and his inadvertent union of these pagans with the rest of England, the homily symbolically accomplishes what the tenth-century reformers could not—the conversion and incorporation of a region "regressive" in its resistance to the institutional Anglo-Saxon church.[79] Moreover, through the pun on Ælle and Allejuia, a region set apart from Ælfric's reformist England becomes enabling in the slave-boy tale, by contributing to the sense that the English margin of the world is special.

Along with the visual pleasures enabled by the white bodies of the boys, the names of the slaves' erstwhile nation, tribal-kingdom, and king enable several linguistic pleasures, as Gregory puns on "Angle," "Dere," and "Ælle." And this ostensibly foreign vocabulary list fuels a series of philological misrecognitions quite like the fantasy of transcending whiteness articulated by Gregory earlier. His ingenious puns suggest how the strange words referring to the youths' particular national, tribal, and secular affiliations also point to the slaves' Christian destiny. Like their white bodies, the Angle slaves' original allegiance to Ælle of Deira fantastically partakes in a Latinate Christian signifying system. The legend thus at once singles out the English for their unique vernacular language and legitimizes that native tongue, by asserting its inherently sacred character. Small wonder, then, that the slave-boy story may have played a central role in the imagining of a shared English language. Peter Clemoes has suggested that the legend served as a "set text" for teaching the vernacular.[80] While Clemoes is speculating here, the slave-boy story certainly would have offered Anglo-Saxon teachers such as the grammarian Ælfric a powerful pedagogic and ideological tool, as it would have at once helped train students in English and helped authorize the very spread of vernacular "literacy." Gregory's puns suggest that writing and speaking in English, far from constituting a turn to an illicit and pagan mode of communication, signal instead the use of a language as legitimate and holy as Latin.

Crucially, the puns do not merely figuratively integrate these specimens of Englishness into a universal community of Christians; rather, through those ingenious translations, Ælfric bestows upon the English a privileged relation to Christianity as a result of their ethnic identity. The first pun is most instructive here: claiming that the slave boys' status as "Angles" suggests that they are also "Angels," Ælfric links the youths with a category of Christian identity that distinguishes them—and, more generally, the English—from the ordinary ranks of Christian men. As Ælfric himself puts it in his homily on creation, angels are both *swiðe strange* or very strange and "closer to God than men."[81] Insofar as the boys' angelic identity inscribes a kind of difference upon the Anglo-Saxons, it returns us to the issue of geographic alterity. As Massimo Cacciari writes, "the dimension of the Angel is ou-topic. Its place is a Land-of-nowhere."[82] In the same manner in which the angels inhabit a *mundus imaginalis* or "nowhere" distinct from the physical world, the cherubic youths before Gregory hail from another kind of "nowhere," the *alter orbis* of England. Thus, unlike their enslavement and heathen status, the boys' affinity with the angels points to the empowering aspects of geographic difference. Like the aristocratic identity suggested by their aristocratic coifs, the boys' cherubic qualities demonstrate how even as alterity proves fearsome in the slave-boy story, difference also elevates the Anglo-Saxons. While from one perspective isolated England is a wild and barbaric world frontier, from another perspective the isolated island constitutes a holy and singular otherworld, a land of men akin to the *æþelduguð* or noble host of angels described in Cynewulf's *Christ*.[83]

The pun on Angle and angel also intersects with the boys' white bodies. Christian thought, of course, imagines angels as bodiless, as Ælfric himself points out when he writes in his creation sermon that the nine hosts of angels made by God "have no body but are all spirit." Yet the Anglo-Saxons, like other members of the faithful, nevertheless ascribed form to angels. Indeed, immediately after he describes them as all spirit or *ealle gastas,* Ælfric goes on to tell us that the angels are "beautiful, formed with great fairness."[84] Ælfric's use of the noun "fægernes" to describe the angels hints at their conception along white Anglo-Saxon lines, as does Cynewulf's *Christ,* which describes the angelic host present at the Last Judgment as "white and heavenly bright [hwit ond heofonbeorht]."[85] Perhaps the clearest indicator of a racialist angelology at work in Anglo-Saxon Christian culture emerges in the full-color images of angels on Anglo-Saxon manuscripts. Angels with blonde tresses, for example, appear both in the crucifixion miniature that adorns the Durham gospels and in the pictorial frontispiece of the New Minster charter.[86] Moreover, in the illustration of the fall of Lucifer and the evil angels in the Old English illustrated Hexateuch, we find a striking analogue to Gregory's construction of white angelic Anglians and a black devil. The upper half of the image centers around God in a mandorla surrounded by angels, all of whom have wavy blond hair, while the lower portion of the illustration portrays a black-haired Lucifer surrounded by black-haired fallen angels in hell.[87] That contrast between "angels and devils . . . white and black" obtains as well in Cynewulf's portrayal of the Last Judgment.[88] These and other portrayals of embodied and fair-haired angels in Anglo-Saxon illustrated manuscripts render explicit Ælfric's implicitly racialized linkage of Anglo-Saxon whiteness not merely with Christian virtue but also with a sublime and angelic identity.

By disengaging "Angle" from its vernacular referent and attaching it to the image of an angel, Gregory asserts the supremacy of this Christian meaning. But in imagining Gregory doing so, Ælfric also raises the question of the vulnerability of these national signs to other refigurations. What may seem, from one point of view, to secure the English vernacular within a master Latin signifying system may also appear as an indicator of linguistic instability from another perspective—whether that of a twenty-first-century poststructuralist, or that of a tenth-century reader of the Old English riddles and wisdom poetry that circulated during Ælfric's time. That is, the very pun-work that legitimates the vernacular, and transforms the barbaric and marginal English into white angels on the edge of the world, also foregrounds the misrecognitions that undermine such resignifications. For what makes a pun work, but its display of its own founding on misrecognition? What troubles this fantastic inclusion of the slaves in a Christian semiotic system is its very representation of Gregory playfully displaying the vulnerability of all signs to appropriation. In the same way that the Old English riddles delight in the capacity of signs to mislead, to mean doubly, so do Gregory's puns.[89]

To be sure, Ælfric does his best to assure his readers of the authoritativeness of Gregory's readings. Indeed, more than any of his sources, Ælfric concerns himself as much with generating his audience's faith in this anecdote as with bolstering their Christian belief. For one thing, unlike Bede and his vernacular translator, Ælfric presents the episode not as a product of tradition, but as an actual event arising out of Gregory's everyday life.[90] Moreover, Ælfric formally situates the encounter within the larger English plot of the homily so as to render it *the* decisive event in England's Christian conversion.[91] Coupled with his efforts at giving the legend a crucial place in England's Christian history are the pains Ælfric takes to establish Gregory's credentials as a master reader. Through devices that range from his assertion that the Greek name "Gregory" means in Latin "Vigilantius," and "in English, watchful [wacolre],"[92] to his emphasis upon Gregory's reputation in Rome as an unsurpassed intellectual, Ælfric includes (from Paul the Deacon) lines attributing superlative perceptual powers to the pope.[93] Moreover, unlike all of his sources, Ælfric carefully underscores the role of Gregory's gaze in the episode itself. In Ælfric's homily, Gregory travels in the marketplace as a spectator—"Gregory went along the street to the English men, *looking* [*sceawigende*] at their things," while his sources indicate that Gregory merely went to the Forum.[94]

Through these and other references to Gregory's matchless intelligence and discriminating gaze, Ælfric strives to deem conclusive those meanings that the Roman monk ascribes to the boys' bodies and their native language.[95] Writing, as we have seen, during a time when "Christian England" was threatened from within and without, Ælfric produces Gregory's authoritative gaze as a means of naturalizing English Christianity. By the end of the Gregory homily, this strategy becomes even clearer, when Ælfric contends that the bishoprics established by Augustine of Canterbury throughout England "have continued to prosper in God's faith to the present day."[96] Blatantly occluding the real discontinuous history of organized Christian religion in England, Ælfric offers the Anglo-Saxons a means of imagining themselves as inevitably belonging to a collective and special Christian English past.

By representing Gregory in the act of generating universal meanings for the boys' bodies and their native language, Ælfric's version of the slave-boy legend constitutes a scene of reading. As such, the narrative inadvertently displays how the meaning of Englishness is not universal, but the product of interpretation—and thus always ideological and open to contestation. Yet I also want to emphasize that, as in any powerful and enduring national fantasy, there is "something more" to the slave-boy story that exceeds its symbolic character. That is, despite their construction as "always already" Christian, a supplement of the strange and pagan pleasures embodied in these beautiful boys remains. Although Ælfric's English fantasy displays, through a Roman medium, the interpretative overcoming of the spiritual, "racial," and ethnic alterity of some Angle boys, its initial representation of that very otherness never quite disappears. Even as the legend seeks to rewrite Anglo-Saxon history in the familiar image of Christianity, it memorializes Anglo difference.

## Coda

Seven centuries after Ælfric wrote his *Catholic Homilies,* this lingering alterity within the Gregory sermon would be taken up in earnest by another writer. I refer here to a text produced during a time marked not by Scandinavian aggression but by British imperial ambition, a period when the English were not enslaved, but enslaving others: Elizabeth Elstob's 1709 edition and translation of Ælfric's Gregory homily.[97] Elstob, whose Anglo-Saxon scholarship reflects the vogue in Anglo-Saxon studies that developed after the Reformation and waned in the early eighteenth century, makes a number of legitimizing claims for her edition in the preface to her text; for our purposes, by far the most interesting of Elstob's claims is her perception of Gregory as an exemplary missionary leader in a colonial world:

> His affection was exceedingly remarkable in his buying up English Slaves, and disposing of them in Monasteries, to be train'd up in the Christian Faith for the future Service of their Country. A Zeal fit to be consider'd and imitated by those who are concern'd in the Plantations, who have doubtless a Power of turning many Souls to God, and of rescuing them from that Slavery, under which they are held by the Prince of Darkness; to which I wish the remembrance of our own Conversion to Christianity, may prove an early incitement.[98]

Because Elstob dedicated her edition to Anne, a queen sympathetic to the missionary cause, her emphasis on Gregory's exemplary missionary status is not surprising. What is more remarkable, however, is her implicit homology between the spiritual enslavement of the slaves in the British colonies and that of the Anglo-Saxons before Augustine's mission. Against those supporters of the missions who yoke conversion with conquest, asking colonists if it can "seem an indifferent Thing, a *small Matter*" whether a potentially "mighty *English* Empire" is Christian or not, Elstob troubles English imperial identity, reminding her readers they too were once enslaved Others.

To strengthen her comparison and further enable colonial empathy for slaves of color, Elstob echoes Gregory's lament over the Angle slaves' subjection to "the Prince of Darkness" in the legend itself. Elstob is here deliberately misreading Ælfric's text, in which, as we have seen, Gregory refers to a "sweart deofol" and not the "ðeostra aldor" referred to in his sources.[99] Elstob must engage in such resignifications, of course, because the "racial" fantasies inherent in Ælfric's phrase would work against her missionary argument. Yet her deployment of Ælfric's text points to something circulating in the legend that works against its "racial" and nationalist tendencies. For although Elstob's stance on colonialism is far from liberating, she does, radically, suggest an alterity within the English that would potentially upset English claims for imperial dominance and privilege. That the story of Gregory's encounter with the Angle boys could be marshaled in such an effort is noteworthy, and makes clear how, even as a narcissistic drive to overcome difference enables one reading of this "school boy's tale," the pleasure of the strange remains.

# CHAPTER TWO

# GERALD DE BARRI AND THE GEOGRAPHY OF IRELAND'S CONQUEST

We know of only one English world map that emerged during Ælfric's lifetime, the Cotton map. Indeed, that Anglo-Saxon mappa mundi constitutes the sole sign not only of world cartography, but also of any English mapmaking whatsoever after the notably active phase of the seventh and eighth centuries.[1] That apparent period of cartographic stagnation would cease by the twelfth century, when the state of English mapmaking drastically altered.[2] We know of at least a dozen maps from that century, many which were detailed mappae mundi. These include both extant maps such as the Duchy of Cornwall fragment (ca. 1150–1220), the late twelfth- or early thirteenth-century Sawley map (fig. 11), and the Vercelli map (ca. 1200); and lost maps such as the world map given to Durham Cathedral Priory in 1195 by Bishop Hugh le Puiset, and the mappa mundi that the man scholars know now as Gerald de Barri (ca. 1146–ca. 1223) claims Hugh of Leicester gave Lincoln Cathedral in 1150.[3] In the following century even more world maps would emerge, maps that range in size from the tiny Psalter map (ca. 1225–50; figs. 12–13) to the colossal Hereford map (ca. 1290; fig. 5).[4] Rendering this high medieval outpouring of English maps particularly noteworthy are two factors. First, many of these maps form one interconnected group.[5] Second, these maps represent the very apogee of medieval world cartography; at no other time and in no other place in the premodern West do we witness anything approaching the world maps created in high medieval England, in terms of both quantity and quality. It was, in other words, the island deemed to be beyond the world that most often made images of that world during the Middle Ages.

**Fig. 11.** Sawley world map, late twelfth or early thirteenth century. Cambridge, Corpus Christi College MS. 66, p. 2. By permission of the Master and Fellows of Corpus Christi College, Cambridge.

**Fig. 12.** Psalter world map, thirteenth century. London, British Library, Additional MS. 28681, fol. 9r. By permission of the British Library.

**Fig. 13.** Drawn facsimile of the Psalter world map. Taken from Konrad Miller, *Mappaemundi: Die ältesten Weltkarten,* vol. 3 (Stuttgart: J. Roth, 1895–98), tab. III.

## National and International

Why did England come to occupy such an outstanding position in medieval world cartography during the twelfth and thirteenth centuries? In part, the English's leading role in world mapmaking reflects how England had become, as Robert Bartlett ventures, "more closely enmeshed with the European and Mediterranean world in this period than it had been at any time since the days of the Roman Empire."[6] It was in this period that England was governed by the family of the counts of Anjou, rulers possessed of territories that made England part of what scholars now refer to as an "Angevin Empire" that extended into France and beyond.[7] Of course, not only their aristocratic rulers but also their Christian identity bound the English to the world; the Latin learning of the church and its system of patronage as well as religious-inspired activities such as crusade and pilgrimage brought England into contact with the whole of the Latin West. These secular and religious influences, as well as related factors such as trade and warfare, all fostered what we can with some accuracy call cosmopolitanism on the part of the English and other western intellectuals. Elizabeth Salter's assertion that during the twelfth century cities such as "Paris, Chartres and Canterbury, Palermo and Catania were points on a map which had no need to concern itself with national boundaries" certainly satisfies the classical definition of the cosmopolitan as *kosmos* and *polis,* that is, world city.[8] Thus both of the probable areas in which Richard de Bello appears to have fashioned the world map ascribed to him, Herefordshire and Lincolnshire, served as, in M. T. Clanchy's words, "meeting places of languages (Welsh, English, French, and Latin) and of cultures (Celtic, Anglo-Saxon, Anglo-Norman, and cosmopolitan)."[9] English cosmopolitans were not always confined to their homeland but inhabited what seems to have appeared as "a completely open western world," as the epitaph of Richard Palmer ("England bore me, France schooled me, Sicily cherished me") demonstrates.[10] We witness such mobility in the career of the purported creator of the Ebstorf world map, Gervase of Tilbury (ca. 1160–1235), an English-bred man who was educated in Bologna, and whose service to William of the White Hands, William of Sicily, and Otto IV took him to Rheims, Palermo, Rome, Arles, and Brunswick.[11] While serving as a provost for an abbey in Germany, Gervase authored or commissioned the world map linked to him. The lives and works of Gervase, Richard, and other English intellectuals go far in supporting Salter's claim "that the fullest sense of English culture during the twelfth century must be conveyed by the phrase 'international exchange.'"[12]

Those intellectuals' access to internationalism both within and without their homeland helps account for the global perspective of medieval English cartography. But the English mappae mundi of the twelfth and the thirteenth centuries were not simply cosmopolitan or universal in character. Far from suggesting a universalism transcending local, regional, and national distinctions, those geographic documents reveal a variety of attachments to particular sites, including England. Distinguished by its location apart from the *oikoumené* in the world Ocean, what these maps variously identify as *Anglia, Albion,* or *Britannia* stands out in terms of its size and in-depth rendering. In the Hereford map, in particular, the topographic detail, large landmass, and global geographic marginality allotted England prevent the island from figuring as just another region of the known world (fig. 14).

We can partly explain these maps' emphasis on Britain by looking at medieval cartographers' early sources. Pliny the Elder, for example, singles Britain out in book four of his *Natural History* as "famous in the Greek records and in our own."[13] And Isidore highlights Britain as a site sundered from the entire world, an *insula interfuso mari toto orbe divisa.*[14] While they do not always go as far as Solinus does in singling out Britain as an other world, these and other writers such as Orosius and Bede give Britain a privileged placement at the start of their descriptions of islands.[15] The stress placed on England in mappae mundi, then, simply may be something that English cartographers

Fig. 14. The British Isles on the Hereford world map, ca. 1290. Hereford Cathedral. By permission of The Dean and Chapter of Hereford and the Hereford Mappa Mundi Trust.

straightforwardly adopted from their sources. Yet if we turn to the writings of high medieval English intellectuals, we find that their traditional geographic identity was something the English did not unthinkingly adopt but instead consciously manipulated. England's global isolation, for example, proves crucial to the national aims of William of Malmesbury's *History of the Kings of England* (1125). Reflecting how, as Adrian Hastings puts it, the post-Conquest Normans came to depend "less on domination than upon assimilation" for their survival, William's chronicle fosters notions of English unity.[16] In part, that national aim emerges in William's emphasis on continuities between the Norman present and Anglo-Saxon past; in other words, like Henry of Huntingdon's *History of the English People* (1154) or Geoffrey Gaimar's *History of the English People* (1140), William's text is written for the ruling elite but fashioned specifically as an

English history.[17] Coupled with this production of temporal cohesion in William's chronicle is a more spatial idea of national unity. As Robert Stein has pointed out, William combines English geographic otherworldliness with a sense of sacred cohesiveness that overcomes the fraught nature of sociopolitical life after the conquest.[18] For example, according to William, heavenly concern over the faith of a nation situated almost beyond the world (*natio pene extra orbem posita*) leads to a disproportionate number of uncorrupted bodies of dead saints on the island matched "nowhere else on earth."[19] Shoring up the unique geography that unites the otherwise disparate inhabitants of an island located "at the ends of the earth" (124–25), William produces England as a land set apart and over other Christian spaces. Robert the Englishman, with the help of Geoffrey of Monmouth, would offer a different version of William's elevation of the British otherworld in his commentary on Sacrobosco. Opposing those who think that because "almost all England is outside a clime" the island must be unfit for habitation, Robert expounds upon the "unfailing fertility" of England and cites the goddess Diana's praise of Britain to its mythic settler, Brutus.[20]

The writings of William of Malmesbury and Robert the Englishman support what critics such as Salter, Clanchy, and Susan Reynolds have argued: that the internationalism of the High Middle Ages did not eliminate national impulses.[21] More specifically, the two writers provide a helpful gloss on mappae mundi, suggesting how their stress on England is not merely a holdover from the ancients, but instead comprises part of a contemporary enlistment of geography to celebrate England. On one hand, as artifacts offering a global geographic perspective, the maps register an English appreciation of the cosmopolitan, a desire to be a part of an international sociopolitical order. As "Angevin" imperialists, the English looked beyond their insular boundaries toward a world they sought to blend with and even dominate. On the other hand, as artifacts highlighting England's isolation from the world, mappae mundi point to an investment in national belonging, a desire to bind the English not to the world but to each other. At the same time that the English turned outward to the world, they also turned inward, toward themselves and the geographic remoteness that seemed to unite and even elevate them above other peoples. The great world maps of high medieval England bear witness to assimilationist drives that are at once national and international.

But what of other isolated European communities? The English held no monopoly on geographic marginality in the West. As Solinus notes, Britain is "environed with many Iles, and those not unrenowned."[22] For instance, the Orcades (Orkneys) appear just beyond *Britannia Insula* in the Sawley map and the Hereford map. The latter document's North Atlantic is dotted with many more islands such as: Man (the Isle of Man); *Insula Avium* and *Insula Arietum* (the legendary islands of birds and sheep described in Saint Brendan tales); *Ysland* (Iceland); and *Fareie* (the Faroes). And the island virtually synonymous with "land's end," "Ultima Tile" or Thule appears north of Iceland on the Hereford map.[23] Most prominent among Britain's insular neighbors, however, was Ireland. Not only, as Bede writes, "the largest island of all next to Britain [insula omnium post Brittaniam maxima]" (18–19), Ireland is also, in Orosius's words, *propior* or quite close to Britain.[24] Owing to its size and proximity to England, Ireland stood as a kind of geographic double to its eastern neighbor. The resemblance between Ireland and Britain, of course, only extends so far. Above all, because, as Pliny notes, Ireland "lies beyond [super eam]" Britain, that island exceeded its eastern neighbor in terms of its geographic remoteness.[25] Thus in the Psalter, Hereford, and Sawley maps, *Anglia* or *Britannia* is nestled in a huge bay-like inlet of the ocean carved into northwestern Europe. Ireland, however, appears directly in the watery border of the world, a location making it clearly the more distant of the two islands.

In this chapter, I analyze the books and maps of Gerald de Barri to demonstrate what the high medieval English made of the heightened isolation of their Irish neighbors. Gerald wrote two books on Ireland: the *Topography of Ireland* (first recension ca. 1187), a description of the Irish, their land, and their history; and the *Conquest of Ireland* (first recension 1189), an account of Ireland's English conquest.[26] By the time he began writing his Irish books, Gerald was a well-traveled cosmopolitan, whose education had taken him repeatedly to Paris.[27] During that period Gerald had also entered royal service at Henry II's request and, as Bartlett points out, explicitly sought the favor of English kings "by praising them in his writings and dedicating his works to them."[28] Gerald's Irish books clearly show how he was "a spokesman for the English point of view."[29] Taken together, the *Topography* and *Conquest* render Gerald the prime apologist of the invasion of Ireland and, moreover, a writer who inaugurated conceptions of Irishness that would inform English discourses well after the Middle Ages.

Those imperial projects reveal Gerald's strong geographic inclinations, as the writer included descriptions of places in his Irish books and even included in those texts maps, one of which descends from mappae mundi.[30] Most important, for our purposes, Gerald devoted special attention to issues of geographic remoteness in his works on Ireland. The *Topography*, for example, begins with Gerald asserting that his book on Ireland describes "what nature has hidden in the western and extreme limit of the earth, for beyond those limits there is no land, nor is there any habitation either of men or beasts—but beyond the whole horizon only the ocean flows and is borne on in boundless space through its unsearchable and hidden ways."[31] That stress in the preface of the *Topography* upon Irish isolation introduces a geographic issue that informs the entirety of both the *Topography* and the *Conquest*. No English-identified writer offers us a better gauge of English attitudes toward the extreme Irish margin of the world than Gerald de Barri.

I argue that Gerald's Irish books demonstrate how, while twelfth-century writers could hail England for its sublime isolation, the high medieval embrace of geographic marginality foundered on the heightened remoteness of Ireland. In other words, insofar as the English imagined that they were set apart from the world because they were a chosen people, the Irish, with their more extreme geographic marginality were potentially possessed of an even greater degree of spiritual election. The traditional status of Ireland as a "holy island" from which hailed a multitude of evangelizing saints suggested as much. Repressing such sacred implications of Irish isolation, Gerald de Barri instead lays stress upon the links between remoteness and barbarism. Too far from the cosmopolitan centers of the world, incapable of crossing beyond their own personal boundaries to create a civic society, the Irish of the *Topography* and the *Conquest* are possessed of a savagery that corrupts their pristine homeland and licenses their conquest and colonization by the English. Repressing the geographic isolation of England, Gerald endows the English with a civilizing centricity the wild Irish lack. Gerald's Irish books thus evince how English writers used the marginality of Ireland as a means of suppressing their own geographic isolation and urging their crucial place within the international Christian community. If not for Ireland, in other words, the marginality of the English would be absolute and hence insurmountable.

The implications of Gerald's project for an expansionist construction of English identity are considerable. Gerald's colonial logic not only positions Ireland as periphery to England's metropole, it also reorients England's relationship to that most renowned and powerful of world centers, Rome. That strategy is epitomized in the map of western Europe Gerald created to illustrate his Irish books. In the final section of this chapter, I analyze this map to demonstrate how Gerald uses the conquest of the Irish as a means of imagining the English as alternately allied with, comparable, and even superior to the Romans. In other words, by seizing upon the relatively greater remoteness of England's Irish neighbors, Gerald imagines the English sharing centrality with Rome, and achieving the "westering" of empire famously attached to the ancient capital. Gerald's Irish projects thus reveal how geographic fictions of English identity during the twelfth century emerged in large part through vexed relations to both the eternal city and the island of saints.

## Irish Angels on the Edge of the World

There is evidence that the Irish did, like the English, locate in their remoteness grounds for national exaltation. A Gaelic life of Saint Patrick, for example, compares Ireland to an equally marginal earthly paradise.[32] The question, however, of how the Irish put their own geographic isolation to national uses is a topic for another book. What matters for this investigation is how sensitive the high medieval English were to the sublime potential of their Irish neighbors. Largely due to the legacy of Bede (ca. 672–735), English intellectuals were inescapably aware of how the Irish could be seen as possessors of a privileged geographic isolation. An English writer who devoted special attention to the Irish in his *Ecclesiastical History* (731), Bede was a monumental figure in English intellectual life during the period of Ireland's English conquest. As Antonia Gransden puts it, the twelfth century "was the great age of copying for the *Ecclesiastical History* and also the age that, more seriously than any other book, took its text as a programme for action."[33] Gerald de Barri thus makes explicit reference to Bede's text in the opening pages of his *Topography,* as does William of Malmesbury, who describes Bede in the first sentence of his *History of the Kings of England,* as a *uir maxime doctus* or most learned man (14–15). Due both to his profound impact on later historians and cartographers, and to the special consideration he gives the Irish, Bede's work must serve as the starting point for any discussion of high medieval English notions of Irishness.

Bede not surprisingly ascribes geographic importance to Britain in the *Ecclesiastical History,* which begins with a lengthy *descriptio* of the island. But this introductory description of Britain segues to that of the island *ad occidentem* or to the west of Britain—a still more remote place whose inhabitants enjoy more temperate weather, greater ethnic uniformity, and broader political freedom than their eastern neighbors. In terms of climate, Ireland figures as a demi-paradise that abounds in milk and honey. Western counterparts to the Hyperboreans of classical lore, a people who "enjoy . . . perfect conditions" in their home at the northernmost edge of the earth, Bede's Irish "inhabit a 'pocket' of climatic tranquility" in their uttermost corner of the world.[34] Possessed of a "healthier and . . . a much milder climate" than Britain, Ireland is devoid even of snakes and serpents.[35] The purity of the Irish for Bede extends beyond their lack of reptiles to their ethnic homogeneity. While the first inhabitants of Britain include the tribes of the Britons, the Picts, and the Irish, early Ireland hosts only the tribe after which the island is named. The relative diversity of Britain's inhabitants only intensifies over the course of Bede's text, as it narrates the arrival of the conquering Romans and then, later, the Anglo-Saxons on the island. Heightened geographic distance, it appears, keeps Bede's Irish protected from the foreign immigrations and conquests to which the Britons are subject.

This is not to say that Bede always considers the geographic exceptionalism of Ireland in a favorable light. Indeed, many of his most overt references to Irish isolation appear when he is criticizing the Irish for diverging from certain aspects of Roman Christian practice and, in particular, the Roman dating of Easter.[36] The chronicler thus commends a letter to the Irish from Pope Honorius "urging them with much shrewdness not to consider themselves, few as they were and placed on the extreme boundaries of the world, wiser than the ancient and modern Churches of Christ scattered throughout the earth; nor should they celebrate a different Easter."[37] Bede applauds Honorius for his rhetoric of might makes right, whereby the pope "with much shrewdness" suggests how its tremendous size and geographic expanse authorizes the beliefs of the Roman church, while *their* geographic isolation and small numbers undercut the doctrinal opinions of Irish clerics.[38] But elsewhere Bede uses geographic isolation not to censure but to excuse the dating of Easter by the Irish, writing that because the Irish were "so far away at the ends of the earth" they did not receive synodal rulings on paschal observance.[39] And while this compassionate invocation of geography only slightly modifies Honorius's censorious citation of Irish isolation, at other times Bede implicitly reads the marginality of Irish religious in a manner that directly counters that of the pope. At odds with Bede's censure of the Irish church is his warm appreciation of the Irish as possessors of a laudably otherworldly spirituality.

Namely, Bede admires the Irish for their monastic austerity. For example, he praises the Irish monk Aidan as a man who "neither sought after nor cared for worldly possessions" to the extent that he "used to travel everywhere, in town and country, not on horseback but on foot."[40] And when Finan, Bede tells us, constructed his church at

Lindisfarne, he builds it after the "Irish method not of stone but of hewn oak, thatching it with reeds."[41] The primitivism of Irish religious suggests their adherence to the "themes of desert holiness" in monasticism, whose founders rejected the refined trappings of civilized life.[42] Eschewing civic centers such as Rome, Anthony (ca. 250–ca. 357), Jerome (ca. 340–402), and other early Christian monks sought to live in remote and unpopulated regions. A monk himself, Bede clearly values the austerity of Irish monks and appreciates Ireland as a holy wilderness conducive to Christian asceticism. In contrast, England, despite its own otherworldliness, is no such haven in Bede's text. When English men seek to engage in prayer, fasting, and scriptural contemplation they go to Ireland.[43] Ireland, indeed, figures in the *Ecclesiastical History* as nothing less than an otherworldly stepping stone to the afterlife for the English, a place where, as Bede writes with respect to the priest Ecgberht, a man exiles himself "so that he might reach his heavenly fatherland."[44]

By no means, however, are Bede's Irish confined to a life of isolated contemplation. Rather, the Irish monks about whom Bede writes are men who travel to England to aid their eastern neighbors spiritually. Exposing how the Roman mission headed by Augustine of Canterbury left much unfinished business in Northumbria, Bede writes that the Anglo-Saxon King Oswald sends to the Irish for a "bishop by whose teaching and ministry the English race over whom he ruled might learn the privileges of faith in our Lord and receive the sacraments."[45] The arrival of Aidan initiates a period of Irish monastic evangelization in England: "From that time, as the days went by, many came from the country of the Irish into Britain and to those English kingdoms over which Oswald reigned. . . . Indeed they were mostly monks who came to preach."[46] Thanks to the missionary work of Irish monks, the Anglo-Saxons of the *Ecclesiastical History* gain a Christian identity. Due to Aidan's instruction, King Oswald and his English subjects "learned to hope for those heavenly realms that were unknown to their forefathers.[47]

Scholars often posit that Bede's notably favorable representation of the Irish results precisely from their Christian edification of the English.[48] But the Irish piety and evangelism that generated gratitude in Bede's work posed problems for other English writers. By representing England as the object of Irish missionary work, Bede shored up some of the most troubling ramifications of English isolation. In contrast to Ireland, which seems so sublimely otherworldly as to constitute a catalyst to paradise, England appears so barbarically marginal as to require foreign spiritual intervention. Viewed by their first Irish evangelist as *homines indomabiles et durae ac barbarae* or an intractable, obstinate, and uncivilized people, the English desperately need the prudent spiritual guidance of Aidan and his successors.[49] As a text written long before the conquest, moreover, Bede's chronicle added the temporal problem of belatedness to its troubling of rhetorics of English geographic exceptionalism. The holy English island made special for the preserved bodies described by William of Malmesbury, for example, was outdone by its Irish neighbor which, well prior to the conversion of the Anglo-Saxons, was the birthplace of Christian saints. And long before the Angevin kings of England embraced an expansionism that led to the conquest of numerous territories, the evangelists of Ireland had demonstrated a certain expansionism of their own, one that led them to convert peoples in England and beyond.[50] The odd combination of otherworldliness and expansionism that could potentially distinguish high medieval England only repeated a pattern already established by the Irish. Twelfth-century efforts to exalt England broke down over the example of Ireland established by Bede.

## Representing Ireland in the High Middle Ages

In some respects later English writers continued to advance the notion of an idyllic Ireland. Citing Marianus Scottus, the early twelfth-century historian John of Worcester thus recounts how "Ireland, isle of saints, was considered sublimely enriched with very many holy miracles."[51] Writing during the mid 1150s, Henry of Huntingdon remarked along similar lines in his English chronicle that God has blessed Ireland with "a multitude of saints for its protection."[52] The responsibility of the Irish for spreading the faith in a pagan England persisted as well. William of Malmesbury acknowledges how the *doctrina Scottorum* or teaching of the Irish rendered the infant-like Christian faith in England *adultam* or fully grown, and Henry of Huntingdon refers to the way "the faith grew and was zealously taught by monks coming from Ireland."[53]

There were, however, limits to how far later chroniclers would go in their celebrations of the Irish.[54] A passage from Bede on Aidan proved particularly troublesome: "With such a man as bishop [Aidan] to instruct them, King Oswald . . . gained from the one God who made heaven and earth greater earthly realms than any of his ancestors had possessed. In fact he held under his sway all the peoples and kingdoms of Britain, divided among the speakers of four different languages, British, Pictish, Irish, and English."[55] Thanks to the religious guidance provided by Aidan, Oswald manages what no English king managed before, the union of *omnes nationes et prouincias Britanniae*. Bede's notion that the English owe not only their Christian identity but also their national unity to the Irish would prove unacceptable to later historians. Henry of Huntingdon, for example, revises the aforementioned passage in his account of the miracles of Oswald, specifying that "King Oswald, by his singular power, had taken all the English, British, Pictish, and Irish kingdoms into his dominion."[56] When he refers to Oswald's governance of a realm with wider frontiers than the previous king, William of Malmesbury similarly suppresses the contribution of Aidan, as does Roger of Wendover in his reference to Oswald's dominion in Britain.[57]

As these revisions of Bede indicate, while later English writers did acknowledge the Irish's reputation for England's Christian conversion, they were not willing to go so far as to claim that the English owed their very national unification to the Irish. By the High Middle Ages, Ireland clearly appeared to certain English intellectuals as less a benefactor than a rival. William of Malmesbury thus exposes his own desire to place the Irish under the English when, late in his *History of the Kings of England,* he exclaims, "What would Ireland be worth without the goods that come in by sea from England?"[58] Such efforts to assert the supremacy of the English over the Irish would reach their full flowering toward the end of the twelfth century, the period that witnessed a change in the political relationship between England and Ireland that was nothing less than monumental. When, in 1166, Diarmait Mac Murchadha arrived in England hoping to regain his kingdom of Leinster in exchange for fealty to Henry II, he set in motion what amounted ultimately to the English invasion, conquest, and colonization of Ireland.[59] In 1169 knights and barons began to occupy Ireland and, in 1171, the king himself landed to assert his lordship. However attenuated and uneven, England's initial invasion of Ireland stands as a crucial and formative event in Irish history.[60] In terms of attitudes toward Irish geographic identity, the conquest inspired texts that exhibit an unprecedented desire to counter the image of the Irish promulgated by Bede. The erstwhile sublime otherworld emerges as none other than the home of barbarians, Christian only in name.[61]

Thus Roger of Wendover offers in his *Flowers of History* (1235) the following account of the conquest: "At this time Henry, king of England, sent a solemn embassy to solicit pope Adrian's permission that he might invade and subdue Ireland, and bring into the way of truth its bestial inhabitants, by extirpating the seeds of vice among them. This request was gladly acceded to by pope Adrian, who sent the king the following charter." Wendover goes on to cite the much-queried papal privilege *Laudabiliter,* which similarly represents the Irish as a savage people.[62] The writer who would offer the most thoroughgoing of such accounts was Gerald de Barri. For example, in his *Topography of Ireland,* Gerald asserts that the Irish are "a barbarous people, and truly barbarous [gens Barbara, et vere Barbara]" (3.10, 102). Among peoples, Gerald proclaims, the Irish are the foulest or *spurcissima* (3.19, 106); they "live on beasts only, and live like beasts [gens ex bestiis solum et bestialiter vivens]" (3.10, 101). And the *Conquest of Ireland* takes as its subject what Gerald describes as "the taming of the ferocity of a very barbarous nation in these our own times [tam barbarae nacionis feritatem his nostris temporibus edomitam]."[63] More than any previous work, Gerald's two Irish books promote an image of Ireland not as an *insula sanctorum* but as an *insula barbarorum*.

Of late, scholars have increasingly attended to that rhetoric of Irish barbarism in the work of Gerald and his contemporaries.[64] Often, this scholarship has viewed the emergence of a brutally primitive and spiritually corrupt Ireland as a crucially formative moment in the history of English colonial stereotyping. John Gillingham, for example, has well demonstrated how the condescending portrayals of a wild Irish made by the English in the Renaissance and beyond owe much to twelfth-century culture, and in particular de Barri, who "well and truly established" themes on which later writers did "little more than play."[65] Similarly, Robert Bartlett notes in his biography of Gerald that "the picture that the Anglo-Normans built up of the native Irish in the twelfth century was still at work among their Elizabethan descendants."[66] On the question of the ideological work performed by Gerald and other writers who demonized the Irish, scholars typically point to the exigencies of imperial expansion. As Gillingham notes, Henry II's "aggressions were normally justified by a claim to have hereditary rights to or over the territory in question."[67] Lacking such an ancestral privilege over Ireland, Henry turned to what Jeffrey Jerome Cohen describes as "a tactic already ancient by the twelfth century: An indigenous people are represented as primitive, subhuman, incomprehensible in order to render the taking of their lands unproblematic."[68] Like their Roman and Greek imperial predecessors, or their German imperial contemporaries, the English viewed their object of conquest as barbarians needful of their civilizing aid.[69]

Their construction of the Irish as savages, to be sure, did serve for the English as, in Robert Bartlett's words, "a hostile stereotype to salve their consciences and justify their conquest."[70] But of course representations of Ireland after the conquest, like all forms of colonial stereotyping, also go beyond those immediate and straightforward imperial desires. While the bold strokes of the imperial imagination may seem to transcend particular times and places, imperialism is in fact a complex practice that alters depending upon the specificities of history, setting, and population. And as trite as the stereotype appears, it is in fact, a nuanced and vexed production of an equally nuanced and vexed colonial process. In the case of Gerald de Barri's Irish books, we can begin to consider the contradictions and complexities of their stereotyping of the Irish by examining how they respond to long-standing notions of both Ireland and England. Images of a barbarously marginal Irish not only mark a "harsh metamorphosis" but also signify a nuanced endeavor possessed of a certain historical and geographic self-consciousness. Through both his *Topography* and *Conquest,* Gerald fully engages in the kind of revisionist historiography and geography that writers as early as William of Malmesbury had begun. A full understanding of the English conquest of Ireland, as we shall see, requires us to redefine it as an event that provided English intellectuals with a prime means of reinterpreting a territory whose alleged sublimity had become increasingly irksome.

## The Geography of Purity and Danger in the *Topography of Ireland*

We might best begin our exploration of the revisionist impulses at work in twelfth-century demonizations of the Irish by attending to the manner in which Gerald de Barri reworks long-standing paradisal notions of Ireland. Most visible is his revisionist account of Irish temperateness as memorialized by Bede and others. While for Bede, their temperate climate complements the spiritual purity of the Irish, for Gerald the even greater clemency of Ireland serves only to intensify Irish horridness. That heightened clemency emerges in the first section of his *Topography,* where Gerald describes how Ireland lacks poisonous reptiles, and says more astoundingly, "if a poisonous thing is brought (to Ireland) from elsewhere, the island cannot and never could, endure to keep it."[71] It is not, in other words, Ireland's lack of snakes that inspires admiration in Gerald's *Topography,* but Ireland's lack of toxins altogether. Ireland is the most temperate or *temperatissima* of lands, a place whose air contains "no disease-bearing cloud, or pestilential vapor, or corrupting breeze."[72]

On the question of why Ireland is so temperate, Gerald points to its distance from the East: "The well of poisons brims over in the East. The farther therefore from the East it operates, the less does it exercise the force of its natural efficacy. And by the time it reaches these farthest parts, after having traversed such long distances, losing its force gradually, it is entirely exhausted—just as the sun, the farther from the zodiac it sends its rays, the less does it exercise the force of its heat."[73] Constructing the binary of purity and danger on a global scale, Gerald's opposition of a pure Irish world border to a noxious eastern world border reflects the tendency of medieval intellectuals "to create an unusually deep chasm between the clean and the unclean."[74] While, as Mary Campbell has pointed out, the societies analyzed by Mary Douglas in *Purity and Danger* tend to marginalize the unclean by positioning them in places that "are usually part of the local habitat," medieval cosmographers placed the unclean on the very edges of the world.[75] That projection of danger onto the borders of the world, in turn, reflects the climatic theories of classical cultures. John Block Friedman writes, "The Greek and Romans imagined themselves to be at the center of the civilized world" and bound that centricity closely to an ideal of moderation: "The farther from the center, the more extreme a thing was, and therefore the more a 'vice' it was."[76] In climatic terms, this meant that at the Greek or Roman center of the world, temperateness reigned, and at the borders of that *oikoumené* existed regions so toxic as to be uninhabitable by humans. Thus Pliny claims, "In the middle of the earth" there exists "a healthy blending" of the elements that contrasts with "the savagery of the nature that broods over" outlying regions.[77]

"Not surprisingly," Friedman points out, "each European nation thought of itself as the 'middle people,' superior in climate," and he cites Gerald's *Topography of Ireland* as an example of how "on occasion, this view was openly stated."[78] But, in Gerald's book, far from being central, the temperate Irish are supremely marginal. Gerald's representation of Irish temperateness does not merely repeat the usual theories of geographic influence but instead uniquely redeploys those theories. Namely, while the centrist ideology of the Greeks and Romans demonizes most geographic margins for their barbaric distance from the temperate center, Gerald fixes danger in one particular, eastern location. Contagion and danger characterize the East, where "all the elements" place man in mortal danger.[79] By singling out the East for its supreme toxicity, Gerald manipulates the logic of geographic distance in such a way as to suggest that it is not central places such as Greece or Rome that are most temperate, but that farthest of western territories, Ireland.[80]

Gerald had ample contemporary support for his demonization of the East. The Crusade culture of the High Middle Ages generated an unprecedented amount of propaganda that succeeded in making the Muslim "the fundamental enemy" of Christendom, the supreme other.[81] From the period of the First Crusade onward, western Christians specifically deployed a rhetoric of purity and danger in their representations of Muslims. Prior to the Crusades, the massive reform movement of the eleventh century had centered on the purification of a corrupt western church. But with the onset of the First Crusade, the church redirected its energies from the Christian West to the Muslim East. "Pollution," as Tomaz Mastnak puts it, "was now seen as existing outside the Church, and outside Christendom. Now it was the pagans who became the 'dirt.' . . . the Holy Land had been occupied by 'unclean races'; the holy places were 'polluted with their filthiness' and defiled with 'their uncleanness.'"[82] Writing not long after the fall of Jerusalem and the onset of the Third Crusade, an event on behalf of which he himself preached in Wales, Gerald was intensely aware of the threat represented by the Muslim Other. His *Conquest of Ireland* even represents the arrival of the patriarch of Jerusalem in England to ask Henry II to go to the Holy Land, which is "now desperately afflicted by the infidels [abhostibus fidei jam desperanter afflictae]" (2.26, 295). By fixing upon the East as the *fons venenorum* or fountainhead of poisons, Gerald enlists the orientalist discourse of crusading Christian culture—a culture in which he participated—for his own occidentalist ends.

And those ends concern the demonization of the Irish, via yet another revision of traditional climatic theory. Influential during the Middle Ages was a largely Macrobian notion that, as Friedman phrases it, the "distinctive features" of "various nations or races of men . . . were a result of their native climates."[83] Thus Pliny contends that in a temperate clime, where there is "a healthy blending of both elements," men's "customs are gentle, senses elastic, intellects fertile . . . and they also have governments, which the outer races never have possessed . . . on account of the savagery of the nature that broods over those regions."[84] Bede adheres to this traditional intertwining of persona and place, whereby Ireland's monks exhibit a spiritual purity that matches that of their environment. If Gerald had followed this logic, attending his deployment of orientalist geography to intensify as never before the purity of the Irish climate would be a similarly unprecedented stress on the purity of the people.

Gerald, however, radically separates the Irish from their physical settings, thus rendering their barbarism as disturbing as possible. For all their failings, the barbarous or even monstrous races of the classical and premodern worlds do not menace but instead complement their wild, rugged, and even uninhabitable settings. But in the case of Ireland, we witness a filthy people contaminating their otherwise pristine environment. Even as Gerald's Ireland is a natural haven far from the well of poisons seeping westward from the East, the many vices of Irish people suggest the domestic presence of that very danger. In stark contrast to their clean natural environment, the native inhabitants of Ireland are "the least clean of peoples, the people most enveloped in vice [gens spurcissima, gens vitiis involutissima]" (3.19, 106). Above all, the Irish are given to the barbaric sexual practice of bestiality, which (despite his references to it as *nefandum* or unmentionable) Gerald goes into some detail describing, telling the reader of women who sleep with goats and lions, and kings who have ritual intercourse with white mares.[85] An *abominabile* or abominable act, bestiality epitomizes the unclean, as Gerald's citation of Leviticus 20.16 attests (2.23, 75; 2.24, 76). The Irish native improperly crosses into or infects the natural world by sleeping with an animal, by mistreating a creature "created not for abuse but for proper use [non ad abusum sed ad usum creata]" (2.23, 75). Ireland bears witness, on the one hand, to natural perfection, and, on the other hand, to human corruption and perversion.

Through this opposition, Gerald transforms the natural purity that, in Bede, serves as a tool by which the writer elevates Ireland, into a means of demonizing the Irish. Applied only to the land, in other words, purity renders the monstrous practices of the Irish all the more reprehensible. Like the holy land polluted by the Muslims, Ireland is a pure territory contaminated by its filthy inhabitants. In the same way that the corrupting presence of Muslim "dirt" in Jerusalem demands Christian "cleansing," the atrocious habitation of a bestial Irish in a land of milk and honey requires foreign intervention.

## Barbarous Monasticism and Urban Piety

A contradiction thus lies at the heart of the *Topography*'s colonial revision of Ireland's traditional identity as an otherworldly demi-paradise. While the writer retains the historical chestnut of a pure, snake-free Ireland, through his emphasis on Irish barbarity he makes the island both clean and filthy. Gerald's paradoxical representation of the Irish evinces how, in Homi Bhabha's psychoanalytically informed account of colonialism, "the chain of stereotypical signification is curiously mixed and split, polymorphous and perverse, an articulation of multiple belief."[86] In the same way that, for example, the "black is both savage (cannibal) and yet the most obedient and dignified of servants (the bearer of food)," Ireland is both pristine and contaminated.[87] A similar strategy obtains in Gerald's response to the long-standing religious image of Ireland as an island of saints. In the same way that his Ireland is at once pure and dirty, Gerald's Irish are simultaneously pious *and* pagan. On the one hand, faced with a reputation for holiness on the part of the Irish too celebrated to ignore, Gerald refers in the second and third portions of the *Topography* to some of Ireland's famous saints. Not only does he describe various miracles ascribed to Colman and other Irish saints, but also he lays stress on the asceticism of the Irish religious. When Gerald describes how Saint Kevin would spend Lent "in a small cabin which warded off from him only the sun and the rain," and commends the Irish clergy for practicing "a considerable amount of abstinence and asceticism in the use of food," he recalls Bede's approbatory accounts of the primitive and austere monastic piety of Irish religious.[88] But by the end of *Topography*, Gerald has turned monasticism on its head; the monastic inclinations of the clerics hailed by Bede render them reprehensible.[89]

Gerald reinterprets Irish monasticism by embracing precisely what monks traditionally reject: civic values. That emphasis upon civic life and culture most clearly emerges in the geographic explanation Gerald provides for the barbarism of the Irish: "Since conventions are formed from living together in society, and since they are so removed in these distant parts from the ordinary world of men, as if they were in another world altogether and consequently cut off from well-behaved and law-abiding people, they know only of the barbarous habits in which they were born and brought up, and embrace them as another nature."[90] While its distance from the East makes Ireland a natural paradise, the remoteness of the Irish from civilizing cultures makes them a socially backward people who "have not progressed at all from the primitive habits of pastoral living. While man usually progresses from the woods to the fields, and from the fields to settlements and communities of citizens, this people despises work on the land, has little use for the money-making of towns, contemns the rights and privileges of citizenship, and desires neither to abandon, nor lose respect for, the life which it has been accustomed to lead in the woods and countryside."[91] Gerald's denigration of the rural tendencies of the Irish and his concomitant appreciation of social convention and "law-abiding" civic culture promote a geopolitics that directly counters that of the monastic ideal. The very distance from civic culture so central to the elevation of Ireland by the monk Bede is cause for censure in the text of the secular cleric Gerald, a man whose multiple adverse experiences with monks would lead him to include in his litany of prayers, "From the malice of monks, Good Lord deliver us."[92] Doubtless reflecting interests not only national but also personal, Ireland emerges in the *Topography* less as a holy wilderness akin to the remote abodes of the desert fathers than as a land barbarously marginal to civilization.

In embracing civic culture, Gerald received support in the ancient writings embraced during the twelfth-century "renaissance." Greco-Roman ideology conceived of humanity as inextricably intertwined with the *polis* or *urbs*. As Friedman writes, "the city conferred humanity, for it gave its citizens a shared setting in which to exercise their human faculties. . . . Men who lived outside cities, since their lives were guided by no law, were not really human."[93] Early on, Christianity adopted the classical view of the city, a theme developed in Augustine's *City of God*.[94] That Augustinian emphasis upon the city in Latin Christendom would receive further stress during Gerald's life, which witnessed a massive urban renewal. While during the eleventh century city populations grew considerably, by the twelfth that urban expansion rapidly accelerated.[95] By 1300, most cities with a population exceeding 20,000 in 1000 had at least doubled in size.[96] With that expansion of urban centers, city values—the importance of civility, economic development, cultural refinement, and so on—received new emphasis. In particular, Christianity itself was increasingly conceived along urban lines. Intellectuals imagined heaven not in the rural image of the Garden of Eden but in the civic image of the New Jerusalem.[97] And, with respect not to heaven but earth, "townspeople, by and large, exhibited a piety that was more vibrant and intense than that of the peasantry and aristocracy," whereby, for example, the "most famous saint of the era, Francis of Assisi" hailed from a town.[98] The period as well witnessed the valorization of a city-based religious practice of social contact: the rise of mendicant orders, who lived out their apostolic ideal in towns, where they preached and otherwise ministered to the populace.[99]

Seizing upon his culture's intellectual and religious prizing of city life, Gerald reinterprets those aspects of Irish religious culture that are idealized in Bede, and transforms them into lamentable evils. In Gerald's urban-identified text, the monasticism behind Ireland's reputation as a sublime *insula sanctorum* constitutes a regrettable religious fixation responsible for a lethal anti-sociality on the part of Ireland's religious. It is none other than their monastic roots that, according to Gerald's *Topography*, accounts for the prime failing of Ireland's prelates, their neglect of pastoral duty: "Since nearly all the prelates of Ireland are taken from monasteries into the ranks of the clergy, they scrupulously fulfill all the obligations of a monk. But they omit almost everything to which they are obliged as clerics and prelates. They care for and are mindful of themselves only, but they omit or put off with great negligence the care of the flock committed to them."[100] Occluding the evangelicalism of Ireland's monks, Gerald links monasticism solely with contemplation and insularity. Thus, by citing Ireland's prelates for fulfilling only their monastic obligations, Gerald maps the geographic isolation of the Irish onto their religious orders. In contrast to the *Scotti vagantes* of Bede, an Irish religious so expansive as to venture actively beyond their insular homeland to spread the Christian faith, Gerald's Irish prelates are as cut off from other people as their homeland is barbarously cut off from the civilized world.

In the same way that the geographic remoteness of the Irish laity requires overcoming through their incorporation into civil society, the Irish prelacy must put an end to their unhealthful monastic insularism. By meeting only their monastic obligations, Ireland's prelates fail to realize the dual dimensions of their duties. Prelates by nature are a divided folk, Gerald stresses in the *Topography*. Troping off of Matthew 10:16, Gerald writes that they "take certain traits from their monastic identity and others from their clerical identity, as monks, they learn a dove-like simplicity; as clerics, the shrewdness of the *serpent*."[101] With his use of the image of serpent to characterize clerical acumen, Gerald recalls the fabled clemency of Ireland. The monkishness of Irish prelates thus duplicates the snakelessness of Ireland's climate. But while Ireland's lack of serpents is part of a beneficent natural remoteness, the "snakelessness" of Ireland's prelates is part of a dangerous social isolation. In other words, by decrying Ireland's prelates for failing to embody their proper clerical-monastic hybridity, Gerald suggests how in human terms the Irish need to open themselves to the serpentine and mingle in the world. Implicitly contrasting Ireland's monastic heritage with the apostolicism of the mendicant friars, he decries how Irish prelates "neither preach the word of the Lord to the people, nor tell them of their sins, nor extirpate vices from the flock committed to them, nor instill virtues."[102]

Due to their own spiritual solipsism, Ireland's religious fail to rectify an immoral solipsism on the part of an Irish people too lazy to extend themselves outward to their fellows, even their own babies, who are "for the most part abandoned to nature [cuncta naturae relinquuntur]" (3.10, 100). Paradoxically, then, the monastic hyper-investment of Ireland's religious in spiritual purity—what Gerald describes as a *columbina simplicitas* or dovelike simplicity—leads to spiritual degeneration, the fostering of an impure Irish laity. Indeed, Ireland's prelates' monastic self-centeredness contributes to a religious disaster of national proportions. "Of all peoples," Gerald proclaims in the *Topography*, the Irish people "is the least instructed in the rudiments of the Faith."[103] The insularity of Ireland's regrettably monastic religious is such that certain pockets of Ireland are in fact ignorant of Christianity altogether, so that "although all this time the Faith has grown up, so to speak, in the country, nevertheless in some corners of it there are many even who are not baptized, and who, because of the negligence of the pastors, have not yet heard the teaching of the Faith."[104] Gerald goes on to describe how sailors encounter in Connaught a skiff manned by primitive hunters and gatherers who "had as yet heard nothing of Christ and knew nothing of him."[105] With his construction of Ireland as what Bartlett terms a "virtually pagan" site, Gerald redefines the extreme geographic isolation that made Ireland a land famed for its nuanced national purity.[106] The barbaric solipsism of the Irish laity and the spiritual solipsism of the Irish religious show how

Irish isolation—whether in terms of the geographic remoteness of the land or the insularity mapped onto Ireland's people—is not sublime but excessive, not otherworldy, but dreadful.

## Ireland, Rome, and the Geometry of English Empire

By signifying a remoteness that exceeds the world and its civilizing effects, the heightened Irish isolation that threatened to undermine rhetorics of English geographic exceptionalism suggests in Gerald's Irish books the benefits of England's relative proximity to the world. Embedded more deeply within Christendom and its city centers, the English are poised to aid the Irish and, in so doing, invert the old relationship between the Irish and English edges of the world. Transferring the role of evangelist and civilizer to the English, Gerald describes in the *Conquest* how, while in Ireland, Henry II "became fired with an ever greater desire to increase the glory of God's church and the worship of Christ in those parts."[107] Thus the very English people who are obliged to the Irish for the original spread of Christian practice in their land now place the Irish in their debt. Quoting from the conclusion of the constitutions of the synod Henry convened at Cashel in order to make a public inquiry into "the enormous offences and vile practices of the people of that land," Gerald writes, "Indeed both the church and the realm of Ireland are indebted to our glorious king for the boon of peace and the growth of religion, so far as they have achieved these up to the present. For before his arrival in Ireland, evil practices of many kinds had arisen there from remote times. These have now fallen into disuse thanks to his power and his efforts."[108]

Gerald endows the English with the Christian civility the isolated Irish lack by emphasizing England's connections to that "mother" of city centers in western Christendom—Rome. For the classicizing intellectuals of twelfth-century England, to celebrate English civilization was necessarily to link it with the urban excellence of Rome. Hence essential to William fitz Stephen's ca. 1170–83 celebration of London as one of "the noble and celebrated cities of the world" is his frequent comparison of that English city to Rome.[109] Contemporary Rome also set the standard for high medieval English civilization; thus the English monk Lucian's 1195 text praises the church of St. Peter at Chester by comparing it to St. Peter's at Rome.[110] Like these writers, Gerald appreciates Rome as a civil standard that the English meet—although, for both Gerald and his contemporaries, "the idea of Rome," as Gransden puts it, also "provoked the competitive spirit."[111] Thus even as fitz Stephen acknowledges Rome as a benchmark of excellence he also asserts that "London, as historians have shown, is a much older city than Rome."[112] Gerald similarly is both an appreciator and an aggressor of Rome. Everywhere in his Irish books he displays an appreciation of things Roman—from the Latin language he employs, to his "ready use of Roman authors," to his representation of Henry II as a son of the Roman church; but in those same texts Gerald also imagines the English usurping the very imperial authority of Rome.[113]

The most arresting cartographic example of Gerald's promotion of England's ties to Rome appears in a ca. 1200 manuscript copy of both the *Topography* and the *Conquest* (National Library of Ireland MS 700). In this unique map of western Europe, England occupies a central position, with Ireland and Rome at the top and bottom margins (plate 2). With its manipulation of cartographic space to engage the question of England's relationship to both Rome and Ireland, the map shores up the crucial role geography plays in Gerald's production of Englishness. In particular, as a document that samples from and revises mappae mundi, the map in the National Library of Ireland (N.L.I.) 700 encapsulates how the writer's justifications for conquest ultimately hinge upon the reworking of long-standing notions of global cultural geography.[114]

That the N.L.I. 700 manuscript "spent a long time with Giraldus" or Gerald is clear.[115] Less apparent is the relationship of the map in N.L.I. 700 to the Irish texts with which it shares manuscript space. Such factors as scale inconsistencies between the map and the *Topography*'s descriptions of Britain have inspired Thomas O'Loughlin to consider the map as separate from Gerald's Irish books.[116] Gerald's map and writings may diverge in certain factual respects. But in terms of their *cultural* production of English, Roman, and Irish geography, these artifacts all complement and comment on each other. While, according to O'Loughlin, "the map's connection with Giraldus *is not textual*," as a discursive tool, an artifact that makes places meaningful in a social medium, that map, like all maps, is itself "textual." A document that invests the sites of Ireland, Rome, and England with particular social meanings, the map in N.L.I. 700 engages in the same sort of cultural work performed by the books it illustrates.

We might best begin to understand this triangle of representation by considering the map's placement directly after the *Topography* and before the *Conquest*.[117] The sandwiching of the Europe map between the *Topography* and the *Conquest* in N.L.I. 700 suggests its importance as a cartographic bridge between those texts. As a document focusing upon Europe and the British Isles, the map in N.L.I. 700 takes up where the *Topography* leaves off. Gerald's text begins by evoking an *oikoumené* in which Ireland is blessedly distant from the poisonous eastern edge of the world. Only in the third and final distinction of that book does Gerald compare the Irish to more centrally located (and hence more socially advanced) peoples. Reflecting that geographical shift from relating the Irish favorably to the whole world to relating them unfavorably to that world's civilized portions, the Europe map in N.L.I. 700 focuses solely upon the territories of the Latin West.

But it does far more than register the movement in the *Topography* from globe to region. The map in N.L.I. 700 clarifies the Roman question that is only implied in the text it follows. Rome, that is, is something of a shadow presence in the *Topography*. In chapter thirty-two of distinction three, for example, Gerald describes how an *ecclesiae Romanae clerico* blames Irish prelates for the atrocities of the country, thus hinting at the status of Rome as a standard of Christian civilization and religious propriety to which the English subscribe. Only in the *Conquest*, however, does Gerald make England's Roman affiliations clear. Thus in the account of the Cashel Synod that appears in chapter thirty-four of the first book of the *Conquest*, Gerald describes how, while

Henry II summoned the Irish clergy for the gathering, a papal legate presided over it, demonstrating how the synod occurred under the auspices of a partnership between England and the Roman Curia. And chapter five of the second book of the *Conquest* features a full citation of the much-debated papal bull called *Laudabiliter.* Supposedly drawn up for Henry II by Pope Adrian IV, the document identifies the English king as Adrian's "most well-beloved son in Christ," and as a man devoted to "checking the descent into wickedness, correcting morals, and implanting virtues, and encouraging the growth of the faith of Christ" in Ireland.[118] The English thus overtly appear in the *Conquest* as upstanding members of the Roman church more than capable of "planting virtue" in an otherwise uncultivated and underdeveloped region. The links between England and Rome, indeed, are such that, as Gerald points out in the version of the *Conquest* that appears in N.L.I. MS 700, the papal author of the *Laudabiliter* is *de Anglia oriundo* or sprung from England: Adrian IV (1154–59), whose given name was Nicholas Breakspear, was the only Englishman in history to become pope.[119]

We might best understand how the map in N.L.I. 700 looks toward that emphasis on Rome by considering its sources. Gerald may have derived his map from the mappa mundi donated to the local church at Lincoln where he lived during the 1190s, or another world map he saw during his European travels.[120] Whatever its precise identification, the world map or maps from which the map in N.L.I. 700 emerged constituted the most powerful visual memorials in high medieval England to Roman power. In the Hereford map, for example, as W. L. Bevan and H. W. Phillott point out, Rome "occupies a conspicuous place, being represented by a grand edifice" near the center of the map. A written gloss, in leonine verse, explains the significance of Rome's cartographic prominence: "Roma caput mundi tenet orbis frena rotundi."[121] In the portion of the world it takes from such mappae mundi, the map in N.L.I. 700 similarly promotes Rome. For one thing, its symbol for Rome—a crenellated box—is almost double the size of the next largest icon denoting cities.[122]

The central placement of Rome in world maps does not obtain in the map in N.L.I. 700. But Gerald's sampling from mappae mundi nevertheless accords Rome a place of privilege. Gerald's map represents only the European section of world maps, namely the area bounded in the southeast by Italy, the south by the Mediterranean, the west by the world ocean, and the north by Scandinavia. By citing this portion of the map, Gerald is able to center Rome at the top of the map, thus imaging its status as *caput mundi.* The fact that this map offers us an image only of the Latin West underscores all the more Rome's great consequence. Moreover, due to its uppermost positioning, Rome serves as the primary point of orientation for the map. David Woodward has pointed out how cartographic orientation always carries with it a meaning greater "than simply showing the reader which way a map is to be read." As much emerges in the term "orientation" itself, which stems from "primitive societies' preoccupation with the east as a primary means of ordering space."[123] In the same way that world maps register the significance of the earthly paradise by orienting themselves around its supposed eastern location, the map in N.L.I. 700 asserts the importance of Rome by using that city as its point of reference.[124]

Ireland's positioning in the map further emphasizes Rome's importance. The map in N.L.I. 700 exaggerates Ireland's distance from Rome, making it seem as extreme as Ireland's distance from the East is at the beginning of the *Topography*. In contrast to the first section of the *Topography*, which conjured up a world bounded on one side by a pernicious East and on the other by a clement Ireland, the map in N.L.I. 700 offers an image of Europe bordered on one side by the civilized Romans and on the other by the barbaric Irish. Centered at the very bottom margin of the map is *Hybernia*, portrayed by the mapmaker as a large bow-shaped island whose southern half dips into the world ocean. Revising and transferring the logic of ultimate distance witnessed in the first section of *Topography* from a global to a regional register, Gerald's Europe map makes Ireland's troubling distance from civilized life specifically a problem of Ireland's separation from Rome.[125] Thus, in the same way that the *Conquest* ignores the contemporary evidence of the vital faith and Petrine ties of the Irish church, the map in N.L.I. 700 deploys a distorted version of western Europe in order to single out Ireland as a site outside of Roman Christendom.

The N.L.I. 700 map effectively offers, as Brian Harley puts it with respect to early modern cartography, a "socially constructed perspective on the world," a perspective that entails not only the production but also the suppression of information, that is, "political silences."[126] Indeed, at the same time that the map in N.L.I. 700 plays up the problem of Irish geographic marginality as much as possible, it represses the way that problem could extend to Ireland's English neighbor. In the world maps from which the map derives, of course, England and Ireland are linked by their shared global marginality. The status of Britain and Ireland as geographic doubles emerges graphically in the Sawley world map, which depicts the two islands as parallel elliptical territories. With the edges of Ireland curved eastward and Britain westward, the two long and narrow landmasses appear to stand facing each other, ready to hug or to wrestle. The geographic intimacy of those territories begs a question that undermines Gerald's colonial project: if the Irish are wild because "they are so removed in these distant parts from the ordinary world of men, as if they were in another world altogether," are the otherworldly English barbaric as well? Making that potential English incivility a reality was the behavior of Henry II himself, whose invasion of Ireland coincided with the Becket controversy. At the very time in which Henry journeyed to Ireland to "tame" an Irish people barbarically divergent from church practice, Roman legates were traveling to England to investigate the king's own wild behaviors with respect to a high church official. As a man notorious for the murder of a notably pious personage, Henry suggested that England, like its Irish neighbor, was a barbarous and unlawful world border.[127]

Gerald, however, suppresses that geographic and cultural doubling in both his Irish books and his map of Europe. Thanks to the space it devotes to the western world ocean and Ireland, the map in N.L.I. 700 transforms Britain from world margin to regional center.[128] Britain appears near the middle of the central vertical axis of the map in N.L.I. 700, directly below Rome and above Ireland. Through that strategic positioning, Gerald urges the status of the English as the conduit through which Roman spirituality flows to Ireland. Near the Irish but also not far from the Romans, the English are perfectly situated to "plant" on behalf of the pope the "offshoot" of the faith in Ireland as outlined by the privilege *Laudabiliter*.[129] The fiction of cartography authorizes a new geographic vision of England as an expansionist world center.

At the same time that Gerald's Europe map works together with his Irish books to ally England with Rome, it also points to the contradictory nature of that English-Roman alliance. Gerald's stress on the English's ability to transport Roman society and culture, after all, is only the means to an end that has little to do with civility and moral virtue.[130] Gerald's textual and cartographic Irish works represent the desire of the English to use Roman authority for an act that is ultimately about *English* power. Thus, at the same time that Rome's placement at the top of the map and its unusually large symbolization assert the value of that city, other factors draw the viewer's eye to the British center of the map. Britain stands out not only because of its disproportionately large size but also because of the manner in which it is framed on its sides and from above by the horseshoe-shaped European coastline, and framed below by the islands of Iceland and Ireland. Moreover, Gerald devotes the bulk of the physical space of his Europe map to Henry II's holdings. Covering all the territory held by Henry at the height of his imperial dominion, the map represents not only Ireland, but also Gascony, Normandy, Brittany, and Anjou (called in the map Gascon[ia], Norman[n]ia, Britan[n]ia and Andegavia); and provides names and city symbols for such Angevin centers of power as Angers (Andegav[en]is), Rouen (Rotomag[I]), Poitiers (Pictavia), and Tours (Turon[icensis]).[131]

Through such cartographic attention to Henry's Angevin holdings and his native England, Gerald does not simply demonstrate, as O'Loughlin puts it, "the way that power and authority flow directly from Rome to the British Isles."[132] England appears not only as a Roman conduit but also as a competitor with Rome in the Europe map, a site bent less on bringing Rome to Ireland than absorbing Roman power for English ends. The map thus images a rivalry with Rome evident in the patriotic address to Henry II near the end of the *Topography:* "Our western Alexander, you have stretched your arm from the Pyrenean mountains even to these far western bounds of the northern ocean."[133] Like the great Greek emperor, Gerald proclaims, his English king is possessed of a vast dominion, territories extending to the Irish limit of the western world. In Gerald's version of *translatio imperii* or westering of empire, not the Romans but the English inherit Alexander's imperial mantle.[134] Gerald's Europe map offers the cartographic counterpart to that literary appropriation of Rome's imperial standing, by placing England at the center of a western empire. Indeed, the low-middle positioning of Britain duplicates with remarkable precision the placement of Rome in the Hereford map and other mappae mundi such as the Cotton, Psalter, and Sawley maps.

If, in Gerald's Irish works, Britain takes on the traditional imperial standing of Rome, it is of course Ireland that assumes the traditional positioning of Britain vis-à-vis Rome. While "furthest of all" in the ancient Roman Empire, as Catullus remarked, live "the horrible Britons," at the edges of the emerging English empire are the barbarous Irish.[135] Gerald's conquest rhetoric entails multiple, linked, and at times contradictory acts of geohistorical revision. Through his map and Irish books, Gerald combines and thus manages two geographical challenges: the centrality of Rome and the remoteness of Ireland. By overcoming Ireland's sublime marginality, Gerald surmounts the problem of Rome's world supremacy. By asserting Ireland's barbaric isolation, Gerald suppresses that of Britain. With their reinterpretations of Irish and Roman cultural geographies, Gerald's Irish works realize in explicit form the dual impulses we've located in high medieval mappae mundi. It is no coincidence, in other words, that the English came to dominate the Irish at the same time that they came to dominate the production of mappae mundi. Thanks to a geographic ambivalence lying at the heart of England's emergent identity, the twelfth-century English turned, as never before, to fictions of both world cartography and regional imperialism.

The foregoing analysis of Gerald's Irish books does not—and cannot—offer the whole story of their engagement with issues of geography and identity. As scholars have rightly stressed, Gerald was an unusually multifaceted individual, and his cultural productions register that complexity. Thus, at the same time that his careerist impulses lead to celebrations of Henry II in both the *Topography* and the *Conquest,* his family ties to the Marcher invaders of Ireland, in Bartlett's words, "occasionally led to criticisms of Royal policies," some of which appear in those Irish books.[136] A native of the Welsh coastal limit of Britain, Gerald was, like other scholars hailing from hybrid border cultures, a man who resists easy classification.[137] Yet to read Gerald in light of regional border disputes alone, is at some level to accept the fiction of geographic scale exemplified by the map in N.L.I. 700. While Welsh border identity has proven a useful subject of analysis in recent medievalist work, in the case of Gerald his peripheral identity is part of a larger issue as well: that of the fluid, historical relationship between world margins and centers. As we have seen, we can unpack notions of English centrality not only by looking at regional borders but also by adopting a far wider scope. That is, if we adopt a global perspective England itself emerges as a border, situated uneasily between the Roman metropole and the Irish world border. For all his official production of the English as a sovereign and centralized people, that is, the Irish books of Gerald de Barri ultimately reveal the English's contradictory nature. The example of Gerald's books and maps exposes "England" or "Britain" as a site whose high medieval adumbration grew visible through a series of triangulated border crossings—a pushing and pulling of the English across their frontiers to Ireland on the one hand and Rome on the other. In registering the spatial nature of Gerald's colonial rhetoric, we find the means of interrogating an influential and early production of English centrality.

# CHAPTER THREE

# LOCATING ENGLAND IN THE *POLYCHRONICON*

Around the middle of the fourteenth century, an English mapmaker, possibly hired by the monks of Ramsey Abbey, Huntingdonshire, produced a mappa mundi that celebrates, in an unprecedented manner, the English world margin: BL Royal MS 14. CIX, IV–2 (plate 3). In no previous world map does England (called *Anglia*) enjoy such a large size with respect to the world.[1] The map also departs from earlier mappae mundi in terms of the toponymic detail (no less than fourteen place names and icons) it devotes to England.[2] Finally, the color red distinguishes *Anglia*.[3] To be sure, the cartographer also reddens other sites, namely Jerusalem, an act (along with the placement of the holy city near the center of the world) that reflects the Christian uses of mappae mundi. Yet even as the red-tinged Jerusalem beckons the reader's attention, it finds its rival in the crimson image of *Anglia*. Occupying the northwestern corner of the oval-shaped map, England lies directly across the world from the Red Sea, whose two hydrographic prongs extend diagonally along the map from the southeast, leading the eye beyond Jerusalem to England.[4] Through its use of proportion, toponymic detail, and color, the Ramsey Abbey map makes the English corner of the world its focus.

Until recently, the aforementioned document was not known as the Ramsey Abbey map, but as the Higden map. Of all of the twenty-one maps that we know were included in manuscripts of Ranulf Higden's *Polychronicon* (ca. 1327–ca. 1360), it is the two-page map that begins the manuscript of the chronicle owned by Ramsey Abbey that traditionally has been associated with Higden.[5] And, in certain respects the Ramsey Abbey map merits its preeminent identification with the chronicle. Far more than any other *Polychronicon* map, Ramsey Abbey corresponds to the issues of English identity and marginality that, as we shall see, are crucial to Higden's work. In effect, the *Polychronicon* offers us a textual version of what the map visually displays: how an artifact of universal scope nevertheless can imagine a sovereign England.

To be sure, there are obvious reasons why we would be inclined to view Higden's text as not a national but a universal history. The text, after all, does cover the world past from Genesis to the reign of Edward III, and Higden did write his chronicle in that great universal language of the Christian medieval West, Latin. Such universalizing aspects of the *Polychronicon* have incited both Peter Barber to claim that it is "not at all nationalist" and John Taylor—the preeminent scholar of Higden's chronicle—to contend that "what gave Higden's work its distinctive character was its treatment of *world* history and of the ancient world in particular."[6] Yet the "universal" aspects of Higden's work by no means prevent it from offering other, more particular meanings. As Andrew Galloway has recently demonstrated, due to its historical authority, "universal" Latin played a key role in Higden's self-fashioning as a definer of "England."[7] Still more aspects of the *Polychronicon*—namely, its form, content, imagined audience, and influence—urge the Englishness of that text.[8] While Higden covers world history starting with creation, the chronicler organizes the universal past from the Anglo-Saxon period onward, "slanting," in Peter Brown's words, "his structure and content in order to emphasize Britain's place in the development of world history."[9] Hence though key biblical events do end books two and three, the respective arrivals of the Saxons, Danes, and Normans close books four through six; and book seven ends with "our age [aevum nostrum]," meaning the reign of Edward III.[10] That reference to Edward's reign, importantly, points not only to the national structure the *Polychronicon* assumes, but also to Higden's imagined national audience. Higden's use of the first person plural in reference to the era of an English monarch shows how the monk imagined his text would be produced for and read by Englishmen, fellow members of the generation of Edward III.[11]

That the *Polychronicon* indeed was perceived as a national text obtains in the history of both its translation and its influence on later medieval writers. As if to remedy Higden's famous lament regarding "the debasement of the native language [nativae linguae corruptio]," the *Polychronicon* itself came to be a "valued vernacular text" in the Middle Ages.[12] First John of Trevisa in 1387 and then later an anonymous fifteenth-century translator produced two separate Middle English versions of Higden's text.[13] Trevisa's version exists in at least fourteen complete manuscripts; among national chronicles in Middle English written during the late medieval period, only manuscripts of the prose *Brut* exceed this number.[14] The *Polychronicon* also influenced such devotional Middle English texts as *Jacob's Well*, Mirk's *Festial*, and *The Stanzaic Life of Christ*;[15] while vernacular writers Thomas Usk, Chaucer, John Wycliffe, and Lydgate all demonstrate either an indebtedness to the chronicle or at the very least a familiarity with Higden's text.[16] The popularity of the *Polychronicon* extended into the early modern period. Presses issued copies of Trevisa's translation into the opening decades of the sixteenth century.[17] Reformation antiquaries plumbed the chronicle for evidence supporting an Anglican church.[18] Higden and his *Polychronicon* would even be featured in Thomas Middleton's *Hengist King of Kent* (ca. 1619–20), a historical tragedy in which "Raynulph Munck of Chester" whose "policronicon . . . raises him as works doe Men" opens and closes the play as chorus.[19]

Yet perhaps the most powerful gauge of Higden's success in singling out his national past in the *Polychronicon* emerges in its impact on other historians. That influence was immense: at least twelve chronicles written during the second half of the century either were composed as extensions of or borrowed extensively from Higden, a fact that spurred Taylor to remark that "in the second half of the fourteenth century history was written as a continuation of the *Polychronicon*."[20] What is especially important about Higden's influence on historiography is the fact that, with one exception, it was not universal chronicles for which the *Polychronicon* served as either foundation or source, but major national chronicles such as that of Walsingham, the Westminster chronicle, the chronicle of Adam of Usk, and the *Vita Ricardi Secundi*. Like the vernacular translations of Higden's chronicle, the many national chronicles that continued the *Polychronicon* demonstrate its reception as an English document intended for English readers.

As we shall see, the stress on English marginality evident in the Ramsey Abbey map goes far in explaining why Higden's "universal" chronicle enjoyed such a "national" appeal in medieval England and beyond. Just as that mappa mundi privileges the English world border as no earlier map does, the sheer frequency with which Higden refers to English isolation in his chronicle sets him apart from other medieval English writers. No less than seven times does Higden refer to the status of England as, alternately, a corner of the world, an other world, and a nation located almost beyond the world.[21] In this chapter, I first demonstrate how the prefaces to the *Polychronicon*—key portions of Higden's text where this compiler of authorities appears at his most original—subtly intertwine marginality and exceptionalism as two mutually constitutive traits that define England as the most special place described in the chronicle (1:26). I then examine the representation of Britain in Higden's first book, his description of the world. In this literary mappa mundi, Higden tropes on the advantages of geographic marginality in order to construct England as a land of divine wonders and natural plenty. Finally, I consider the complex relationship that obtains in the chronicle between Britain and the other site to which Higden devotes inordinate attention, Rome. Through both the form and content of his chronicle proper, Higden links Britain and Rome in a manner that implies that his island on the edge of the world merits the same historical prominence accorded the great classical empire.

## On the Border of the Border of the World

As with earlier historians hailing from borderlands such as Welsh writers Geoffrey of Monmouth and Gerald de Barri, Higden's emphasis on English marginality emerges partly in relation to his own local identity as a Cheshire man. English isolation finds its parallel, in microcosmic form, in Cheshire isolation. In the same way that, as Higden puts it at the beginning of book one, England is an angle of the world, so too, as Higden later writes in the forty-eighth chapter of book one, is Cheshire "on the border of England."[22] Not only geography but also politics made Cheshire a kind of world apart from England. The new status of the county as a palatinate in the thirteenth century "stimulated in Cheshire both a sense of community and a sense of differentiation from the rest of England," whereby the men of Cheshire came to treat county custom as distinct "at most points from the law of England," and the charter of liberties of past earl Ranulf Blundeville as a "constitutional guarantee."[23]

The geographical and political distancing of Cheshire from England helps account for the local patriotism evident in Higden's chronicle, in which the narration of English history is peppered with references to the earldom. Furthermore, in the initial descriptive section of the *Polychronicon,* the River Dee receives special attention in a chapter on the marvels of England, as does Chester in a chapter on English cities (2:26–29). In the latter instance, Higden refutes William of Malmesbury's claims about a lack of resources in Chester both by stating that the Norman chronicler "might have dreamed [somniaverit]" of that paucity, and by describing the abundance of corn, fish, and other resources in the city. A poem in praise of Chester even ends the chapter (2:78–85). The local pride Higden evinces here and elsewhere may well indicate the extent to which a distinct communal identity can arise in border communities. But even as their marginality could have contributed to the people of Cheshire's sense of themselves as distinct from the rest of England, it could also bind them to their nation as fellow communities faced with the problems and potentials of difference. As a resident of a county on the edge of his nation, Higden may well have been more inclined than other Englishmen to invoke in his writing the positioning of his nation on the edge of the world.

As we have seen in the examples of Ælfric and Gerald, geographic alterity is double-edged insofar as it always carries with it not only the threat of wildness and regression but also the potential for independence and sovereignty. Yet it was, above all, the adverse associations of geographic marginality that marked Higden's county in the decades leading up to the first recension of the *Polychronicon.* As the coincidence of Edward II's deposition in 1327 with the completion of Higden's first version of his chronicle makes clear, the *Polychronicon* emerged during perhaps the most volatile moment of English political history in the fourteenth century. The king's demise formed the climax of a period of political instability and social distress, a time marked by an inept monarchy, civil war, and poverty. Sparked initially by the powers the king bestowed upon his Gascon favorite, Piers Gaveston, baronial discontent erupted throughout Edward's reign and at times resulted in civil war. The king's powers consistently were encroached upon, at first by the Ordainers, later by Thomas of Lancaster, and finally by Roger Mortimer. Additional national turmoil took place after the disaster at Bannockburn in 1314, when the Scots raided the north counties. And, as if matters were not bad enough, poor weather and land overuse led to a series of natural disasters during the initial decades of the century: the great famine of 1315–17; exceptionally poor harvests in 1320 and 1321; the prevalence of cattle and sheep murrains in 1319 and 1321. These natural disasters in turn led to disease and starvation; in some parts of the British Isles, the last catastrophe even may have led to cannibalism.[24] Higden wrote his chronicle for a nation that was, physically as well as politically, in acute distress.

Not only Higden's national community but also his local community would have suggested to the monk the associations of marginality with the uncivil and even the savage. Evidence of the advantages of Cheshire's distinct status in England belonged, by and large, to the past. During the reign of the centralizing Henry II, Ranulf III, the ruler of the Norman earldom, was the envy of his contemporaries for his unique capacity to maintain his territorial holdings and even achieve in Cheshire "a regality equivalent to, but under, that of the king."[25] And throughout the Welsh wars that led to its palatinate status in the early thirteenth century, the county was valued and fostered as an essential asset to the realm. However, after the appropriation of North Wales and the death of Edward I at the start of the fourteenth century, "the course of events," as Geoffrey Barraclough notes, "showed the disadvantages, rather than the advantages, of the special status of Chester," as the county fell into disrepair and "remained backward and disorderly for upward of two centuries."[26] The abuses of the now largely absentee earl led to insurrection in the county, culminating in the 1353 rebellion.[27] Partly due to the presence of "hardened criminals" among the soldiery of this military recruitment site, Cheshire became a notably lawless county, populated by both individual and bands of outlaws.[28] Once distinguished from the rest of England in terms of its unique political powers, Cheshire was now notorious for rebellion, villainy, and regressiveness.[29]

As a monk at St. Werburgh Abbey in Chester, Higden by no means would have been secluded from the social unrest occurring in a county Adam of Usk called a "nest of wickedness."[30] Because of the dominant role the well-endowed abbey played not only in the religious but also in the social and economic affairs of Chester, St. Werburgh did not protect its brothers from the upheavals of their marcher environs.[31] Indeed, the disorderly state of the abbey itself during Higden's tenure there from 1299 to his death around 1363 reflected and contributed to county discord. The abbot of St. Werburgh from 1324 to 1349, William de Bebington, caused dissension in the abbey when he obtained a papal exemption from the jurisdiction of the diocesan bishop at Lichfield. Bebington disturbed the monks so much that four of them complained directly to the king that their abbot impoverished the abbey through the ounce of gold per annum the exemption required, ejected all monks who opposed him, and obtained the exemption "so that he might the more freely give himself up to dissolute living."[32] The troubles brought upon the abbey by Bebington pale, however, when compared to life at St. Werburgh under his successor, Richard of Seynesbury (abbot in 1349–62). In 1350, a monk accused Seynesbury of forcing him to carry off by force 60s. of agricultural property from a local village.[33] Two years later, the abbot was indicted for imprisoning a boy in the abbey; in 1356 Seynesbury led a dozen men in an assault on the men of the parson of one of the abbey churches, during which £1,000 in goods were stolen and the church rectory was burned; and in the same year, the abbot and thirty-seven other men attacked a married woman. As a member of a household of forty brothers at the most, Higden could not have helped being aware of the internal troubles of his abbey. Surely St. Werburgh's upheavals partly inspired him to contrast the fine governance of Cern Abbey in Anglo-Saxon England with "our time in England," when greed, gluttony, and pride reign.[34]

By insisting in his chronicle upon the identity of England as an other world, Higden could acknowledge England's social problems. But, as the Higden map suggests, geographic marginality could also imaginatively resolve such problems. The unrest characterizing Higden's nation, county, and even abbey remind us how periods of social unrest provoke national texts such as the *Polychronicon,* how writers imagine a united and sovereign national culture when that culture is itself divided. Thanks to the twofold meaning of geographic marginality, Higden could use geography to exalt his otherworldly homeland during a time when social tensions threatened to substantiate the barbaric implications of English isolation. Edward III, for one, appears to have considered Higden's chronicle a socially responsive text. A Close Roll entry records that Edward summoned Higden to appear in court on August 1352 "with all of your chronicles and those in your charge to speak and treat with our said council concerning matters to be explained to you on our behalf."[35] We do not know on what state issues the monastic chronicler was asked to consult with the king. The Close Roll entry does underscore, however, how stories of the past such as the *Polychronicon* can speak to the present needs of a nation. Edward summoned Higden during the middle years of his reign, a time when the king was improving the state of the realm (and consolidating monarchic power) through military advances, legal reform, reconciliation with magnates and ecclesiastics, and cooperation with parliament. Higden's summons signals both the king's perception of historiography—and in particular the *Polychronicon*—as a useful political tool, and his view of Higden as a man capable of aiding none other than the most powerful public official in England in matters of state.[36]

## Beginnings

But how did Higden want his chronicle to be used and interpreted? Did he see his text as performing the sort of social function I have suggested? We cannot fully answer these questions, of course, but we can begin to explore them by examining one of the most overtly authoritative elements of the *Polychronicon,* Higden's prefaces. While throughout his chronicle Higden tends to play the role of compiler, in the three chapters that precede the text proper he appears, if still somewhat conventional, at his most original. Here, in what Gérard Genette would call the paratext, Higden describes the genesis of his project, its rationale, uniqueness, traditionalism, accuracy, and sources.[37] Taken together, these prefatorial elements construct a meaning for Higden's chronicle before its readerly consumption, and hence provide perhaps our best indicator of his ambitions as a public figure. To be sure, Higden's prefaces cannot be equated with the *Polychronicon* per se; they are, like England, marginalized structures located on the border of another (textual) body. Yet, like England, too, these border structures are also sites of power. The preface, along with other aspects of the paratext (such as the title, subtitle, and afterword), constitutes "a fringe of the printed text which in reality controls one's whole reading of the text."[38] Through close analysis of the three prefaces to the *Polychronicon,* we will find that they produce Higden's text as a chronicle that is above all about England, a nation that is close to the chronicler's heart.

Higden explains to us in his first preface why he wrote a universal history. The example of previous historians, he begins, inspired him. By memorializing the great deeds of the ancients, historians use examples to instruct their readers, laying out for them the *forma vivendi* or right way of living (1:2–5). Higden's evocation of the moral utility of historiography, while conventional, is not inevitable.[39] History is not always a matter of telling great deeds. It is the oppressions of the past, for instance, that are recorded in a classical source of the *Polychronicon*, Orosius's *Seven Books of History against the Pagans*.[40] And an even-handed approach to historiography is offered by one of Higden's British historiographic sources, Bede's *Ecclesiastical History* (731). In his preface, Bede articulates a twofold task accomplished by history: not only does it "tell of good men and their good estate" to encourage "the thoughtful listener . . . to imitate the good," but also "should it record the evil ends of wicked men" so that "the devout and earnest listener or reader is kindled to eschew what is harmful and perverse."[41] Higden, unlike Bede or Orosius, emphasizes only good deeds, I would argue, because of his national attachments. These English sentiments are revealed immediately after Higden's encomium to history, when he tells us that the example of past historians inspired him "to write some sort of treatise, compiled from the labors of different authorities, about the state of the island of Britain, for the edification of future readers."[42] *De statu insulae Britannicae:* the *Polychronicon,* it appears, was intended originally not to be poly at all, but to focus solely on the British past. And presumably since Higden claims to follow the example of the historiographic tradition he praises earlier in the preface, the British history he originally intended to write would have memorialized British greatness. Thus even as the preface begins with the *laudatio historiae* common to historical prefaces since the classical period, it complicates this convention by using it for an implicit *laudatio Britanniae,* in which Britain possesses a past worthy of recounting in that tradition of historical writing. If earlier historiographers memorialized the past because of the "example of admirable actions [spectabilium actionum exemplaria]" (1:4–5) it offers, Higden's prompting to write a specifically British history by example of those writers implies the value of the British past as a storehouse of "great deeds [magnifica . . . gesta]" (1:2–3). Higden's inclusion of his initial British historiographic intentions renders what otherwise would be a straightforward homage to history an indication of national feeling.[43]

It is only *after* Higden establishes his initial intent to write a British chronicle that he explains the presence of the universal elements of the history he ultimately wrote. According to Higden, his Benedictine *sodales* or fellows urged their brother to write instead "about the more famous stories of the world [de famosioribus orbis historiis]" from the beginning of time to the present (1:8). It hardly surprises, if this meeting actually did happen, that it is the *Polychronicon* and not a specifically British chronicle that is prefaced by this story of a meeting between a would-be national chronicler and his universalist brothers. Intrafraternal obedience lies at the very core of Benedictine life, whereby, according to the rule, "the brethren must . . . obey one another, knowing that by this path of obedience they shall come unto God."[44] Moreover, for a literary monk at St. Werburgh, the duty of obedience was particularly pressing: since 1277, obtaining the permission of the abbot had been required for brothers planning to write a book.[45] However, Higden never fully renounces his British interests in the *Polychronicon,* as he demonstrates in the second preface when he refers to Britain as the site "for the sake of which his entire history has been produced [cujus gratia tota praesens lucubrata est historia]" (1.26). Thus Higden's account of his fellow monks' desires does not serve the same function that similar moments do in classical *exordia*. Typically, such requests confer authority on the classical writer, who explains that he has embarked upon his enterprise to further not his own interests but those of his dedicatee or audience.[46] Higden's desire to suggest his own impartiality may explain his description of his meeting with his *sodales;* yet when we consider the positioning of this account after his explanation of his original national intentions for his chronicle, another reason emerges, one that has less to do with authorial objectivity than the uniquely complex nature of the scope of Higden's history. Together, these stories constitute a kind of opening dialectical movement, whereby the monk first intends to write a national history but then modifies his plans according to the universal desires of his colleagues. Through this sequence Higden alerts his readers to the status of the *Polychronicon* as a national/universal hybrid, a compromise text authored by a man divided by his own national interests and the universal concerns of his brethren. Neither a universal nor a national history outright, the *Polychronicon* straddles the line between a cosmopolitan view of the world and the particular achievements of Britain in that world.

After relating his monastic brothers' request, Higden describes his trepidation at the thought of tackling a universal chronicle. He asserts his own lack of intellectual ability to accomplish this massive task, one that he likens to that faced by Daedalus in the labyrinth (1:8–9). Higden's humility at his brothers' impossible demand provides his readers with an intensified version of the "modesty formulas" of judicial oratory, which, as Ernst Curtius observes, "achieve an immense diffusion . . . in the Latin . . . literature of the Middle Ages."[47] For Higden, as well as other late Latin and medieval Latin writers, the classical author's expression of the difficulty of his job has given way to the medieval author's expression of utter incompetence, of a hopeless discrepancy between the writer's capabilities and the brilliant achievement of his predecessors. Painfully aware of his own poverty (*meam paupertatem*), Higden, like Persius, dreads "after such trumpeters," to whine through his nose with his own "barren speech."[48] He asks: "Who would not laugh, or rather who not mock, if after the work of Hercules, and after the strife and jousts of the Olympics had been entirely finished, a pigmy readied himself for battle?"[49] Taken at his word, Higden provides ample support here for the possibility that the tremendous authorial anxiety voiced in medieval exordia testifies to "a general feeling of unworthiness before great predecessors experienced by the authors of late antiquity and the Middle Ages."[50] Of course, through his registration of the problem of authorial belatedness in his preface, Higden does in a sense overcome that dilemma. By voicing his fears at the very beginning of the *Polychronicon,* he at least gains over his readers the precursory power that previous scholarship denies him. That is, in his preface Higden enjoys the position of coming "before" denied him as a postclassical writer. Yet its prefatory location cannot completely mitigate the content of his words here, their registration of the anxiety of belatedness felt by an author writing after his predecessors' achievements. What interests us even more, however, is how Higden's complaint over his own belatedness richly suggests a problem specific to his identity as a historian of

Britain. Even as the authorial "poverty" he fears will produce only "barren speech" suggests the anxieties of any medieval writer conscious of his classical predecessors, it also allegorizes the particular problems associated with writing in England, an island as synchronically marginal to the civilized world as Higden is diachronically marginal to the classical past. That is, the anxious alienation from earlier writers that spurs Higden to call himself a barren and fragile writer parallels the dangers posed by Britain's status as a wild outback territory, far from the world's religio-cultural centers.

Allusions to geographic marginality appear more than once in Higden's complaint. For the cartographically minded medieval reader, the monk's reference to Hercules' feats could not help but conjure thoughts of the pillars (that is, the straits of Gibraltar) set up by the demigod during his tenth labor as a memorial to his journey to the western end of the known world. Throughout the Middle Ages, Hercules' pillars were memorialized in mappae mundi; they make one of three appearances in the first book of the *Polychronicon,* not long after the first preface, when Higden describes the longitude of the habitable world from East to West as the distance between India and the *columnas Herculis* (1:44–45).[51] On mappae mundi, the pillars typically appear at the very bottom of an eastern-oriented world, just to the right of Britain and Spain. Thus, at the same time that Hercules' memorial demonstrates the might of the demigod, it also recalls the frontier status of the classical and medieval West so troublesome for Higden. For it is of course Gibraltar's distance from classical civilization, its status as an outpost, that merits Hercules' memorial to himself. As Higden puts it in his description of the islands of the world ocean, at Gibraltar, "Hercules set his pillars, as it were, in the extremity of the earth (which is) wondrous and noteworthy."[52] Far from marking out the worthiness of the border *space* of their placement, the pillars signify the powers of their Greek (and hence centrally located) assembler, Hercules.

As if to underscore Hercules' status as representative of the powers ascribed to peoples hailing from the classical center of the world, Higden contrasts the labors of Hercules and other Greek feats—the labyrinth of Daedalus and the Olympics—with the diminutive efforts of the Pygmies, the dwarfish people who comprised one of the "monstrous races" perceived to inhabit either the eastern- or southernmost margins of the world.[53] The Hereford mappa mundi, for example, locates the Pygmies in India, on the world's eastern border. As we have seen, at the edges of the world, where the Pygmies and other monstrous races lived, lay "barren or savage landscapes" inextricably connected to the less-than-human status accorded their inhabitants.[54] Thus Albertus Magnus describes the Pygmy as an instinctive creature who lives in the wilderness and is uninterested in civilization.[55]

By comparing his failings with respect to classical writers to the Pygmies' inadequacies with respect to Hercules, Higden not only raises the problem of writing a universal history, but also highlights the challenges facing a chronicler of England, an island whose inhabitants, like the Pygmies, occupy the fringes of the world. How can his homeland possess a past worth emulating when it constitutes a kind of desert? Johannes Fabian has taught us that the location of a culture far from perceived centers of civilization carries with it not only a sense of spatial isolation but also temporal separation, whereby the contemporary western anthropologist views the native as inhabiting a primitive "past."[56] A similar collapsing of time and space under a rubric of distancing obtains implicitly in Higden's preface. The problems of belatedness facing a medieval writer and those facing a nation remote from the classical centers of civilization are the same: each has to do with an anxiety over how such distances, whether diachronic or synchronic, evoke problematic lacks: to be "barren," to be "fragile," and to "degenerate" (1:10–11).

## A Verbal Mappa Mundi

How does Higden overcome the challenge of English geographic marginality that he raises in the first preface? One crucial answer lies in yet another place where he yokes the spatial and the temporal: the verbal mappa mundi that forms the first book of his universal history. Higden was not alone in introducing his chronicle with a description of place. Orosius spends the second chapter of book one of his influential *Seven Books* briefly describing the three perceived parts of the medieval world (Asia, Africa, and Europe) as well as their regions, bodies of water, and peoples.[57] One century before Higden wrote the *Polychronicon,* we see the continuing importance of linking space and time in the historiographic work of Vincent of Beauvais, who not only describes the world à la Orosius but also surveys the natural resources of its various parts in his *Speculum Historiale* (1244), the most famous universal chronicle of the thirteenth century.[58]

The presence of these chorographic introductions in primarily chronological texts demonstrates how, for many medieval historians, the comprehension of past cultures requires knowledge not only of occurrences but also, as Orosius tells us, "of their geography as well" (1:34). In his third preface, Higden echoes Orosius's logic as he explains that the *descriptiones locorum* or descriptions of places contained in book one are one of the eight things necessary for a full understanding of past cultures (1:30–31). Why is space so important to these medieval historians? What does geography add to the understanding of the history of a people? The imbrication of space and time in Higden, Orosius, and other chroniclers demonstrates, as Henri Lefebvre has taught us, that space plays a crucial role in the constitution of societies. To enable his readers to imagine that cultures of the past actually existed, the medieval chronicler must project or inscribe those cultures within a definable space. "Otherwise," Lefebvre writes, "they remain in 'pure' abstraction."[59]

As cultural geographers such as Edward Soja suggest, the addition of a topographic component to a historical work is hardly a straightforward process. Far from serving only as, in Soja's words, "history's mirroring container," space is dynamic and rich, and uniquely contributes to the production of cultures.[60] We might best understand the constitutive function of geography in medieval historiography by turning to Higden's native sources. Several of those English sources—namely, the chronicles of Bede, Geoffrey of Monmouth, and Henry of Huntingdon (1154)—comprise part of a national tradition, initiated with Gildas's history of the Britons (564), of beginning histories by describing British topography.[61] These national histories offer no explicit rationale for

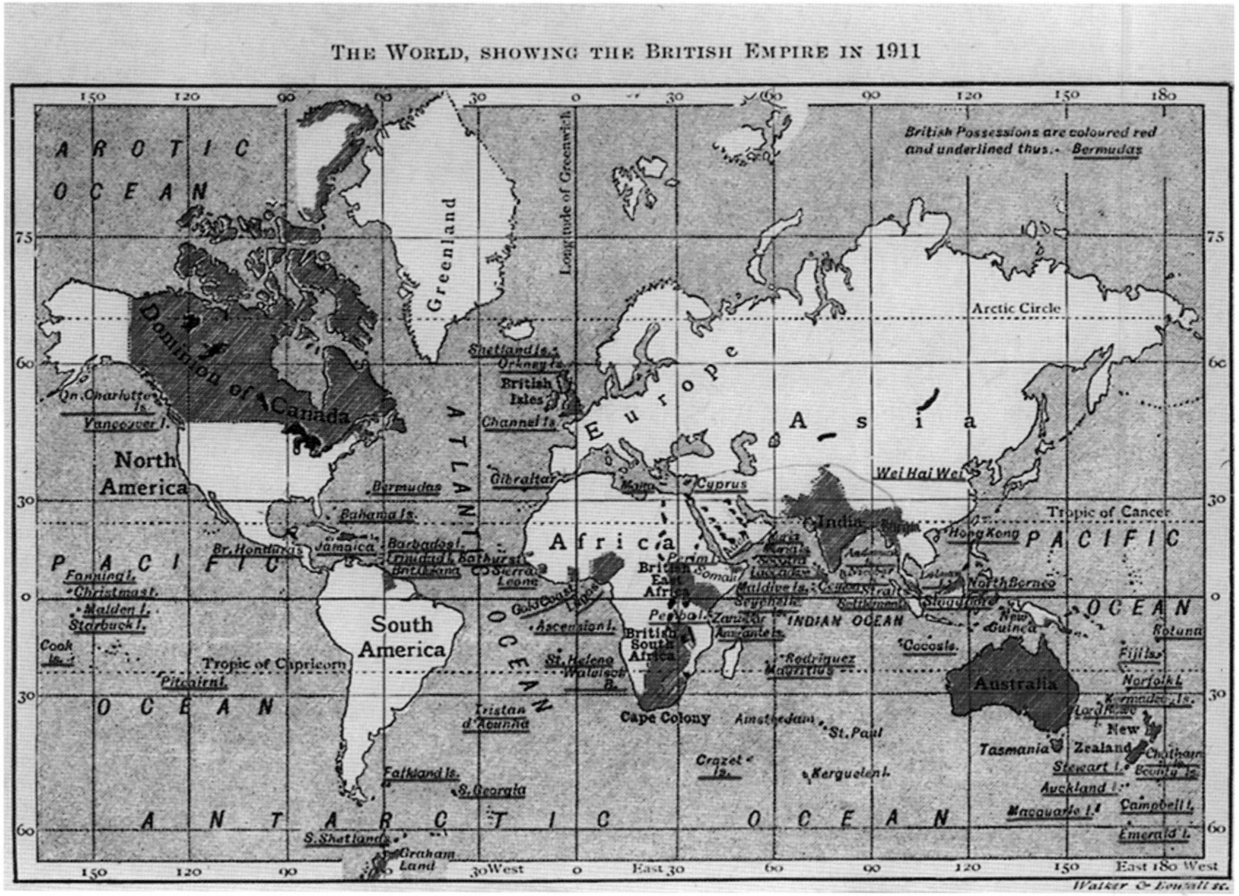

Plate 1. World map by Emery Walker and Walter Boutall for the frontispiece of P. H. Kerr and A. C. Kerr, *The Growth of the British Empire* (London, 1911).

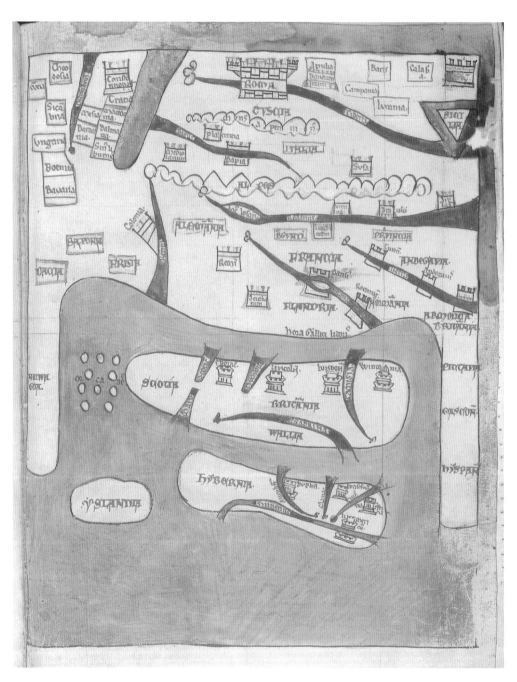

**Plate 2.** Map of Europe by Gerald de Barri, ca. 1200. Dublin, National Library of Ireland, MS. 700, fol. 48r. Property of the Trustees of the National Library of Ireland and reproduced with their permission.

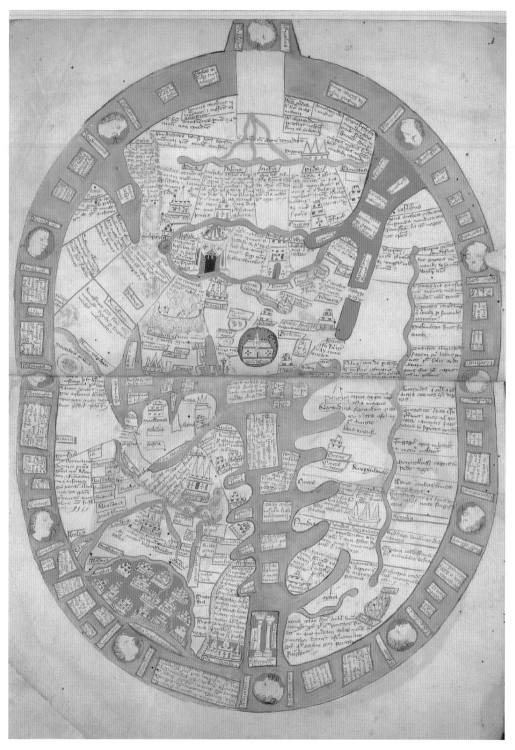

**Plate 3.** World map illustrating a copy of Higden's *Polychronicon*, Ramsey Abbey, late fourteenth century. London, British Library, Royal MS. 14 C.IX, 1v–2r. By permission of the British Library.

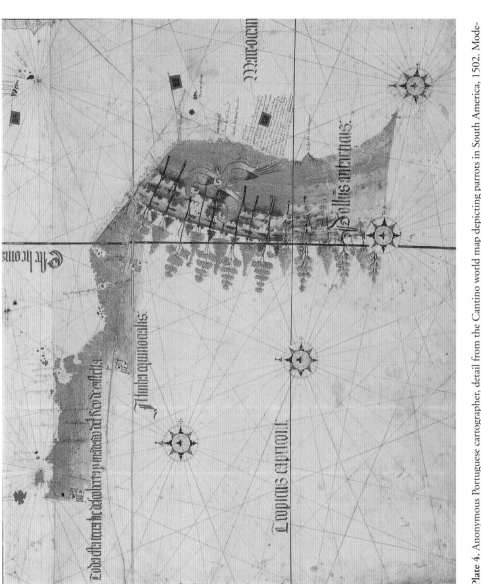

**Plate 4.** Anonymous Portuguese cartographer, detail from the Cantino world map depicting parrots in South America, 1502. Modena, Biblioteca Estense. By permission of the Ministry for Cultural Assets and Activities (Ministero per i Beni e le Attività Culturali).

their geographic prefaces, yet they clearly do more than merely augment temporal with spatial knowledge. In particular, descriptions of Britain not only provide a sense of place, but also celebrate the place that is Britain. Going beyond the mere survey of climate and location found in universal chronicles to detail natural resources, cities, counties, language, and even the character of the inhabitants of Britain, the descriptive prefaces offered by Bede, Geoffrey, and Henry construct England as a supremely worthy and exceptional territory. Geoffrey, for example, calls Britain "the best of islands" that "provides in unfailing plenty everything that is suited to the use of human beings . . ."[62] And Henry describes Britain as "truly an island of the utmost fertility," and a "celebrated island," in which "corn, milk, and honey, fuller shed their stores . . . than over all the isles."[63]

Through their very emphasis on the excellence of British topography, these chroniclers show how the spatial provides, as Soja puts it, no "stable and unproblematic site of historical action."[64] For by celebrating the land itself, these chroniclers complicate the image of Britain provided in the histories proper that dominate their texts, in which the nation is signified preeminently not by territory, but by people (namely, monarchs and ecclesiastics).[65] Because the diachronic matter of Bede's, Geoffrey's, and Henry's histories celebrates the deeds of kings and saints, it often presents a hierarchic image of human relations on the island. But by focusing on geography, medieval English historiographers set aside such ecclesiastical and monarchic tendencies for the sake of celebrating Britain itself. While the Britons and the English are vertically linked to their religious and secular leaders in the diachronic matter of these texts, their geographic prefaces construct the inhabitants of Britain as a people horizontally united and blessed by their shared climate ("very temperate and healthy" in Henry's history) ample resources, and insular boundaries.[66] By invoking space, in effect, the historiographers imaginatively transform the hierarchically structured populace portrayed in their chronologies into a community leveled and bound by the land.

Higden's chorographic first book epitomizes the incipient Englishness of his native chronicle sources, as the length alone of his description of Britain attests. Until Higden, Henry of Huntington offered the most extensive national chorography in an English chronicle. Higden, however, devotes about four times more space to describing Britain than does Henry. It may appear curious that the tendency to include celebratory descriptions of Britain culminates with the *Polychronicon*. For while Bede, Geoffrey, Henry, and other national chroniclers focus solely on Britain in their chorographies, Higden prefaces his universal text with a description not only of Britain but also of the rest of the known world and thus risks reducing his home to yet another region among the many described in book one. But Britain of course really is never just another place in universal geography. As Vincent of Beauvais writes in the geographic preface to his *Speculum Historiale,* "Britain is an island of the ocean with the sea surrounding it cut off from the whole world."[67] The erasure of particular identities threatened by the adoption of a universal geographical perspective does not figure in the case of a marginalized Britain.

Of course, whether British marginality is worth celebrating is another matter. As we have seen, Higden first hints at the status of Britain as a marginal island in his initial preface, where his anxiety over his own authorial belatedness figures the problems of an island on the edge of the world. Later, in his third preface, while explaining the rationale behind the structure of the *Polychronicon,* he alludes yet again to English marginality, but in this case he emphasizes the advantages of the border positioning of England: "The first book of this work, in the manner of breaking down of the genus into species, will describe the regions of the world. Next the world will be divided into its more significant parts. Third, each particular region is treated in succession, until the text will have reached Britain last of all, as if the text will have reached the most special sight, for the sake of which the entire chronicle at hand assiduously was produced."[68] Close philological analysis of this passage reveals the careful attention to the issues of geography, alterity, and Englishness that underlie Higden's first book. The monk's own use of classical sources, his probable role as "official custodian of the abbey's library" as well as the preeminence of the Benedictines as, to borrow Beryl Smalley's phrase, "classicizing friars," all suggest that he would have been well aware of both the ancient and medieval connotations of his Latin prose in the above passage.[69] *Novissimam* means not only "last," but also "furthest"; hence when Higden tells us that book one reaches Britain "last of all" he connotes the geographic marginalization of Britain in cartography.[70] The mingling of geographic content and literary form further obtains in Higden's use of verbs of motion such as *percurrere* ("to run through, hasten through, traverse") and *pervenire* ("to come to, arrive at, reach a place").[71] By using this language of travel to indicate the placement of Britain at the end of book one, he suggests how his chorography structurally mimics the shape of the world itself, whereby the act of reading offers an imaginary journey across the world, until, at its extreme edge, one "arrives" at England. The arrangement of places in Higden's narrative of world topography, roughly speaking, does indeed follow the placement of lands on medieval world maps. In the same way that Paradise appears at the top and the British Isles appear at the bottom of such maps, book one begins its description of the parts of the earth with Paradise and ends with Britain. Yet there are also telling differences between the sequence of descriptions in the *Polychronicon* and the arrangement of territories in the world. As we saw in our analysis of Gerald de Barri's Irish books, it is Ireland that lies furthest on the earth's western edge. Higden in fact relies upon Gerald for his descriptions of both Ireland and Wales in his chorography. But those descriptions *precede* that of England. Implicitly transferring the supreme marginality of Ireland to England, Higden makes his homeland the terrain that his readers reach last of all.

*Novissimam* does more than conflate time and space in the *Polychronicon.* Defined as "novel, strange, singular, unusual, unaccustomed, or inexperienced," the stem of the superlative, *novus,* reflects the various meanings of geographic alterity. "Unaccustomed" and "inexperienced" recall the inept and marginal Pygmies as well as a backward British world frontier. "Singular," however, suggests an English people set apart from the world because they are exceptional. It is that latter definition that Higden perhaps has in mind when he writes that book one ends with "Britain last of all, as if the text will have reached the most special sight."[72] Reminding the reader of his original national intentions, Higden further writes that it is "for the sake of" England that "the entire chronicle at hand assiduously was produced." By alerting the reader to the intense work out of which the *Polychronicon* has arisen and attaching that labor specifically to the English elements of the history, he appropriates the weight of his universalist labor ("the *entire* chronicle") and attaches it to the national construct, "Britain." Through his invocation of the voice of the toiling and even affectionate chronicler, Higden reiterates that he has saved the best for last.[73]

## Eternal Isolation

It is one thing for Higden to tell us in his preface that his description of England is the most important one offered in the *Polychronicon;* it is quite another matter for him to succeed in showing his readers the excellence of the island in the chronicle itself. Of course, Higden's predominant status as compiler in his chronicle complicates matters further. How can we locate anything like authorial agency in a work based heavily on the gathering of previous sources, sources that are themselves difficult to pin down? Yet no compilation is neutral. As Peter Brown has pointed out, Higden is indeed a compiler, but he is a compiler with a method.[74] That method emerges with particular clarity when considered in terms of his prefaces. That Higden's unique arrangement, expansion, and abbreviation of sources produced a description of Britain with exceptional national appeal is suggested by the considerable number of Englishmen who decided to translate or print vernacular versions of Higden's national chorography independently of the rest of the *Polychronicon.* In 1440, Osbern Bokenham translated those portions of Higden's chorography dealing with England into a vernacular text he termed *Mappula Angliae* (in apparent imitation of Higden's terming of book one mappa mundi); and, in 1480, Caxton printed an adaptation of Trevisa's translation of Higden's description of Ireland, Scotland, Wales, and England.[75] Entitled *The Discripcion of Britayne,* Caxton's text reversed the organization of Higden's account of Britain, "putting," in A. S. G. Edwards's words, "the priority where he felt his London customers would want it."[76] The *Discripcion* was reprinted in 1498 by Wynkyn de Worde.[77] Editions would continue to appear as late as 1528, and manuscript chorographies based on Higden would be made up to 1530.[78] As we have seen, many Latin descriptions of England by Bede, Geoffrey of Monmouth, and other writers preceded that of Higden. But of all these works, it is only that found in the *Polychronicon* that is consistently deemed appropriate for vernacular translation for a national lay audience. Both the translation and separate publication of Higden's description of Britain indicate how, well into the sixteenth century, up to the eve of the Reformation, the literary/geographical work of imagining England as a place was identified above all with Higden. The monk's influence would continue well into the early modern era, when his chorography would form the basis of William Harrison's decidedly patriotic description of Britain in the introduction to Holinshed's *Chronicles* (1587).[79]

Small wonder that later writers and printers embraced Higden's chorography, as it provides an appealing image of English geographic marginality, one that overcomes a host of challenges to national identity. As Andrew Galloway has shown, Higden shores up a problematic variety or *varietas* that troubles the notion of English unity. From the diversity of the English language, to that of English society, to that of the multiple conquerors of England, "*varietas . . .* becomes both an encompassing principle of all history and a broadening 'now' in [Higden's] locatably English act of writing."[80] As much emerges in Higden's chorography of Britain, which covers chapters thirty-nine to sixty of book one. Questions of space dominate the chorography, yet the section is hardly divorced from the chronicle of historical events it precedes. Instead the description offers, as Higden puts it in his second preface, contextual or introductory information related to the books it precedes (1:28–29). Thus in addition to relating the dimensions, principal parts, major waterways, and cities of the island, the chorography also surveys the history of the kings, bishops, and peoples of England. Those historical aspects of the description undermine the production of a unified and supreme English identity. For example, English history is one of successive disruptions in chapter fifty-one, where a united Britain disintegrates into a Roman colony; and Anglo-Saxon England is divided into seven kingdoms and later united under Athelstan, only to be disrupted by the Danes and then by the Normans (2:96–99).

The disjunctive nature of English history pervades even the geographic material of the description. In particular, Higden's emphasis on the various names attached to places throughout English history reminds the reader of Britain's recurrent conquest by different peoples speaking different languages. For instance, Higden includes from Geoffrey of Monmouth Brutus's establishment of Trinovantum as the principal city of Britain, and Lud's renaming of the city Caerlud, and then himself adds that later the English called the city London and still later the Normans renamed it Loundres (2:56–57). The history of place-names—whether of cities, rivers, highways, or shires—in the *Polychronicon* suggests the instability of identity on the island, an instability that pervades the text of the *Polychronicon* itself, as Higden's description of the roads, cities, or principal parts of his country is interrupted consistently by his inclusion of the past names of various features of the isle he describes. The fragmentation of the text itself by the unsettled nature of the British past perhaps obtains most clearly in a passage on the cities of the island taken from Alfred of Beverly: "These were the names of the cities: Caerlud, that is, London . . . Caerthleon, or Caerlegion, that is the city of legions, which was later called Legecestre(?), but now is called Chester . . . Caerpaladour, that is Septon, which today is called Shaftesbury."[81] Here, as elsewhere in his chorography, Higden's compulsion to provide past place-names renders his writing nearly unreadable.

But such indications of British historical discontinuity are mitigated by manifestations of spatial continuity in Higden's work. For example, in chapter forty-five, on the principal highways of England, Higden (following Henry of Huntington) describes four roads that stretch throughout the island ("per insulam strui," 2:44) linking all of its inhabitants, from the north, south, east, and west. By describing the cities traversed by British roads—and by describing, in chapter forty-six, the cities traversed by British rivers—Higden shows his readers how they not only inhabit a local community but also belong to a larger island to whose cities they are bound by various roads and waterways. And while the names of the cities connected by the rivers and roads of the island may have changed, these urban centers—above all, London—do at least remain in the same location. Above all, what provides a cohesiveness to English identity that transcends the fragmentary quality of the English past is *haec terra*—the land itself. To be sure, the names of the land may change, as is evinced even by the heading of the first chapter of the description: "On Greater Britain, otherwise called England."[82] Yet the land itself remains and retains its unique properties.[83]

Foremost among the unique properties of *haec terra* as it is described in the *Polychronicon* is its marginality. Higden mentions British geographic isolation at least seven times in book one. Three of these references appear at the beginning of the description, in the account of the various names of the island, which he abridges from Bartholomaeus Anglicus's *On the Properties of Things*:

> First this island was called Albion because of the white cliffs around the shore of the sea which could be seen from afar; later, after having been conquered by Brutus, it was called Britain; after that it was called England by the Saxons (or English) who had taken possession of it; others say that it was called England because of a queen of the island for many years named Angela, who was the daughter of a most noble Saxon duke; or, as Isidore states in book fifteen of his *Etymologies,* it is called England because (the island) is an angle of the world; or, as Bede states in book one of the *Ecclesiastical History,* the blessed Gregory seeing some English children for sale at Rome, and he—alluding to the name of their country—said: "truly they are English, for their faces shine like angels; for the nobility of the land shined forth in the faces of the children." Alfred. English Britain is called another world, which formerly Charlemagne called his own chamber because of the great abundance of good things there. Solinus. For the coasts of France would be called the end of the world, if Britain did not deserve the name of almost another world.[84]

The history of names offered here yet again suggests the instability of the English past, its history of conquest after conquest. Moreover, the various explanations offered for the appellation "England" appear to deny any stable etymological underpinning to the final name given the island. Yet Higden uses geography to recuperate the chronologic differences facing the imagining of an English community. Above all, the insistent reference to the island as an *angulus orbis* or an *alter orbis* points to a national geographic marginality that provides the very cohesive and unified identity denied by the fragmentary past of England. The status of the English as geographic "others" forms a kind of refrain in this passage that binds its apparently discordant elements together. While the names of England alter, the land always remains an *alter orbis.* To be sure, the barbaric implications of geographic isolation obtain in the reference to the enslavement of the heathen English boys for sale at the Forum. Yet the passage ultimately suggests how the marginality of the English is less a matter of their brutality than their supremacy. Gregory's Latin pun on *Angli* and *angeli* implies that English otherness is less about *dis-*

*tance* from civilization than about *proximity* to the angels. Crucially, the account of the slave-boy story, taken here from Bartholomaeus, does not merely repeat the English/angel pun, but adds to it, by having Gregory remark that the "nobility of the land shone forth in the faces of the children." This imbrication of territory and body through a kind of prosopopeia reinforces the superlative valence of English isolation. The strange isle inhabited by the English slaves is also a *terra nobilita,* an excellent land whose reflection in the boys' visages overcomes the problem of their enslavement and barbarity. Moreover, the binding of land and body in turn connects the final appellation offered here for the island with the first. The English children's bright visages bespeak the excellence of their birthplace, reflecting the whiteness of the cliffs of Albion. The turn to geography appeals to the reader's senses, allowing her to envision imaginatively a land apart from the world and admire the white cliffs of Dover, topographic signs of a national integrity that transcends historical disruption.

After this etymology of the island, Higden elaborates on the bounty of resources ("omnium bonorum copia") that spurred Charlemagne to call Britain his own chamber. While Higden follows here the precedent set by Bede, Henry of Huntington, and other English chroniclers, he departs from them when he explicitly identifies English natural resources as signs of English distinction (the chapter is titled *De praerogativis insulae attollendis* or On the Privileges of that Island to be Exalted) and expounds on those resources in unprecedented detail. Throughout the chapter (in which Higden combines his own original entries with citations from Bede, Pliny, William of Malmesbury, Alfred of Beverly, and Isidore) a vocabulary of natural plenty and productivity reigns. Using adjectives such as *abundus, copiosus, ferax, foecundus, praeclarus,* and *spatiosus,* Higden indicates the abundance and beauty of the flora, fauna, and minerals upon the island. The chapter culminates in a poem, indebted to sources including Hildebert, Alfred of Beverly, and William Fitzstephen, proclaiming that

> England is a fruitful land and a fertile corner of the world. England is full of amusements, (and) a free people worthy to be amused; independent are her people, to whom (belong) a free mind and a free tongue, but the hand is better and freer than the tongue. England, the worship and flower of all regions that border it, is satisfied by means of the fertility of its goods. It restores and refreshes depleted foreign people, when hunger strikes them. When it has the blessing of peace, the pleasant land fully thrives due to its good fortune of amazing fertility. The havens of the English are known East and West. England has fleets that help many places. Both food and wealth are shared here more than in other places. . . . Indeed, blessed by far-famed splendor, in terms of its brilliance, its lands, its well-known milk, honeys, and cheese, that island rises above all others and whose help the whole world needs. It is a very plentiful island, which does not need the entire world, and the power of which the whole world is in need. It is a very plentiful island, the delights of which Solomon may marvel at, the riches of which Octavian may desire.[85]

The final phrase of the first line, *fertilis angulus orbis,* encapsulates the apparent project of Higden's first descriptive chapter on England: the production of the world margin as a site of natural plenty. The abundant resources of the land allow the remote English to enjoy the self-sufficiency, supremacy, and renown typically identified with world centers. Supporting Benedict Anderson's insight that the nation is imagined as "'the best'— in a competitive, comparative field," the poem proclaims that the fertile English corner of the world does not need the entire world (*toto non eget orbe*), it is a land of milk and honey that surpasses (*supereminet*) all; its havens are renowned from East to West (*novit et ortus*).[86] The bounty of England in these verses also includes an abundance of pleasures (*Anglia plena jocis*) that are intertwined with the plenteous nature of the English themselves, who are described as a *gens libera.* The adjective *libera,* repeated several times in the poem, refers to several qualities, among them nobility, generosity, freedom, and independence. Binding together English independence and English pleasure, the poem shows how, as Slavoj Žižek has taught us, the nation, like the subject, "fully 'exists' only through enjoyment."[87]

Through its emphasis on the self-sufficiency of and freedoms enjoyed by an English *locus amoenus,* the poem produces the edge as a site of power, preeminence, and autonomy. Yet anxieties over geographic alterity remain. After all, Higden wrote during a time when famine and other forms of acute physical distress made England more a wasteland than anything else. His linkage of fertility and peace ("Commoda terra satis mirandae fertilitatis / Prosperitate viget, cum bona pacis habet") binds the natural disasters of early fourteenth-century England with its political upheavals, suggesting that the resolution of the former problem hinges on overcoming the latter. Moreover, Higden appears to respond to the historical problem of England's multiple invasions. Imputing to the Other the "theft of enjoyment," the poem implies that many peoples have entered the island because of the riches and delights it possesses.[88] England in the poem is a site whose abundance the rest of the world needs. That identification of England as a haven, however, exposes the contingent nature of national fantasy. For all its emphasis on the independence of the English, the poem also registers the wish that the nation be desired by others. In particular, isolated England requires the validating desire of authorities hailing from world capitals. King Solomon and Emperor Octavian represent the geopolitical might of Jerusalem and Rome, which both appear at or near the center of the world on medieval mappae mundi. England cannot authorize itself, it appears, but requires the legitimizing approval of the center.

## Angels at the Center of the World

Above all, in the *Polychronicon,* what England needs is Rome, which follows closely on the heels of England as the object of Higden's attentions. Insomuch as he emphasizes Roman history, Higden mirrors the conventional Roman bias of Christian universal historiography.[89] Theoretically, of course, universal history conceives of a past dominated not by any worldly people but instead by the Christian God. The universal scope of Christian history signifies both God's status as the providential force behind all of history, and the promise of all world peoples' Christian redemption. But as thinkers on history such as Hayden White, Tzvetan Todorov, and Fredric Jameson have shown, any reference to the past involves equivocation.[90] Such equivocations began in universal historiography with Eusebius of Caesarea. An early fourth-century writer whom R. A. Markus has called the "greatest publicist of the first Christian emperor," Eusebius claims that the empire under Constantine fulfilled certain messianic prophesies, such as the oracle's promise to Abraham that "He shall become a great and mighty nation, and in him shall be blessed all the nations of the world."[91] Eusebius's "imperial theology" became embedded in the late classical popular imagination and, even after the sack of Rome in 410, his perception of Rome as God's chosen instrument continued to be promoted by Orosius.[92] Emphasizing Augustus over Constantine, Orosius asserted a special bond between Christianity and Rome in his *Seven Books,* a view that was passed on to medieval writers due to the chronicle's popularity.[93] To be sure, not every writer supported this promotion of the Roman Empire. Most notably, Augustine in his *City of God* insisted that no earthly entity, not even Rome, could enjoy a privileged relationship with God. But Augustine's views proved far less influential than the Roman schematizations of world history offered by Eusebius and Orosius. For medieval Christian historians, Rome, as the last of the four empires envisioned by David, was from its inception and would be until the end of time the central player in history.[94]

In many respects, Higden accepts the universal historians' elevation of Rome. Beginning with his account of the legendary foundation of Rome in book two, the monk narrates in detail the development of the empire. During chapters forty-one through forty-four of the chronicle's third book, Rome even becomes the principal topic of the *Polychronicon,* as Higden recounts the eras of Julius Caesar and Octavian. Higden's assessment of these Roman figures, while at times critical, is often celebratory. The chronicler praises, for instance, Caesar's swiftness in battle, his remarkable learnedness, and his outstanding patience.[95] Higden bestows even more praise on Octavian. Reflecting the high esteem that had been placed upon the emperor in chronicles since the appearance of the *Seven Books,* he recounts Augustus's claim that he had found Rome brick and left it marble, and writes that the Romans admired the emperor so much that they would have made him a God if he had let them.[96]

Yet Higden's emphasis on Rome should not be read at face value. The placement of the Roman episodes in the *Polychronicon* suggests that there is more to the story. Higden's account of the Roman past begins book two, which covers world history from the creation to Nebuchadnezzar. In the book's twenty-sixth and twenty-seventh chapters, Higden directly follows an account of Aeneas's wanderings after the Trojan War and his conquests in Italy with a chapter focusing upon the Brutus legend. By juxtaposing the myth of Rome's Trojan origins with that of Britain's Trojan beginnings, Higden urges his readers to consider Rome and England in relation to each other. The contiguity of these founding stories, in particular, suggests that the moment of the production of British identity is of such consequence that it merits consideration along with the creation of the great empire. The writer continues to juxtapose Rome and Britain throughout the chronicle. Higden's third and fourth books focus on Rome, with some British history interspersed among these imperial episodes increasingly until book five, where

Britain supplants Rome as the prime focus for the rest of the chronicle. That temporal juxtaposition suggests a kind of *translatio imperii* at work in history, whereby some of what was special about Rome is being carried on by Britain.[97]

Yet, as with the poem on the bounties of England, Higden's national appropriation of Rome also suggests the monk's vexed attitude toward English geographic isolation. Higden's ambivalence most clearly emerges in moments when he doesn't simply juxtapose Roman and British history, but instead blurs the line between them. In the crucial transitional stage of the chronicle, near the end of book four, at whose conclusion the balance of history shifts from the affairs of Rome to those of Britain, one episode stands out: Higden's long biography of Constantine. What makes this episode especially interesting for our purposes is the historiographer's support for the myth of Constantine's British ancestry. While he mentions Ambrose's contention that Constantine's mother Helen was French, Higden's account of Constantine's life ultimately supports the mythic claim, first made by Geoffrey of Monmouth, that Helen was a Briton, whom Constantine's Roman father Constancius married after restoring Roman rule in Britain (cf. 5:96–97; 5:136–37). Indeed, the monk refers to the emperor's British bloodline no less than three times in this section of the chronicle.

While Higden takes the emperor's British roots from Geoffrey, his uses for Constantine differ from his source. As Robert Hanning has demonstrated, Geoffrey's "Britishing" of Constantine is largely a secular and British matter. While Geoffrey tells us that Constantine served Britain well during his reign there, we learn nothing of his role as the first Christian Roman emperor; rather, Geoffrey only emphasizes the disastrous consequences for Britain of Constantine's imperial ambitions, as he relates the emperor's efforts to crush a rebellion against Roman rule on the island.[98] While Higden does relate Constantine's efforts to overcome the rebellion of Octavius in Britain, he departs from Geoffrey by stressing Constantine's beneficial role in Christian history. Higden's account of Constantine consumes more space than that of any other emperor described in book four, and by and large that account is celebratory. While he does follow his relation of the donation of Constantine with excerpts from Gerald de Barri and Jerome about the secular corruption of the church, Higden spends more time complimenting than criticizing Constantine (5:130–31). He relates both mythic and historical accounts of Constantine's life, recounting such episodes from the emperor's *vita* as his vision of the cross the night before the defeat of Maxentius at the Milvian bridge, his miraculous catechism by Sylvester, and his pity for pagan infants. The book even closes with citations from Gregory the Great, Ambrose, and Isidore on Constantine's gracious end, his great merit, his reward before God, and his Greek feast day. Both the space and praise allotted Constantine in the *Polychronicon* point to the status of his life as the Christian imperial climax of book four, which begins with the life of Christ and culminates in the Christian conversion of the empire.[99] According to the *Polychronicon*, then, at the apex of Roman history ironically sits no Roman at all, but a Briton. The Britishing of Constantine reveals an attraction on Higden's part to the authority of the center so great that he imagines the movement of a man from the British border of the world to its Roman capital, where that Briton assumes nothing less than the role of the world's first Christian emperor. Even as Higden is invested in the coherent national identity that geographic isolation affords England, he is also drawn to the idea of a Briton breaking past his island's limits and enjoying the centricity and global supremacy embodied by the Roman Empire.

## Cosmopolitan Nationalism

For a reader interested in the English aspects of the *Polychronicon,* most remarkable perhaps is Higden's sensitivity regarding the role of fantasy in nation building. In chapter six of book five, Higden briefly turns to the career of the legendary figure whom we most identify with the incipient nationalism of medieval England, King Arthur. After mentioning some of the details of Arthur's life and death, Higden queries the Arthurian legend as it appears in Geoffrey's *History.* While Geoffrey describes Arthur overcoming both the king of France and the emperor of Rome, Higden remarks, no Roman or Frankish histories record such Arthurian exploits. While Geoffrey wonders at the absence of Arthur in the work of Gildas and Bede, Higden tells us that he marvels at Geoffrey's extensive praise of a man ignored by credible and established chroniclers.[100] Yet he not only wonders at but also offers a rationale for Geoffrey's account of Arthur. We may understand the presence of an unbelievably mighty Arthur, Higden tells us, if we consider how such heroes may be constructed not for their own sake but for the sake of a nation:

> But perhaps it is the manner of every nation to extol in excessive praise some one from their members, as the Greeks do their Alexander, the Romans their Octavian, the English their Richard, the French their Charles; and thus it follows that the Britons overly exalt their Arthur. That happens often, as Josephus says, for the beauty of the story, for the pleasure of the readers, or to praise their own blood.[101]

As John E. Housman remarked in his 1947 reading of this astonishing passage, Higden "realizes that every nation is prone to extol certain of its heroes excessively."[102] Part of the work of history, Higden admits here, is that of giving pleasure, of offering a fiction that imaginatively creates a sovereign nation. His remarks provoke a strident rebuttal by his Middle English translator John Trevisa, a Cornishman who is clearly an Arthurian enthusiast.[103] But Higden's thinking on the tendency of nations to render their heroes larger than life also proves so powerful as to even make Trevisa both concede that "it may wel be þat Arthur is ofte overpreysed and so beeþ many oþere," and refer to Augustine's remarks on the overvaluation of Greek heroes (5:338–39).

Higden's analysis of the patriotic impulses that lead to scarcely credible assertions within classical and medieval historiography appears to place the chronicler outside of the very dynamic he outlines. While Higden registers the tendency of national chronicles to indulge in the legendary, he fails to acknowledge his participation in such fantasies. Indeed, he appears here as a man invested in destroying English identity by, on the one hand, demystifying Richard the Lionhearted and King Arthur as exaggeratedly heroic characterizations and, on the other hand, separating the Britons from the English as individual peoples lacking a shared past. It is no doubt moments such as these in the *Polychronicon,* instances when Higden presents himself as an objective chronicler of the world past, that prompted John Taylor emphatically to distinguish Higden's chronicle from the only other fourteenth-century chronicle to exceed its popularity— the *Brut.* According to Taylor, while their wide appeal links these chronicles, "it would be difficult to imagine two more dissimilar histories": "While the *Brut* gave a legendary account of British history based upon the story of Geoffrey of Monmouth, the *Polychronicon* offered to the most educated and learned audience in England something which they had never previously known, a clear and convincing picture of world history. Whereas in its early chapters the *Brut* provided fiction and romance, Higden struggled with a mass of classical and medieval sources to give a true picture of the Roman world."[104] The contrast drawn here between the "romantic" *Brut* and the "clear and convincing" *Polychronicon* tells us less about those texts than about Taylor's desire to establish Higden as a "solid" historian. Taylor's claim about the "truth-value" of Higden's text is bound up with his emphasis upon its status as "the first chronicle written in England to treat world history on an extended scale."[105] Taylor thus links the truth/fiction binary he constructs with another, national/universal binary, whereby the narration of national history is a suspect and legendary matter, while the telling of world history is a far more objective and scholarly enterprise. The "cosmopolitan" shift to the world, Taylor implies, prevents the universal chronicler from succumbing to the patriotic storytelling to which national historians are prone.

Taylor's valorization of Higden resembles the celebrations of various forms of world thinking (multiculturalism, cosmopolitanism, and so on) that have circulated prominently in critical debates in recent decades. Just as the medievalist Taylor views Higden's shift to the world as a liberating gesture that frees the chronicler of national biases, theorists have interpreted the shift to a global perspective as a useful way of responding to social problems such as racism and nationalism. To be sure, a global perspective indeed can oppose the claims of elitist groups to supremacy. Consider the force of Higden's critique of Geoffrey, a critique so powerful as to give the Celtic patriot Trevisa pause. But we also need to attend to how localized forms of sociopolitical bias or prejudice thrive in ostensibly global or multicultural programs. Although certain globalisms can fight the unfair claims and practices of certain social formations, those very social formations can also appropriate global discourses for their own troubling purposes. Timothy Brennen, for example, has shown how U.S. mass culture at times espouses a cosmopolitan ethic on behalf of American national and corporate interests.[106] And Saskia Sassen has demonstrated how "processes of economic globalization" are "concrete economic complexes situated in specific places," that hardly constitute "the terrain of a balanced playing field."[107] As both the Roman biases of universal historiography and the English biases of the *Polychronicon* demonstrate, the shift to the world does not necessarily endow the premodern historian with critical distance on his topic. The assumption of a world perspective always takes place from a particular place in that world. As a result, the biases of the particular remain. A monk writing from the Cheshire border of England, Higden manipulates global geography to fashion his own myth of English identity.

CHAPTER FOUR

# BEYOND ROME

Mapping Gender and Justice in the *Man of Law's Tale*

With charming audacity, William Godwin fulfills in his *Life of Chaucer* (1803) the long-ing of many a critic to know what the poet and Petrarch would have made of each other had they ever met and, in doing so, gives his readers a startling lesson in premodern car-tography. While Petrarch's status as the literary heir of classical Rome fascinates Chaucer, the English poet, Godwin writes,

> was interesting to Petrarca for a different reason. He came from the *ultima Thule,* the *penitus toto divisos orbe Britannos* (Virgil, *Bucolica,* Ecl. I); that country which the wan-tonness of more genial climates among the ancients had represented as perpetually en-veloped in fogs and darkness. To later times the literature and poetical genius of Britain is familiar; no tongue so barbarous, as not to confess us the equals, while in reality we are in intellectual eminence the masters, of mankind. But this was a spectacle alto-gether unknown in the times of Petrarca. The discovery he made was scarcely less as-tonishing than that of Columbus when he reconnoitred the shores of the Western world. . . . He embraced the wondrous stranger from a frozen clime, and foresaw, with that sort of inspiration which attends the closing period of departing genius, the fu-ture glories of a Spenser, a Shakespear and a Milton.[1]

By writing that, from Petrarch's premodern perspective, Britain was *penitus toto divisos orbe* or wholly sundered from the entire world, Godwin troubles his readers' sense of normative Englishness. While for Godwin the English are the intellectual "masters of mankind," for Petrarch as for Virgil, the English were mankind's Others, the backward inhabitants of an isle "enveloped in fogs and darkness." Yet even as Godwin raises the problem of English geographic isolation, he also turns it, through a figure of Roman "classical greatness," into a sign of English "future glories." The marginality of England sets the stage for an "astonishing" discovery: the Italian finds on this isolated isle no savage alien, but a "wondrous stranger." Chaucer's geographic isolation ultimately signifies not his brutality, but his magnificence.[2]

In imagining Petrarch's "astonishing" discovery, Godwin ignores what is perhaps a still more striking characteristic of early English literary history: the self-consciousness that, as we have seen, English writers from Ælfric onward evinced over England's reputation as an island sundered from the world. That Chaucer himself was interested in issues of Englishness and strangeness emerges throughout his most social text, the *Canterbury Tales.*[3] The *Wife of Bath's Tale,* for example, uses a character possessed of a fourfold otherness (the "foul, and oold, and poore" hag) to relate an Arthurian legacy to British national identity (3.1063); the *Franklin's Tale* allows the pilgrims to imagine "Engelond" as a foreign country (5.810); and the *General Prologue* depicts Canterbury as a site both identified with the "straunge" and the "ferne" and capable of attracting a national gathering of England's populace, "from every shires ende" (1.13–15).[4] Chaucer's most extensive engagement with English geographic otherness, however, emerges in the most geographic of the *Canterbury Tales,* the Man of Law's story of Custance (ca. 1394).

The figure of alterity in the *Man of Law's Tale,* of course, is a familiar topic in critical work on the poem, though the primary Other interpreted by Chaucerians is not England, but Custance. As David Raybin has pointed out, Custance herself is geographically marginalized in the tale; she is famed for her many ocean voyages and, when ashore, never ventures far inland.[5] For Raybin, both Constance's spatial isolation and her temporal strangeness—that is, her capacity to transcend the messiness of historical events—render her an exemplary and "hooly" outsider.[6] With his take on Custance, Raybin joins other scholars such as Morton Bloomfield in claiming that Custance's alterity offers a Christian ideal of living in, yet being not of, a fallen world.[7] More recently, feminist critics including Susan Schibanoff, Geraldine Heng, and Kathryn Lynch have linked Custance's alterity to the orientalist tendencies of the tale.[8] Thus Heng writes that "by virtue of its geographical distance and its mythological proximity," the East performs fantasy work "for the West that is proximately similar to the function performed" by women such as Custance in masculinist culture.[9] Along similar lines, Schibanoff notes that Custance becomes intertwined with Others including Saracens and Muslims in the Man of Law's strategy of establishing "Christian fraternity among the pilgrims."[10] All in all, these and other feminist critics have made clear how figures of feminized *and* eastern alterity become the basis of patriarchy in the *Man of Law's Tale.*

Yet Custance and the Syrians hardly constitute the only outsiders in the poem, as the second part of the tale plainly shows. After having transported his fellow pilgrims from Syria to Rome and back, the Man of Law takes his auditors home, as Custance journeys in a divinely navigated ship to Britain:

Yeres and dayes fleet this creature
Thurghout the See of Grece unto the Strayte
Of Marrok, as it was hire aventure

. . . . . . . . . . . .

Er that the wilde wawes wol hire dryve

. . . . . . . . . . . .

. . . into *oure* occian
Thurghout *oure wilde* see, til atte laste

. . . . . . . . . . . .

Fer in Northumberlond the wawe hire caste.

(2.463–508; EMPHASIS ADDED)

While Chaucer's sources, Nicholas Trevet's *Chronique* (ca. 1334) and John Gower's *Confessio Amantis* (ca. 1390), do not mention the specifics of Custance's long journey to England, the Man of Law includes geographic details such as the eastern Mediterranean and the straits of Gibraltar that make palpable the space traversed by Custance.[11] As V. A. Kolve puts it, "the tale creates a residual image that is geographical: a map of Europe with a boat moving upon its waters."[12] But since Custance's journey begins in Syria, the cartographic territory evoked in the tale in fact extends beyond Europe and, more accurately, suggests a map of the world. What form would such a map have assumed for Chaucer and the auditors—actual, imagined, and intended—of the *Canterbury Tales*? By Chaucer's day, Portolan-style world maps, whose use of projections dramatically broke with the method of rendering the world in medieval mappae mundi, may have gained some ground in England. Only five years after Chaucer wrote the *Man of Law's Tale,* for example, maps like the famous Catalan atlas of 1375 were being fashioned as gifts for a newly crowned Henry IV.[13] Yet such new perspectives on global space were, by far, the exception rather than the rule. When the English themselves drew up world maps, they turned to their own venerable tradition of mappae mundi, a tradition whose continued relevance and indeed vitality in England can be gauged by the multiple maps illustrating *Polychronicon* manuscripts as well as both the Aslake world map (ca. 1325–70) and the Evesham world map (ca. 1390).[14] Chaucer's own interest in mappae mundi emerges early in the *Canterbury Tales.* As Sylvia Tomasch has argued, aspects of the *Knight's Tale*—in particular, Theseus's lists—exhibit Chaucer's familiarity with traditional world maps.[15] And, in the case of the *Man of Law's Tale,* its interest in medieval geography is registered near the start of the narrative, by a Latin gloss (appearing in several manuscripts) alluding to the tripartite world (2.161 and note). Along with the *Knight's Tale,* that of the Man of Law merits analysis in light of medieval world geography.

Like mappae mundi, the Man of Law's account of Custance's journey highlights English geographic isolation. With his representation of Custance traveling from Rome and Syria (two sites located near the center of world maps) through the threshold of the straits of Gibraltar (found on the western border of mappae mundi) into the "wilde"

English channel and "fer" into Northumbria, the Man of Law evokes nothing less than England's status as an island on the edge of the world. Full analysis of the representation of alterity in the *Man of Law's Tale,* then, requires our consideration not only of Custance's strangeness and Syrian difference, but also of the otherworldliness of England.

As we shall see, for Chaucer's lawyer, English otherworldliness serves a function akin to its role in Godwin's biography. Just as Chaucer's romantic biographer binds geographic marginality with English magnificence, so too does Chaucer's medieval lawyer. Namely, through Custance's providential journey, Chaucer's lawyer endeavors to affirm the best implications of English geographic isolation: how the English are set apart from the world as God's chosen people. This reading counters a long tradition of viewing the *Man of Law's Tale* as a narrative primarily identified with universal Roman values.[16] In *Chaucerian Polity,* for example, David Wallace describes the Custance story as a tale that "affirm[s] the Rome-centered authority of emperors and popes," while Kolve, whom Wallace cites, asserts that "Rome is the center of the poem's gravity, its geography, and its moral and spiritual meaning."[17] In contrast, I suggest that it is in fact the Man of Law's interest in *distinguishing* England from Rome as a sovereign territory that inspires his performance. As the sheer frequency of references to England and the English language (more than in any other Canterbury tale) in the *Man of Law's Tale* indicates, while Rome certainly has its attractions in that text, so too does England.[18]

Archival evidence supports the status of the Custance story as a national tale. In a late fifteenth-century manuscript held by Cambridge University Library (MS Ee.2.15) a corrupt copy of the *Man of Law's Tale* appears with several other vernacular religious texts.[19] The contents of the manuscript are, in order: a fragment from Mirk's *Festial* on Saints Nicholas and Thomas Becket, the *Man of Law's Tale,* Gower's tale of the three questions, John Lydgate's epic poem on Saints Edmund and Fremund, a poem on Christ's passion, and a prose legend of Augustine of Canterbury. To be sure, as it does in the *Man of Law's Tale,* Rome figures importantly in many of these texts. Gregory authorizes Augustine's mission, Becket died due to his Roman allegiances, and Edmund's parents make a fateful pilgrimage to Rome. But above all, these are English texts, stories written in the vernacular and focused mainly upon saints special to England: while the story on Augustine relates the English mission of England's great missionary and first archbishop, Lydgate's double legend concerns the Anglo-Saxon king and martyr who was the national saint of medieval England (until that honor was transferred to one of the subjects of the *Festial* fragment, Thomas Becket). Constituting something of an anthology of English spiritual narratives, MS Ee.2.15 addresses an English audience implicitly concerned with questions of national community. The inclusion of the Custance story in this particular assemblage of texts shows that, at least for one early reader of Chaucer, the *Man of Law's Tale* signified not in a universal Roman but in a specifically English register.[20]

That a lawyer tells this narrative of geographic exceptionalism is no accident.[21] Due to debates regarding spatially charged issues such as jurisdiction and sanctuary—debates that reflected juridical conflicts between England and the church—English lawyers spoke powerfully to questions of geography and nationalism in the Middle Ages. Namely, by Chaucer's time, the careerist and secular lawyers of England set their home-land apart as a privileged site of juridical practice, asserting that, as Alan Harding ex-presses it, "the eternal principles of law were nowhere better expressed than in the customs of England, as declared by the judges."[22] I argue that the particular legal per-spective on national geography offered by the *Man of Law's Tale* is twofold, and relates intimately to the Man of Law's decision to tell a tale featuring the geographically iso-lated and "hooly" Roman princess Custance. For our lawyerly narrator, the sovereign English patriarchy he espouses is faced with the challenges of the Christian "empire" of Rome on one hand and, on the other hand, the imperial maternity of woman. Situated often at the heart of mappae mundi, possessed of an imposing classical juridical her-itage, and recognized as the home of canon law, Rome links geographic centrality with global juridical supremacy. As the seat of western Christendom and canon law, the Ro-man "mother church" threatened to engulf the English edge of the world within its canonical jurisdiction. To be sure, in the centuries immediately after 1066, canon law served as a kind of nourishing mother to the system of common law so cherished by English lawmen such as Chaucer's lawyer (as evinced by his knowledge of "caas and doomes alle / That from the tyme of kyng William were falle," 1.323–24). Yet, by Chaucer's time, English lawyers strove to extricate themselves from what had become a suffocating *ecclesia mater* not unlike the notoriously "suffocating mothers" represented by the Man of Law via the Sultaness and Donegild.[23] Just as those infamous mothers endeavor to stifle their respective sons' efforts to move beyond their immediate family, the universal church sought to squelch efforts to liberate the English common law from canonical authority.

The imaginative resolution the lawyer offers for those linked problems of empire and maternity emerges in the figure of Custance. As the bearer of divine law, yet also an en-tity whose radical alterity separates her from both Rome and biological womanhood, Custance embodies the paradoxical desires of English lawmen toward both Rome and woman. Passive and pious, Custance represents a sublime juridical conception of woman that contrasts with the lawyer's characterizations of Donegild and the Sultaness, who exhibit a menacing and overweening relationship to patriarchy's legal system.[24] Moreover, insofar as she is less a Roman woman than an angel of God, less an inhabi-tant of the eternal city than a territorial outsider, Custance serves not only as a type of the ideal *woman* under patriarchal law but also as a personification of the sovereign *En-gland* hailed by English lawyers. Through his tale's heroine, in effect, the Man of Law absorbs and reconfigures the charged difference of woman so that she may be imagined to bear the word of the privileged alterity he claims for England.[25] Thus while the *Man of Law's Tale* offers an origin story that differs in many ways from the tale of Gregory and the English slave boys, it resembles that myth in its effort to rehabilitate difference. Just as Gregory's emphasis on the boys' angelic beauty converts those enslaved Others into emblems of English sublimity, the Man of Law's representation of Custance trans-forms that gendered Other into an icon of English election.

Like all binary oppositions, however, the Man of Law's efforts both to divide

England from Rome and to separate the "good" woman Custance from "bad" women such as the Sultaness prove unsustainable. The lawyer's celebration of the English margin of the world is bound up with his attachment to global centers, even as his embrace of woman is founded on his animosity toward that gender. The eventual return of Custance's suppressed physicality in the tale demonstrates how the lawyer's embrace of geographic isolation is troubled by his desire to appropriate on England's behalf the universal authority of the mother church.

## Rome, Eternal Law, and the Question of English Juridical Sovereignty

From the advent of its classical period in the twelfth century onward, canon law came to be a system, according to Frederick Pollock and F. W. Maitland, "even more cosmopolitan than the imperial [system]; the sway of the Roman church was wider than that of the Roman empire."[26] In theory if not practice, canon law served as the key device through which the church leveled its members within a single universal Christian siblinghood. As James Brundage puts it, "medieval churchmen claimed authority over virtually every aspect of human beliefs and actions"; canon law extended in theory to all levels of private and public life and applied equally to everyone, "regardless of gender, class or social standing" and, most important for Chaucer's lawyer, nationality.[27] Key to that juridical universalism was the notion of the threefold nature of the law, namely its divine, human, and natural components. Typology unified these three laws, whereby the laws human and natural each figured eternal law. The unity of the three laws also entailed their hierarchical organization. According to medieval theological and juridical treatises, because human law and natural law merely shadowed forth God's principles, they were subordinated to divine law. Thus Thomas Aquinas's *Summa Theologiae* both stresses how "all things . . . somehow share" in divine law, and emphasizes the supreme dominion of eternal law by characterizing it as "nothing other than the exemplar of divine wisdom as directing the motions and acts of everything."[28] By claiming a monopoly on that divine justice, the church asserted its juridical supremacy, with secular lawyers subject to their spiritual counterparts.

That hierocratic rhetoric met with resistance in certain parts of medieval Europe, including England. Assertions of the preeminence of the English law appear as early as the twelfth century, in the Clarendon Constitutions through which Henry II countered Thomas Becket's rejection of English jurisdictional customs. About seven decades later, we again find the implicit affirmation of the rectitude of English legal tradition in a famous passage from Bracton's *De legibus*. In response to Bishop Grosseteste's demand that the English align common with canon law on the issue of bastardy and the timing of marriage, Bracton writes that "all the earls and barons as many as there were, answered with one voice that they did not wish to change the laws of England which had hitherto been used and approved."[29] To be sure, the opposition to canon law registered by Henry II's constitutions and the collective "no" of Bracton's "earls and barons" is somewhat unusual. By and large, clerics and common lawyers respected, supported, and cooperated with one another during the High Middle Ages. That harmonious relationship, however, would end by Chaucer's time.

Integral to the rising tensions between canon and common lawyers during the late Middle Ages was the fact that lawyers were the first group of professionals to be laicized in England. Since the time of Magna Carta, clerks along with laymen had upheld common law. But, with the union of the bench and the law at the start of the fourteenth century, where "no one could become a justice of the central courts of law . . . unless he had previously been a sergeant at law," the benches of the civil courts began to be staffed solely with laymen.[30] The secularization of the common law and king's benches by 1341, along with the introduction of the vernacular in English courts in 1361, contributed to a real separation between civil and canon law. As William Searle Holdsworth writes, "we can no longer expect to find royal judges who can show an accurate knowledge of papal legislation; nor will ideas drawn from canonical jurisprudence be used to develop our law. On the contrary, it is coming to be a rival—almost a hostile system."[31] As members of a lay profession that was also, as Michael Bennett has shown, markedly careerist, fourteenth-century English lawyers resisted canonical impingements on their authority in a manner that distinguished them from their predecessors.

Indeed, W. R. Jones writes that the late medieval period "witnessed the culmination" of medieval English impingement upon the legal powers of the church.[32] Fourteenth-century England brought forth statute after statute delimiting the jurisdiction of the church and bolstering the legal rights of the king and his officers: the issuance in 1351 and 1390 of Statutes of Provisors (which forbade the Roman court from interfering in the free presentation of English benefices) and the creation in 1353, 1365, and 1393 of Statutes of Praemunire (which banned ecclesiastical appeals of royal court decisions).[33] This period produced as well the first theory of English juridical sovereignty, in the work of that most notorious advocate of the law in England during Chaucer's lifetime, John Wyclif.[34] Wyclif's most important work on the topic emerges in his commentary on the 1378 Hawley-Shakell sanctuary incident, in which he opposes the jurisdictional rights of the abbots who housed these fugitives from the king's justice by claiming that they had offended "In legem Dei, ecclesie et in legem regni."[35] Wyclif's assertion that the fugitives' recourse to a space marked out as a sanctuary *by* the church nevertheless *errs against* the church exemplifies the appropriation of divine authority implicit in English civil claims over canonical legislation. Here as elsewhere in his work, Wyclif urges the theological validity of adherence to English law against canonical authority.[36]

Providing potential support for the English legal cause was the fact that, since the beginning of the fourteenth century, factionalism had made the Roman church not quite the formidable rival it once was. In 1309 Pope Clement V took residence away from Rome, establishing an Avignon papacy that would last until 1377. The reinstatement of the Roman curia by Gregory XI hardly ended Rome's troubles. When they elected Clement VII in 1378, the College of Cardinals initiated the Great Schism, whereby for some fifty years the western church was broken up into multiple territorial seats and claimants to the papacy. Divided thus politically and geographically, deprived of its historic dominance and centricity, the Rome of Chaucer's lifetime was vulnerable as never before to English juridical aggression. This despite the fact that during the Schism England officially endorsed the Roman Pope Urban VI, a decision that had as much or more to do with anti-French feeling than Roman allegiance. The Hundred Years War, which rendered the notion of supporting an Avignon pope ludicrous, made Urban the default option of the English at the outset of the Schism.[37] English support for the Roman curia, moreover, by no means precluded English resistance to canon law. For example Wyclif, in the same text that covers the Hawley-Shakell sanctuary incident, upholds the reformer Urban even as he offers his most striking claim for the preeminence of English law over canon law.[38]

Yet if the contemporary splitting of the rock of Peter may have aided the nationalistic rhetoric of England's lawyers during the fourteenth century, the past achievements of the Roman church suggested otherwise. In other words, the legacy of the early church—like that of Rome's long-dead classical empire—guaranteed that Rome, whatever its late medieval shortcomings, would persist as a force to be reckoned with by the English. The recent troubles of the church could not take away from the authority Rome possessed because of its historical achievements, above all its role in England's original acquisition of divine law. As we saw in the work of Gerald de Barri, Ireland's share in England's Christian conversion troubled medieval notions of English sovereignty, and Rome's role in that project was even more problematic. How could English lawmen assert their autonomy from Rome, when they owed their very religious identity to the mission led by Augustine of Canterbury and authorized by Pope Gregory the Great? As Marcel Mauss's work on the aggressivity of the gift has taught us, Rome's bestowal of Christianity upon England supports the subordinate role that canon lawyers allocated civil lawyers. If, as Mauss puts it, "to give is to show one's superiority, to show that one is something more and higher," Rome's religious conversion of England established the sovereignty of the church over the English and especially English lawyers.[39]

To return to the *Man of Law's Tale*, the interrelation between England's religious conversion and its juridical identity is made clear throughout the text by the lawyer's legal conception of faith: all questions of conversion in the tale hinge on the willingness of barbarians (whether Syrian or Anglo-Saxon) to accept a "newe lawe" (2.337; cf. 2.572). By emphasizing the status of Christianity as a law—the very eternal law understood in the Christian West to be essential to the work of justice—the Man of Law reveals his keen awareness of how the Gregorian mission haunts the Christian exceptionalism espoused by medieval English jurists. Moreover, in the geographic terms crucial to the *Man of Law's Tale,* by telling a tale of England's conversion, the Man of Law can't help but point to the fact that England was not always the privileged legal arena celebrated by common lawyers but was instead once a pagan and lawless backwater. The alienation of a pagan Anglo-Saxon England from divine law is raised by the Man of Law himself, through his implicit comparisons of England and Syria in the tale. The tale pairs the Northumbrian king Alla and the Sultan of Syria through their marriages to Custance. But above all, it is Alla's name—with its uncanny evocation of the God of Islam—that most binds England to Syria. We saw in the slave-boy myth how Gregory's pun on "Alle" and "Allejuia" suggests that the Christian destiny of the English is encoded in the

English leader's name. It is that same Northumbrian king who appears in the *Man of Law's Tale,* but his name hardly affirms the Christian fate of the English.[40] Through his implicit pun on Alla and Allah, Chaucer's lawyer instead shores up the idea that Anglo-Saxon England, like Syria, constituted a "Barbre nacioun" outside of Christendom (2.281).

## "And the woman fled into the wilderness," Rev. 12:6

Yet England is not simply another Syria in the *Man of Law's Tale.* For one thing, the Anglo-Saxon land to which Custance travels is not entirely pagan. Of the Northumbrian region encountered by his heroine, the Man of Law writes, in a passage unique to Chaucer's version of the Constance story:

> In al that lond no Cristen dorste Route;
> Alle Cristen folk been fled fro that contree
> Thurgh payens, that conquereden al aboute
> The plages of the north, by land and see
> To Walys fledde the Cristyanytee
> Of olde Britons dwellynge in this ile;
> Ther was hir refut for the meene while.
>
> But yet nere Cristene Britons so exiled
> That ther nere somme that in hir privetee
> Honoured Crist and hethen folk bigiled.

> (2.540–49)

Far from a united nation, England is torn by a history of conquest that points to its slippery identity as the homeland of the pagan *English* and the "Cristene *Britons*" who beguile them by secretly practicing their faith. Yet in the Man of Law's mythic revision of the Augustine mission to England, those surreptitiously Christian Britons ultimately contribute to the national elevation of England over Syria. That is, the very *incompleteness* of the Anglo-Saxon effort to reterritorialize England and push the Britons to its fringes enables England to preserve a residue of Christian practice absent in the thoroughly heathen space of Syria.[41]

The source of their Roman Christian conversion likewise separates the English from the Syrians. A pope and emperor intent on the "encrees of Cristes lawe deere" (2. 2.237) authorize Custance's journey to Syria. In contrast, God's *sonde* or providence sticks Custance's ship fast in the *sond* (sand) of Northumbria, thus ending abruptly her watery meanderings (2.523; 2.509). God's navigation of Custance's ship obviously reveals His majesty; as with His rescue of Custance from the Sultaness's treachery, God performs such miracles "for we sholde seen his myghty werkis" (2.478). Yet the heavenly navigator of Custance's trip to England also reflects favorably upon that island and its people. While the Holy Roman "imperialism" that mobilizes Custance's journey to Syria renders its occupants the heathen object of Roman spiritual conquest, the divine pilot of Custance's ship to England makes the English less Rome's holy subject than God's chosen people. We might even say that the pun on *sond* and *sonde* suggests a kind of bond between "the wyl of Crist" and the very sand of Northumbria (2.511). Supporting the elect national identity implicitly claimed by English jurists, the Man of Law makes the English indebted directly to God Himself for their religious identity.

Custance, certainly, does bring Roman Christian law to England; yet by rendering his heroine less a Roman emissary than the bearer of God's word to England, Chaucer's lawyer imagines England paradoxically gaining the gift of divine law without the obligations to Rome it entails. Crucial to this strategy is the identity of Custance herself. The Man of Law enlists his heroine as an ally in his national project by subordinating Custance's status as a worldly Roman woman to the transcendent spiritual identity suggested by her name. Insomuch as Custance figures more as an angel of steadfastness than as a Roman emperor's daughter, she enables an origin myth that denies Rome juridical dominion over England. The strategies through which the lawyer emphasizes Custance's spiritual identity include, as Raybin has noted, the Man of Law's persistent characterization of her as "hooly" at crucial moments in the tale, as well as his portrayal of her unflagging capacity to remain "unwemmed" (2.924) regardless of whatever worldly mishap she endures.[42] However, critics have yet to address how the Man of Law's suppression of Custance's historical ties intensifies in the English section of his tale. While the Syrians are well aware of Custance's status as a Roman "Emperoures doghter," the English remain ignorant of her ethnicity. Telling the English that "she was so mazed in the see / That she forgat hir mynde," Custance uses amnesia to mask her Roman origins (2.526–27). Following Gower, Chaucer's Custance refrains even from acknowledging the noble blood in her veins (*Chronique,* 168; *Confessio Amantis,* II.738–39). Rather, the only "family" with which she affiliates herself in England is the holy family. During her trial, Custance prays aloud to God, asking him to rescue her just as he "savedest Susanne / Fro false blame," thus proclaiming her status as a type of the Old Testament heroine Susannah (2.639–40). Typology, or figural interpretation, retrospectively constructs a genealogy between persons in Judeo-Christian history based not on blood but on affective resemblances; the unjust suffering of Custance hence renders her a "sister" to Susannah.[43] The spiritual ancestry declared by Custance finds divine confirmation later in the trial when a disembodied voice tells her accuser before a "general audience . . . 'Thou hast desclaundred, giltelees, / The doghter of hooly chirche'" (2.673–75); and receives further emphasis from the Man of Law, who describes her as a figure of Christ, Jonah, Mary the Egyptian, and David during the English portion of his tale (2.486, 2.500, 2.617, 2.939). By making her a daughter of God and a sister of Susannah and Jonah, the Man of Law inserts Custance into a Judeo-Christian ancestry through which her literal Roman genealogy is overshadowed by the nonbiological structure of descent that typology offers.[44]

The Man of Law's capacity to affirm a sovereign English juridical identity thus hinges on his ability to empty Custance of her biological and physical aspects. Far from invoking the alterity associated with women embedded in the world and its social networks, Custance offers a kind of radical hyper-marginality or divine otherness. As Winthrop Wetherbee notes, Custance is "an essentially 'strange' being," a heroine lacking "a full measure of earthly existence."[45] The stripping of Custance's social and ethnic roots, her ties to a Roman body politic, in turn, enables her to perform representative labor for the English body politic. By dint of her holy alterity, that is, Custance becomes a sign of England's national geographic sublimity. As an "angel" set apart from Rome yet possessed of Christian law, Custance personifies the very divine juridical identity espoused by English lawyers. Possessed of a saintliness that elevates her above the rest of humanity, Custance figures what John Capgrave would call in his fifteenth-century *Chronicle of England* a "Blessed Inglond . . . of Angel nature."[46]

The lawyer's disembodiment and idealization of Custance should seem familiar to us, since contemporary examples abound in western culture. For example, both the Statue of Liberty and the goddess Britannia perform important symbolic work that is predicated on their status as idealized females, unsullied by the physical particulars of embodied, historical existence. That communal use of woman has a long history and was not unique to Chaucer. For example, during the Middle Ages, the English turned to the most idolized woman in western culture for use as a national symbol: the Virgin Mary.[47] King Arthur devotes himself especially to Mary in romances and chronicles beginning with Geoffrey of Monmouth's *History of the Kings of Britain,* where the image of the Virgin on Arthur's shield enhances its protective function.[48] And the Virgin calls England her "dower" and safeguards the island in John Lydgate's plague poem "Ave Regina Celorum."[49] Long before Lady Liberty guarded the eastern border of the United States, the Virgin Mother watched over England and her knights.

The multiple Marian characteristics critics have identified in Custance may suggest how Chaucer's lawyer intends to recall in his tale the traditional linkage of England with the most saintly of Christian women. Yet surely the most striking analogue of Custance appears not among English celebrations of Mary but in the words of the aptly named Lollard, Walter Brute. In a deposition he made the year before his trial in 1392, Brute, like the Man of Law, binds an image of ideal womanhood to the unique geographic standing of England as an otherworld. In his learned response to the charges made against him during his inquisition, Brute claims that since England, famed as a land placed beyond the climates or *positus est extra climata,* has long been considered a wilderness or desert place (*solitudo seu desertus locus*), that marginal land must be the wilderness prepared by God into which the woman of Apocalypse 12 (meaning the Church or True Faith) fled.[50] As in the *Man of Law's Tale,* Brute's national usage of woman engages with global geography: both Holy Church and Custance journey from the eastern portion of the world to its English edge. Moreover, each of the women in the narratives of the Man of Law and Brute is a gendered Other whose idealized, sublime femininity implies the sublime status of her isolated destination. By taking refuge in England, Brute's apocalyptic woman suggests how that remote land, far from being a barbaric hinterland, instead possesses a sanctity appropriate for her own holy persona.[51]

## An English Jeremiad

In combining notions of feminine and geographic otherness to celebrate England, both Lollard and lawyer recall much older, biblical usages of woman and territory to conceive of community. In particular, Walter Brute and the Man of Law evoke the book of Jeremiah, where the prophet (spoken by his Lord) affirms the chosen status of Israel by describing it both "as a bride" that "was holy to the Lord" and as a "wilderness . . . holy to the lord" (2.2–3). Jeremiah, to be sure, does more than merely celebrate Israel; he also, famously, laments its deplorable condition. In a move that displays how the ambivalent meanings of the wilderness lend themselves to social critique, the prophet at once celebrates Israel as a blessed wilderness and warns the Israelites that "the land shall become a waste" (7.34; 2.2). Like that Hebrew prophet, both the Lollard and the lawyer not only assert the elect status of their communities, but also mingle such national elevation with social critique. After all, Brute relates his narrative of English geographic exceptionalism in a deposition made before his own trial in England as a Lollard, a setting that suggests how certain elements of English society make his isolated island anything but a refuge for the holy. The English prove similarly hostile to Custance in the *Man of Law's Tale*. In particular, during a crucial trial scene, not only does an English knight falsely accuse Custance of a murder he himself committed, but also the king himself, who presides over the proceeding, nearly executes our holy heroine. Although King Alla pities Custance, he also is taken by the treacherous knight's testimony, and "caught a greet motyf / Of this witnesse, and thoghte he wolde enquere / Depper in this, a trouthe for to lere" (2.628–30).[52] The knight's influence upon the king even prompts the Man of Law to lament Custance's potential death, complaining that "but if Crist open myracle kithe, / Withouten gilt thou shalt be slayn as swithe" (2.636–37). Far from suggesting the sublime otherworldliness of England, Custance's near-execution binds England's frontier status to danger, misconduct, and injustice.[53] Like the English legal system that threatened Walter Brute, the Anglo-Saxon court of the *Man of Law's Tale* suggests the status of England as a wild backwater that menaces Custance's very life. At the same time that Chaucer's lawyer's tale affirms the sublime potential of England, he also acknowledges its barbarous shortcomings.

The notion that the lawyer's tale constitutes a kind of complaint has been well demonstrated by critics such as Robert Enzer Lewis and Ann Astell.[54] As these readers have shown, Chaucer's unparalleled use of Innocent III's *De Miseria Condicionis Humanae* in his Custance story, as well as his lawyer's frequent use of those figures—*indignatio, conquestio, exclamatio*—that recall the classical rhetorical roots of this medieval genre, both support the Man of Law's role as a kind of Boethian, monitory figure.[55] It is only, however, a *universal* brand of complaint that Chaucerians have located in the *Man of Law's Tale,* whereby Custance's repeated misfortunes epitomize the sufferings that Original Sin entails. Thus for Lewis, the repeated pattern in the tale of "wo after gladnesse," culminating in "joye after wo," offers the universal moral that happiness "comes to him who, through all misfortune, believes in Jesus Christ."[56] But in addition to such a universally applicable brand of complaint, Chaucer's lawyer offers a social je-

remiad focused on the particular juridical issues facing a specifically English community. In a move that most closely resembles that of Gower in his *Vox Clamantis*, whereby
the poet assumes the voice of one crying *in deserto*, or from the wilderness of England,
the Man of Law addresses the juridical problems and potentials of the English world
frontier.[57]

Custance's pertinence to English juridical critique emerges in the allegorical valence
of her name. As Joseph Grennen has pointed out, jurists medieval and modern have
used the notion of constancy to characterize justice, insofar it entails a *constans et perpetual voluntas* or constant and perpetual will.[58] Precisely what the constancy of justice
signifies varies slightly from legist to legist. But, fundamentally, it refers to a jurist's steadfast desire to give each his own due, a notion that resonates with the ideal, found in both
fourteenth-century parliamentary records and the 1346 oath created for English lawyers,
that "justice should be done equally for all men in the central courts and localities."[59]
Chaucer himself binds constancy with the law in his short poem to Richard II, whose
monitory refrain over the "lak of stedfastnesse" in England refers in large part to the
realm's "lak" of justice. As Chaucer's reference to an absence of juridical constancy in
"Lak of Stedfastnesse" suggests, utopian assertions of the law's steadfastness in the fourteenth century were belied by English lawmen's infamous shortcomings. Through such
practices as champerty (a second party's promotion of a suit for personal gain), em-
bracery (efforts to corrupt a jury via threats, promises, money, or other means), bribery,
and most of all, maintenance (illegal support of another's suit), English justices notoriously undermined the law.[60]

The troubling image of a lawless Anglo-Saxon backwater conjured by the *Man of
Law's Tale* thus applied to the England of Chaucer's day, with its corrupt legal officers.
The failings of late medieval England's lawyers hardly went unnoticed; as Jill Mann affirms, "charges of corruption are the most frequent and most fully developed items in
estates treatments of judges and lawyers."[61] Lawyers also constituted a principal object
of rebel aggression in 1381, the year that witnessed the greatest internal challenge to the
welfare of the English body politic in the fourteenth century. As a justice of the peace
and a member of the "Wonderful" Parliament of 1386, Chaucer witnessed first-hand
public censure of the law. Parliament's desire to end the abuses of "lez bonez leyes, es-
tatutz, et custemes de nostre dit realme" manifested itself several times during this ses-
sion, in the Commons' call for the forbidding of maintenance and retaining, in their
impeachment of Michael de la Pole, and in the Commission of Government's outlin-
ing of tasks to a newly appointed parliamentary council.[62] Chaucer's parliamentary service certainly would have impressed upon him the troubled state of a realm whose "good
laws" are spoiled by their practitioners. Custance's very name calls out for what English
law should be, an ideal English justices grossly failed to meet.

Further support for Chaucer's lawyer's interest in commenting on the state of the law
in England emerges in the unique status of Alla as a judge in the *Man of Law's Tale*. In
the *Chronique* and the *Confessio Amantis*, the king meets an already vindicated Constance. Chaucer's inclusion of Alla in Custance's trial—indeed, his decision to have the
king assume his standing as the sovereign embodiment of the law in England and pre-

side over the hearing—lends a certain stress on that episode that is lacking in his sources and is consonant with the juridical aims of the tale's teller. While Trevet and Gower represent their English kings in a relatively unproblematic fashion, Chaucer's lawyer's Alla suggests the *inconstancy* of justice in England. An imperfect chief justice, the English king of the *Man of Law's Tale* is a judge dangerously close to making an unjust decision. To be sure, the legal system the Man of Law criticizes is safely located in the Anglo-Saxon past; to criticize the lawmen of his own time may well hit too close to home for this justice, given the professional flaws intimated by his portrait.[63]

Moreover, the Man of Law criticizes the law in England only as a prelude to his imaginative elevation of England and its legal system. Alla's initial doubts about Custance vanish after the tremendous descent of a hand from above to strike the libelous knight's neck, knock out his eyes, and decry his slander against a "doghter of hooly chirche" (2.675). That marvelous and terrible education leads to Alla's juridical elevation. During the trial and its immediate aftermath, the Man of Law's national appropriation of Custance culminates, as Alla, the very *lex animata* or law incarnate, converts to the Christian law especially offered to his people and unites in marriage with *Justitia* herself, as embodied by Custance. Even as the severe injustice that the king nearly authorizes recalls the corruption of English legal officers, Alla's eventual union with a woman personifying juridical constancy affirms the utopian potential claimed for the English legal system by the Man of Law's professional class.[64]

## Spiritual Gifts, Corporeal Baggage

Custance's marriage to Alla points to the fundamentally incorporative goal of national fantasy. While England resists absorption within the canonical "empire" of Rome, it seeks to fulfill what Lauren Berlant calls "the nation's utopian promise to oversee a full and just integration of persons" within its territorial boundaries.[65] That ideal national inclusiveness emerges, as we have seen, in the Commons' claim that justice should be done for all. By manipulating woman as a sign of the judicial constancy that secures national unity, the Man of Law thus conceals the law's resistance to incorporating within the space of the nation all sorts of historically disenfranchised groups, such as the poor. Above all, the lawyer's apparent celebration of national integration via woman masks a deep antipathy to historical feminine difference. Denying woman any social agency, the economy of patriarchal national fantasy subsumes woman into the body politic on a symbolic or metaphorical level.

As Elsbeth Probyn and other contemporary feminist geographers point out, "the movement of metaphorizing the nation in terms of woman would generally serve to displace actual historical women," and the discourse of medieval jurisprudence is no exception.[66] Such critics as Carolyn Dinshaw, Elizabeth Fowler, and Shulamith Shahar have made clear how, even as juridical discourses on *Justitia* celebrated woman as symbol, the patriarchal legal system of medieval England sought to render historical women public outsiders. As Pollock and Maitland put it, "in the camp, at the council board, on the bench, in the jury box there is no place for them."[67] The Man of Law's idealization of Custance—like most idealizations of woman in the official cultures of the premodern West—serves as a means of ironically imagining the gender excluded from his national culture as, to use Jonathan Goldberg's formulation, a "trope of ideal femininity . . . that secures male-male arrangements and an all male history."[68] Custance's angelic qualities represent English lawmen's desire to detach themselves not only from Rome but also from woman in all her materiality. It is worth noting, indeed, that during the trial episode, more than at any other moment in the tale, the lawyer's claim on the primacy of Custance's spiritual identity over her historical ties most forcefully resonates: Custance may be, as the lawyer reminds the pilgrims, of "blood roial" and an "Emperoures doghter" (2.655), but it is only her affiliation with God as a "doghter of hooly chirche" that stands her in good stead during her judicial ordeal (2.675).

Bodies, however, have a way of resurfacing. Notions of fraternal collectivity founder on the nation's dependence on female physicality for a biological future. Although the Man of Law endeavors to "spirit away" as irrelevant her flesh-and-blood status, Custance's body ultimately does matter. As a result of the ambivalence over woman that paradoxically accompanies every national claim made by the lawyer about Custance, the very body the Man of Law represses nevertheless emerges in his tale, not long after the trial episode. In the space of three lines, Chaucer's lawyer describes how Custance must "leye a lite hir hoolynesse aside" on her wedding night and soon gives birth to a baby boy (2.713; 2.715). The lawyer's assertion that Custance has set aside her spirituality refers directly to her sexuality, a comment that corresponds with the medieval elevation of chastity linked most famously with Jerome's letter against Jovinian and derided so humorously by the Wife of Bath. But the lawyer's words also point to the biological outcome of female sexuality and the maternal role it entails. The notion that a woman's maternity stands in inverse proportion to her spirituality probably would not have surprised the lawyer's pilgrim auditors. As Clarissa Atkinson has shown, medieval mothers often viewed their maternal function as a hindrance to their own piety.[69] And later in the *Canterbury Tales,* it is precisely the degree to which the Clerk's Griselda demonstrates her holy steadfastness that determines the extent to which she strays from her motherly role (4.561–65). In the case of Custance, the loss of holiness entailed by motherhood has troublesome national implications.

Namely, Custance's maternity threatens the lawyer's national project insofar as it represents a danger akin to that posed by canon lawyers' efforts to extend their jurisdictional authority into England. Like Rome's gift of eternal law, the gift of life proffered by woman undermines the sovereignty claimed by English lawmen. To put it in geographic terms, both Rome and the mother threaten to break down the territorial integrity of the nation and the child, respectively. Like the maternal empire, the imperial mother represents the supplanting of independence with union and debt. The tale itself suggests as much. The overbearing mothers of the *Man of Law's Tale,* Donegild and the Sultaness, reveal how a mother's power to bind the child can take a distinctly disabling, even deadly, turn for her offspring. But although here the maternal bond turns lethal, in other medieval texts the debt binding the child to the mother, while still burdensome, emerges as an effect of her capacity to nurture life. Marbod of Rennes thus asks in his *Liber decem capitulorum,* "who . . . makes up . . . with love to match" the "price of bearing a child which the careworn mother pays in bringing us into the light"?[70]

The labor expended by the mother figures in Marbod's text as the most burdensome gift of all, that which cannot be returned. That form of potlatch converges with Rome's gift of Christian law in Custance's maternity. The reappearance of Custance's repressed physicality is also the return of the eternal law's suppressed Roman basis. The body that bears Alla his son Maurice also shores up the historicity of Custance, her status as not the angelic converter of the Anglo-Saxons but a woman whose Roman origins trouble the lawyer's efforts to distinguish England from the universal Christian family.[71]

The geographic ramifications shared by both the maternal potlatch registered by Marbod and the gift of "Cristes lawe" offered by Rome emerge in the geographic association of capitals such as Rome with biological femininity. Both ancient and premodern cultures describe the center of the world as an *omphalos* or navel. Thus an ancient monument at the center of the Roman Forum was known as *umbilicus mundi,* the "navel of the world," and a stone at Delphi signified in classical Greece as the *omphalos* of the world. Similarly, Jerome's Commentary on Ezekiel supports the prophet's identification of Jerusalem as *umbilicus terrae.*[72] What does it mean to characterize the center of the world as a navel? This anthropomorphizing of the world, in part, simply reflects the premodern notion of the unity of nature. In the same way that, for example, medieval writers allotted man's life various "ages" that accorded temporally with the number of seasons, months, days in the week, and so on, they also compared the geography of man's body with that of the entire world. Higden, for example, describes man as a microcosm of the world in the *Polychronicon,* whose anonymous vernacular translator writes that God "impressede" on man or the "lesse worlde" "the similitude of the grete worlde."[73] Given its location, to cite Bartholomaeus Anglicus, on "þe middil place of þe body," the navel was identified with world centers by medieval writers and cartographers.[74] Such a conflation of the world and the body emerges in the massive eastern-oriented Ebstorf map (fig. 15), in which the presence of Christ's head, hands, and feet at the top, sides, and bottom of the world displays, as Samuel Edgerton notes, "both physically and metaphysically the *Corpus Domini*—macrocosm and microcosm united."[75] Located at the center of this map, Jerusalem functions as the divine *umbilicus* of both Christ and the world.

Yet the navel also is a charged site of maternal union and debt. In Elizabeth Bronfen's phrase, the *omphalos* "functions as a sign of bondage" that distinguishes humankind anatomically from the angels.[76] Even more than the breast, the navel territorializes maternal power by memorializing the child's implantation in the mother's uterus. Bartholomeus, for example, compares the umbilical cord to the root joining a plant to the earth when he writes, in a passage taken from Gregory's commentary on Ezekiel 16:4, that "a childe in þe modir wombe fongiþ fedinge be þe nauel, as treen and yerdes fongen priuey liche by morys and rootis humour of þe erþe and ben ifed þerwiþ."[77] To describe a world center as a navel, then, is to appropriate a graphic emblem of the child's

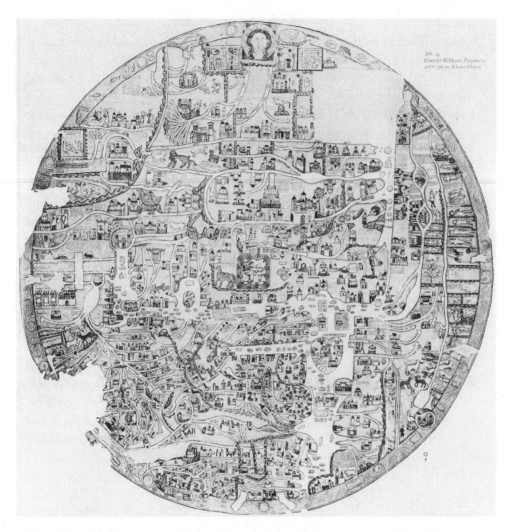

**Fig. 15.** Ebstorf world map, ca. 1235. Destroyed in 1943, the map has been reconstructed from earlier reproductions. From Birgit Hahn-Woernle, *Die Ebstorfer Weltkarte: Dem Kloster Ebstorf und seinen Konventualinnen gewidmet* (Ebstorf: Das Klosterf, 1987), 39. By permission of Birgit Hahn-Woernle.

tie to the maternal body, its biological dependence upon the mother. The status of Jerusalem—or, more pointedly, Rome—as *umbilicus* naturalizes the nonbiological production of that capital; Rome becomes a source of the law (and all the other key elements of civilization) akin to the maternal source of humanity. Above all, Rome as *umbilicus* signifies the enduring connection and subjection of all earthly territories to their religio-cultural "mother." Just as all children are biologically indebted to the mothers who bore them, the English and their legal officers were burdened by their obligation to the mother church.

Insomuch as Custance's maternity calls forth such biological and religious debts, she ceases to signal English sovereignty. In a narrative move suggestive of Custance's transformation from national guarantor into national liability, not long after the lawyer's heroine becomes a mother, she finds herself exiled from England and "fleteth in the see" once more (2.901). It is Alla's own mother, Donegild, who sends Custance and her newborn child Maurice away from England upon the very rudderless ship in which she had arrived. A xenophobic contempt for Custance, we are told, compels Donegild to sabotage her son's marriage to "so strange a creature" (2.700). In her counterfeited letter to Alla, Donegild speaks to a nation's blood anxieties over the foreign woman when she writes that Custance must be an elf, given her delivery of "so horrible a feendly creature / That in the castel noon so hardy was / That any while dorste ther endure" (2.751–53). An endogamous queen mother, Donegild suggests that, as feminist geographic work on nationalism observes, if there is a place for woman in the nation, it is rooted within privatized domestic space.[78] Insofar as its welfare can be said to depend upon the "proper" (that is, racialist and patriarchal) biological reproduction of its members, the nation embraces mothers of national stock grounded firmly within the home and rejects nomadic strangers such as Custance.[79] Indeed, it is worth noting, with Roland Smith, that the "legitimacy had been in question" of the woman whom some readers of the tale and its sources have identified as the historical counterpart to Custance, John of Gaunt's second duchess, Costanza of Castille.[80]

Yet Chaucer's lawyer suggests otherwise—that it is not Custance as foreign queen but Donegild as native queen mother who proves problematic for England. The Man of Law censures Donegild for her behavior and proclaims its "un-Englishness":

> O Donegild, I ne have noon Englissh digne
> Unto thy malice and thy tirannye!
> And therfore to the feend I thee resigne;
> Lat hym enditen of thy traitorie!
>
> (2.778–81)

In this stanza of *exclamatio,* found only in Chaucer's version of the Constance story, Donegild's aggression toward Custance and her child places Alla's mother outside the vernacular, and hence only the devil, according to the Man of Law, can accurately articulate this evil mother's actions.[81] While her libelous predecessor, the English knight, emerges in the tale as an enemy of God, Donegild appears in this diatribe as the foe of both God and England; her treachery so opposes her homeland that its native tongue cannot even "speak" her crimes. By asserting his inability to describe Donegild in English, the Man of Law implies her alterity to England itself. The lawyer thus linguistically endeavors to do to Donegild what she literally does to Custance, when the menacing queen mother orders the constable to "croude hire fro the lond" (2.801). Indeed, the intractable Donegild, after having successfully rid England of the foreign woman in its midst, ends up not only verbally but also physically ejected from English life as her son, playing again the role of judge, executes his mother as a traitor (2.894–95).

Taken together, Donegild's ejection of Custance and the aggression the Man of Law directs at Donegild manifest a narrative strategy of occlusion, whereby an evil woman accomplishes the "dirty work" that, if acknowledged openly as desirable in the tale, would undermine its national appropriation of woman. Donegild's aggression toward Custance, that is, is shared by the Man of Law. As we have already noted, Custance's entry into the world—her laying "a lite hir hoolynesse aside"—disturbs the Man of Law because it brings to light the linked threats of Rome and womanhood that challenge the territorial sovereignty cherished by his juridical class. Just as fourteenth-century lawmen sought to eliminate the church's presence in England, so too does the Man of Law route through Donegild his masculinist aversion to "mother" Custance. That a repugnance toward not only Custance but all women lies at the heart of this national fantasy may be best seen, perhaps, when we consider the fact that all the native English women who appear in the tale are killed. The murder of Hermengild and the execution of Donegild testify to a desire to empty England of living, breathing women. The evacuation of women in the tale suggests the wish that England could flourish without their repro-ductive work. Reflecting the patriarchal bias of his class of legal professionals, Chaucer's lawyer imagines England as a fraternal collective, a site of, to quote Benedict Anderson, "deep, horizontal comradeship."[82] As so often is the case in national fantasy, biological reproduction is replaced with a nonbiological, symbolic, and masculinist production of England akin to Godwin's creation of sublime English identity via Chaucer, Virgil, and Petrarch.

## Beyond England

Throughout this chapter, I have emphasized the desire of English lawmen to move be-yond the forensic reach of Rome and exalt their isolated homeland. The ostensible proj-ect of the *Man of Law's Tale* is to rehabilitate marginality in the name of English juridical sovereignty. Yet the final turns of the tale suggest that our lawyer is not so confident about the benefits of isolation as he seems. After his mother's execution, Alla finds him-self filled with "wich repentance" that he travels to Rome "to receyven his penance; / And putte hym in the Popes ordinance" (2.989–92). Renewed attachment to his bio-logical mother inspires Alla to go to Mother Rome, a journey that demonstrates a cer-tain English attraction to the world *umbilicus* at work in this Canterbury tale. In particular, Alla's pilgrimage reveals how any celebration of the marginal always entails an appreciation of the center. After all, the unique status of England as an isolated is-land appears not through maps of England alone but through mappae mundi that of-fer the global perspective of a Rome-centered world. Moreover, the English *need* Rome not only to perceive their own geographic marginality in the first place, but also, as God-win's use of Petrarch suggests, to authorize their otherness. Although Custance's spiri-tual ties reflect the Man of Law's desire to receive the gift of Roman Christianity without the Roman obligations it entails, it is nevertheless *Roman* Christianity that she brings to England.

The imaginary compensation of stressing centrality over marginality ultimately amounts to the "flip side" of English national fantasy, that is, English imperial fantasy. Even as our lawyer celebrates the English edge of the world, he also wishes, at some level, that the English were less the inhabitants of an isolated island than a global presence, possessors of the very universal dominance accorded Rome. That rivalry with Rome, in turn, speaks to a patriarchal envy of the mother's potential power to obligate, control, and engulf her offspring.

Custance's son, Maurice, evinces the lawyer's imperial desires. The son also of Alla, and a man who "was sithen Emperour / Maad by the Pope," Maurice represents the fantasy of a Roman Empire subject to an Englishman (2.1121–22). To be sure, this aspect of the Constance story is played down by the Man of Law. Trevet writes that "Cist Moris fu apele de Romeyns en Latin 'Mauricius Cristianissimus imperator'" (181), a line Gower translates as "men him calle / Moris the cristeneste of alle" (II.1598). The Man of Law's Maurice, however, lacks such superlative piety, as the lawyer only tells us that he "to Cristes chirche . . . dide greet honour" (2.1123). Among these three versions of the Constance story, the *Chronique* is most clearly invested in English imperialism, as Trevet's version begins not with Constaunce, but with her son, whose Anglo-Saxon paternity Trevet takes pains to clarify (165).[83] While it appears that what is at stake in the *Chronique* is less Constaunce herself than her generation of an English emperor of Rome par excellence, the *Man of Law's Tale* professes its lack of interest in imperialism. Claiming that "Of Custance is my tale specially," Chaucer's lawyer tells the pilgrims, "In the olde Romayn geestes may men fynde Maurices lyf; I bere it noght in mynde" (2.1125–27).

Yet perhaps the English justice protests too much. We may draw this conclusion from the final crisscrossing movements of Custance that end the *Man of Law's Tale*. While, before her reconciliation with Alla, Custance already has trekked from Rome to England and back, after her eventual reunion with her spouse these travels between world center and world edge recur at a frantic rate; whereby, in the space of three stanzas, Custance returns to England and then, after Alla's death, circles back to Rome. That dizzying topographic "splitting" of Custance between England and Rome points to the instability that founds the Man of Law's national fantasy. At once attracted to and repulsed by her maternity, alternately repudiating and embracing Roman authority, both proud of and anxious about his isolated homeland, Chaucer's lawyer exhibits a version of the ideological vacillation and uncertainty that Homi Bhabha and other contemporary theorists associate with nationalism.[84] Even Custance's final settling down in Rome shores up the Man of Law's ambivalence over both England and woman: On the one hand, the tears of joy Custance sheds upon having "scaped al hire aventure" reinscribe England as a land that, from the perspective of the Roman world *umbilicus,* is unappealingly distant and alien (2:1151). On the other hand, Rome does not necessarily emerge at the end of the tale as a sacred world center. As Dinshaw has pointed out, the life led by Custance in Rome is charged "with undertones of incest," including the absence of Custance's mother and the quasi-matrimonial quality of Custance's life with her father, with whom she resides to "nevere asonder wende; / Til deeth departeth hem" (2.1157–58).[85]

Those hints at father-daughter incest trouble the idea that "vertu and hooly almus-dede" characterize Custance's life in Rome (2.1156). Insofar as the emperor and his daughter seem guilty of sexual impropriety, they imply Rome's status not as Mother Church but as the Whore of Babylon decried by Walter Brute. In this light, the depositing of Custance in Rome cleanses England of a certain Roman moral depravity or "unkynde abhomynacions" (2.88). The conclusion of Custance's "aventure," her wanderings, offers no closure to the ideological uncertainties informing her narrative but instead raises yet again her lawyerly narrator's anxieties over both the English margin and the Roman center of the world.

# CHAPTER FIVE

# "FROM THE VERY ENDS OF THE EARTH"

## Medieval Geography and Wolsey's Processions

With its focus upon late fifteenth- and early sixteenth-century English culture, this chapter turns to a period whose traditional designation as "Renaissance" invests that historical era with newness. As Leah S. Marcus notes in a recent assessment of early modern studies, "the term Renaissance implicitly calls for a perception of historical rupture" since "in order to be reborn, a culture"—in this case medieval culture—"must previously have died."[1] In the received account of English cultural history, the Renaissance gave new life to concepts that were unthinkable in the Middle Ages, notions such as selfhood, nationhood, liberty, objectivity, and perspective. Of late, however, scholars have queried the idea that Renaissance England radically broke with its medieval past. Critical analysis of transitional figures such as Cardinal Thomas Wolsey (ca. 1472–1530) has yielded important revisions of periodization. A man who manifested, in the most ostentatiously ritualized manner imaginable, his transformation from an Ipswich trader's son to someone who "rule[d] both the king and the entire kingdom," Wolsey offers an early prototype of the histrionic self-fashioning said to have emerged first during the Renaissance.[2] With their unprecedented combination of theatricality and careerism, the magnificent displays and spectacular public processions of early Tudor England's supreme upstart fascinated and overwhelmed the writers of the time. Jonathan Crewe writes in his gloss on George Cavendish's biography of the cardinal that if Wolsey "looks to Cavendish like a shockingly unprecedented monster of vanity and appetite, all the more does the monster show forth what is in the process of becoming. Wolsey is paradigmatic of the Renaissance life of ambition that has so widely been perceived in recent criticism."[3] As Crewe notes, he is not alone in considering Wolsey prototypical. Stephen Greenblatt's *Learning to Curse,* for example, foregrounds Wolsey in its final chapter.[4] Both Greenblatt and Crewe affirm the status of Wolsey as "the grand

Master of the Revels in a staging of power that is to be repeated throughout the Elizabethan and Stuart reigns."[5]

But at the same time that Wolsey exemplifies the theatrical careerism of the Renaissance, he is also a medieval holdover. As cardinal of York and the most powerful official of the Roman church in England, Wolsey typifies the very old-fashioned religious authority rejected during the English Reformation. Indeed, it is that very "medieval" ecclesiastical identity that his histrionic performances largely served: the "prop" analyzed in Greenblatt's culminating chapter is none other than Wolsey's red cardinal's hat, one of the prime signs of his power as an official of the Roman church.[6] The striking synthesis of the new and the old in Wolsey's self-fashioning undoes the supposed division between the Middle Ages and Renaissance. As a figure who looks toward, as Crewe puts it, "the transformation of the medieval Catholic prelate into a secular, Renaissance master of ceremonies as power-broker," Wolsey exposes how historical "opposition and discontinuity are not complete or fundamental, and cannot be so."[7] The modern and the medieval cannot be opposed in any simple manner.

To stress the contradictory *temporality* of Wolsey's stagings of power, however, is to provide only a partial picture of their unstable and transitional nature. If Wolsey's theatricality offers us a way to reimagine the relationship between the Middle Ages and the Renaissance, that same theatricality emanated from and responded to *spatial* dynamics that were equally fluid and unstable. For one thing, the components of Wolsey's theatricality—like all modes of performance—are always potentially mobile. Theater, that is, travels; it is part of a "social process through which objects, gestures, rituals, and phrases are fashioned and moved from one zone of display to another."[8] By donning a cardinal's hat Wolsey exposes the capacity of such a material object to travel from its "proper" location on upper-class personages to bodies located far lower on the social ladder. By staging his, in Greenblatt's words, "transformation from a butcher's son to a prince of the Church," Wolsey presents a powerful critique of the geography of social privilege, one that reflects social upheavals taking place throughout Renaissance Europe.[9]

What recent scholarship on Wolsey has been slow to recognize, however, is that those performances had particularly English resonances as well. For Wolsey, that is, the enormous "gulf" between his class origins and the ecclesiastical and political heights he sought to attain was intimately connected to another kind of distance, the territorial expanse separating England from the world. As we have seen, since at least the tenth century, England was famed for its extreme global isolation, and the early modern period was no different. Owing not only to the revival of the classics but also to their unusual interest in medieval chorography and cartography, the English would continue to consider themselves inhabitants of a remote *angulus orbis*. Thanks in no small part to Wolsey, however, early Tudor England was endeavoring as never before to overcome the barbarous implications of its isolation and instead assert the sovereignty of the English edge of the world. Binding his own status as social *arriviste* to the brutish standing of his nation as global backwater, Cardinal Wolsey dramatized the magnificence of both himself and what he called the English "angle of the worlde." In a move that looked toward the symbolic appropriations in which his king would engage as Supreme Head of the Church of England, Wolsey appropriated the rituals of Roman Christendom to exalt its English border.

As his use of ecclesiastical "props" such as his cardinal's hat suggests, Wolsey's theatrical elevation of England was fraught. His crafting of a sovereign English world margin at once depended upon and was challenged by the authority of Rome. For the cardinal as for his medieval predecessors, the *oikoumené* bordered by England was a world in which Rome figured as a powerful and richly endowed territorial center. Wolsey's appreciation of Rome, indeed, was such that he evinced an unprecedented appetite for its might, as witnessed by his many unsuccessful bids for the papacy as well as his attainment of the next-highest offices of cardinal and papal legate. Thus in Wolsey's sixteenth-century theater of power, we witness perhaps *the* pivotal moment in the England-Rome dynamic that arose during the Middle Ages. To be sure, we have seen multiple instances when England's rejection of and desire for Roman authority flared, instances such as the late twelfth century, when Henry II figured as both a Roman emissary (to Ireland) and a Roman outlaw (as Becket's murderer). But as both a high officer of the church and the chief counselor to an absolutist ruler, Wolsey pushed at the cleft between Rome and England as never before. More than any Englishman before or after him, Wolsey tested just how much an inhabitant of the margin of Christendom could garner the privileges of its Roman center. Ultimately, I hope to show how Wolsey's contradictory geography and the long-standing medieval dynamic it represents have much to offer recent attempts at registering the ambiguities of history.

## A Pope from "another worlde"?

Graphic evidence of Wolsey's interest in world geography emerges in a mid-sixteenth century inventory of his massive palace, Hampton Court. Among the entries for the Short and Long Galleries appear two world maps: "a lardge platte or mappe of the worlde" in the former room and "a rownde mappe mundi" in the latter.[10] Unfortunately, we do not know for certain what either map—both are lost—looked like. Complicating matters is the fact that, during the some one hundred years preceding Wolsey's rise, the history of cartography witnessed several upheavals, so that the cardinal's maps potentially could have offered any combination of a wide array of possible graphic images of the world.[11] For one thing, one or both of the maps may have used the rediscovered projection of Claudius Ptolemy. The Latin translation of the *Geography* (ca. 160) in about 1406–7 led to an outpouring of maps and atlases whose use of coordinates of latitude and longitude produced a more "scientific" projection of the world than that offered by medieval mappae mundi.[12] For another, Wolsey's world maps may have represented the western territories encountered by Renaissance explorers. Columbus's North American landfall in 1492 initiated a process of "discovery" that would extend the boundaries of the world across the Atlantic and into America and ultimately obliterate the old notion of a tripartite world.[13]

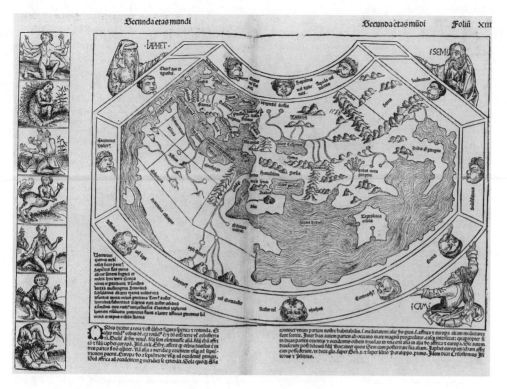

**Fig. 16.** Ptolemaic world map, Nuremburg, 1493. London, British Library, IC 7452. By permission of the British Library.

If Wolsey's maps reflected such changes in the history of cartography, what would they have told the cardinal about the location of his homeland? Was the old medieval notion of the extreme isolation of England a casualty of the "new" geography? Hardly. In the world produced by Ptolemy's mathematical projections, for example, England is still a global other, if one located now on the margins of a northern-oriented world (figs. 16–17).[14] Even more significant, as critics including Jeffrey Knapp, Bernhard Klein, and Lesley Cormack have demonstrated, the new American *alter orbis* did not supplant England as prime "otherworld" so much as it gave English geographic alterity new relevance.[15] As much emerges in "the first modern atlas of the world," the Strassburg *Geographia*.[16] By including England in the northeastern margin of its Terra Nova map, the atlas suggests England's identity as a border of not only the Old World but also the New World (fig. 18).

That Wolsey was alive to the new opportunities confronting his isolated homeland appears in his status as "almost certainly" the man "who was the inspiration for" an English effort to discover a northwest route to China and the East Indies.[17] In 1520 Wolsey offered to pay Sebastian Cabot a generous sum to head up a quest to find the Northwest Passage to Cathay.[18] When Cabot declined, an undaunted Wolsey invited London merchants a year later to take up the enterprise, only to have them reject the daring plan

**Fig. 17.** Ptolemaic world map, Augsburg, 1497. London, British Library, IB 6361. By permission of the British Library.

as well.[19] Wolsey's persistent efforts to erect an English-sponsored exploration program represent a notable, if failed, return to the New World ambitions that characterized Henry VII's reign.[20] During a period in which the English were by and large uninterested in western exploration, Wolsey's aborted Northwest Passage project stands out as an unusual attempt to extend English authority far into the New World.[21]

Given his interest in the newly discovered lands, Wolsey may well have owned one or two maps depicting them. But to do so, the cardinal would have had look to foreign map producers.[22] As E. G. R. Taylor points out, in the history of cartography in Europe there existed "a lag in English geography far behind the standard reached on the Continent."[23] From 1478 on, Italian presses, along with presses in Salamanca, Nuremberg, Augsburg, and Ulm, made Ptolemaic maps. And, after the publication of Giovanni Contarini's groundbreaking drawing of the world in 1506, presses in France, Belgium, the Netherlands, Austria, Poland, the Holy Roman Empire, and, above all, Italy produced some thirty world maps representing the new continent. But up to 1534, no Ptolemaic world map was printed in England. And, with regard to the New World, no world map incorporating it would be published in England until 1576, by Humphrey

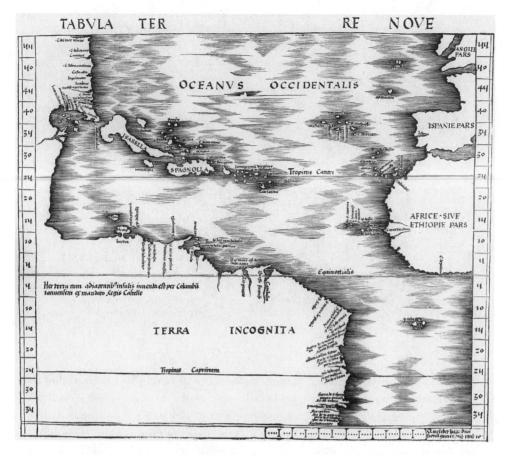

Fig. 18. Terra Nova by Martin Waldseemüller featured in Ptolemy's *Geographia* (Strassburg, 1513), facsimile with introduction by R. A. Skelton (Amsterdam: Theatrum Orbis Terrarum, 1966).

Gilbert. Indeed, only in the eighteenth century would the English come into their own with respect to modern mapmaking.[24]

England's "backwardness" regarding map production suggests a certain national disregard for new images of the world and a lingering national investment in the old medieval image of the *oikoumené*. That attachment to the medieval worldview emerges in the first English book to use printed illustrations, William Caxton's 1481 English edition of a popular scientific book, *The Mirrour of the Worlde,* which includes several T-O maps (fig. 19). Even more telling evidence of England's investment in the old global perspective emerges in the afterlife of Higden's *Polychronicon.* Caxton's 1480 adaptation of Trevisa's translation of Higden's description of Britain—a description that, as we have seen, highlights and expands upon the traditional perception of England as an angle of the world or even other world—was published no less than seven times, in editions as late as 1528.[25] Indeed, the king himself authorized in 1510 the publication of Caxton's *Description* by the royal printer, Richard Pynson (STC 9999). In his account of the popu-

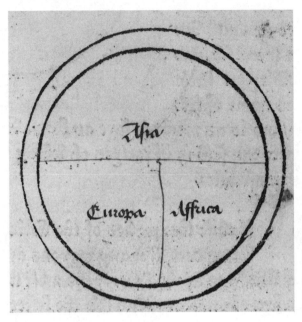

**Fig. 19.** T-O map from William Caxton's *Mirrour of the Worlde* (Westminster, 1481). London, British Library IB.55040, fol. 35r. By permission of the British Library.

larity of Higden into the Renaissance, A. S. G. Edwards notes that in those editions, Caxton's adaptation tends to appear alongside versions of the entire *Polychronicon,* both its world chorography and universal history. Edwards views such a conjunction as an inexplicable "oddity," though we can perhaps make sense of the linkage in terms of the fact that the notion of English global marginality so stressed by Higden requires the adoption of a premodern perspective on the *entire* world. The repeated publication of Higden's description of Britain, along with that of the entire *Polychronicon,* demonstrates how, at the same time that the English proved uninterested in publishing texts promoting the new geographies offered by Ptolemy and the European explorers, English readers—including the king himself—sought out older accounts of the world and England's place in it. During Wolsey's time, in other words, Englishmen retained a distinctly medieval perspective on matters geographic.

Could the maps listed in the Hampton Court inventory have followed the traditional approach given by Caxton and Higden? The characterization of one of Wolsey's maps as both "rownde" and a "mappe mundi" may well suggest as much. Moreover, the geography of Wolsey's political career also makes it likely that his maps observed medieval conventions. Wolsey's one New World endeavor pales when compared to his many engagements with the Old World. Insofar as Wolsey sought to expand the sphere of influence of both himself and his homeland, the terrain of that expansion lay not across the Atlantic Ocean but on the other side of the English Channel. As much emerges in a 1521 letter he sent to Henry VIII during an international conference at Calais, that English continental holding which, as David Wallace points out, "was increasingly used as a 'staging post' to signal English designs to greater Europe."[26] Wolsey's endeavor in this case was to serve officially as a diplomatic mediator between Holy Roman emperor Charles V and King Francis I of France, while *covertly* scheming to accrue power for both himself and his king. In his report to Henry, Wolsey invokes England's Old World marginality to describe his successful clandestine machinations with Charles.[27] Directed "To the Kynges Grace ys owne handys onely," the letter informs Henry that Charles is

> determyned . . . in all hys afferys to take and folowe your cownsell and advyse, and no thyng to do without the same . . . Wherfor, Syre, Ye have cause to geve thanckes to Almygthy Gode, wych hath gevyn Yow grace so to ordyr and conven your afferys, that Ye be nat onley the ruler of thys your Realme, wych ys in an angle of the worlde; but also by your wysdome and cownsel, Spayne, Itally, Almayne, and thes Lowe Cowntres, wych ys the gretest parte of Crystendame, shalbe rulyd and governyd.[28]

Ostensibly in this passage, English geographic marginality affects the identity not of Wolsey, but of Henry, insofar as the king rules from "an angle of the worlde" yet nevertheless garners considerable control over "the gretest parte of Crystendame." Thanks to Wolsey's persuasions, Charles has offered to transfer much of his imperial authority over to Henry's "wysdome and cownsel," making the English king the de facto ruler of "Spayne, Itally, Almayne, and thes Lowe Cowntres."[29] But, as always, Wolsey, who notoriously ruled "as a second king" with Henry, considered his own fate to be intertwined with that of the Tudor monarch.[30] Wolsey's self-description elsewhere in the letter as a "poore parson of wyt, exsperyens, substance, and blode" intent solely on his king's "gret exultation" is belied by the fact that, at the same time he made Henry a closeted Roman emperor, Wolsey strove to secure his own elevation as pope. Wolsey, that is, garnered from Charles support for his candidacy as pope upon the imminent death of Leo X. The grand sphere of continental influence Wolsey describes here refers not only to the future exertion of Henry's royal muscle abroad but also to that of the cardinal himself.

Like his motto, *ubi Petrus, ibi Anglia,* Wolsey's letter to Henry bears witness that the cardinal's ambitions revolved around Rome. The papal machinations Wolsey engaged in at Calais, for example, were no one-time affair: ten years before the conference, he wrote to Richard Fox of the honor his elevation would bring the king;[31] shortly after Calais, when Charles reneged on his promise, Wolsey sought to replace the man who did follow Leo, Adrian VI; finally, in 1529, Wolsey's candidacy was raised for a fourth and last time as a means of resolving Henry's divorce case.[32] Multiple reasons account for Wolsey's particular Roman orientation. As a cleric, the cardinal was certainly sensitive to Rome's status as the capital of Christendom. And as a man who appreciated the humanist learning of his day, he was clearly aware of Rome's grand classical heritage and standing as ancient world capital. When we turn to politics, Wolsey's Rome had gained still another distinction. As the "leading temporal power" in Italy, a region that was "the most contentious area in Europe," Rome had become, as Peter Gwyn puts it, "the diplomatic centre of Europe."[33] Thus dominating Henry VIII's pre-reformation foreign and domestic papers are missives to and from Rome. These communications make manifest

Rome's status as a center that drew to itself not only pilgrims and classical enthusiasts but also representatives of the emerging European nations such as Spain, France, and England. With its newly rediscovered classical pedigree, plus its status as Christian capital and European diplomatic center, it is no surprise that Rome attracted the power-hungry Wolsey.

But as his letter to Henry also attests, Wolsey bound his papal ambitions closely to his national identity. Like early sixteenth-century Rome, early Tudor England was a site possessed of new powers that appealed to a careerist such as Wolsey. Due to the achievements of the previous reign, England had become an absolutist state with all the privileges attending such a transformation. Bent on restoring stability to a war-torn realm, Henry VII heightened the administrative authority of his monarchic government through new advisory and legal committees such as the Privy Council and Star Chamber. That gathering of power within a centralized bureaucracy, along with a massive transfer of local capital to the crown, led to the emergence of a state government that Wolsey would come to lead as lord chancellor. Indeed, even more than his king, Wolsey exhibited the centralizing impulses of the early Tudor absolutist state.[34] Attending the state's consolidation of authority was an expansionist impulse witnessed by such New World ventures as the Cabot voyages and, in the case of Henry VIII's reign, Tudor intervention in the politics of continental Christendom. A notably powerful nation-state, Wolsey's England had become a major player on the world scene. And Wolsey aimed at being nothing less than the arbiter of that international arena.

With its celebration of Henry and himself as isolated Englishmen who nevertheless wield power throughout Roman Christendom, Wolsey's letter well demonstrates the simultaneously insular and expansionist status of early Tudor England. The cardinal's words, indeed, look toward the national geographic rhetoric of England's imperial heyday (1880s–1920s), when patriots would wonder at "tiny" England's mastery over vast territories throughout the earth. For both the Renaissance cardinal and modern imperialists, the geographic marginality of the English renders their world governance exceptional and extraordinary. The early Tudor linkage of geographic isolation with the wondrous, however, was hardly inevitable. One could just as easily label preposterous the notion of the barbarously isolated English ruling the world.[35] That the sixteenth-century Romans, at least, used geography as a means of belittling English global aspirations appears in a letter penned by English ambassadors Richard Pace, John Clerk, and Thomas Hannibal. Sent from Rome during Wolsey's third bid for the papacy, the letter describes to the cardinal the maneuverings of his rivals at the 1523 conclave following Pope Adrian VI's death. On Cardinals Pompeo Colonna and Giulio di Medici, the English ambassadors write:

> The Cardinall Columpna is now clerely agaynst hym [de Medici]; et *ut excitaret non solum odium sed etiam tumultum contra eum hic in urbe,* he hath [therefore]noysyd throughout Rome, that by the said Cardinall [de Medici's] meanys, at the last tyme, Cardinales *elegerunt barbaru[m Fle]mingum in Pontificem, et quod nunc idem conabatur eligere Ang[licum].* And this is certayn, that the sayd Cardynall Columpna is

brother hath reportyd opynly that, if his brother the Cardinall had not been, the Cardinalles had chosyn Pope one beyng absent out in another worlde, meanyng therby an Englisheman, *propter carmen, quod solet esse in ore omnibus "et penitus toto divisos orbe Britannos."*[36]

Through their description of Colonna's own campaign efforts, Pace et al. reveal the identification of geographic isolation with rusticity. Colonna (called Columpna in the passage) decries his rival de Medici by pointing out his role in electing the last pope, the "barbarous Fleming" or *barbaru[m Fle]mingum* Adrian Florenszoon Boeyens. Ignoring Boeyens's own cultured status as the tutor of none other than Erasmus, Colonna portrays Adrian VI as an uncivilized foreigner. The role of a geographic rhetoric in Colonna's production of Adrian's barbarity emerges in his reference to Wolsey's election as an even more horrifying prospect. Wolsey is far worse than Boeyens, because he hails from a land even farther from Rome than the Netherlands: he is "absent out in another worlde." Though elsewhere in the letter, Pace et al. claim they are "in fast and ferme hope to se some good successe ensue" regarding the cardinal's election, the passage reveals that not just Wolsey but any Englishman has little chance of gaining the pontificate, given their reputation from Virgil onward as men *penitus toto divisos orbe.*

That Colonna constructs the fearful image of a barbarian pope via geography cannot be overemphasized. What makes the notion of a Fleming pope and, particularly, an English pope horrible is their contamination of the privileged Roman world center by the geographically alien and otherworldly. Or so the citation of Virgil is meant to explain, with its reference to Rome's classical heritage and presumed cultural superiority. What Colonna suppresses through the quote, however, is the fact that, far from an immutable space, the sixteenth-century city had only recently itself been a wilderness of sorts. As recently as 1500, Rome's classical monuments and edifices were overgrown and abandoned, given over to the use of livestock and the cultivation of orchards and vineyards. Only through the efforts of figures such as the Medici pontiff Leo X (1513–22), who brought Renaissance artistry to bear on Catholic ritual and ceremony, would Rome again attain the eminence of its ancient counterpart.[37] The "medieval village, smelling of cows and hay" merely of late had given way to a city whose classical past and late Renaissance present urged its status as a privileged physical space, an *umbiculus mundi*.[38] And such historical transformations were hardly exclusive to Rome. While England itself was still some one hundred years away from the kind of cultural productivity manifested in Italy, the candidacy of Wolsey (like the election of Boeyens) demonstrated how even foreigners born in the European lands most distant from Rome were gaining new powers. The reconfiguration of authority in Renaissance Christendom stretched from its Roman capital to its English edge.

Colonna's invocation of Virgil thus suggests the powerful appeal of geography as a means of masking how Rome and England, like all places, are subject to transformation and variation. By suggesting that England is still the remote land described by the ancients, Colonna fixes that place as rustic and undeveloped and implicitly renders Rome eternally central and powerful. Through the fiction of premodern geography, the Roman cardinal quells the idea of historical change. Within this geocultural rhetoric of power, the proper person to lead Rome is a native such as Colonna. Conversely, the very last man likely to occupy Rome is Wolsey, the inhabitant of an island geographically isolated from Rome and a place still disconnected from the neoclassical efforts centered on Italy. Indeed, the notion of giving the papacy to a man so far from Rome as to be "absent out in another worlde," is as strange and unthinkable as having a New World native occupy the papal seat.

## The Excessive Processions of "A Bochers Curre"

The Romans were hardly the only people to view Wolsey as a man bent on venturing into places he did not belong. Wolsey's fellow Englishmen also saw him as a man whose acquisition of power violated the bounds of propriety. As John Foxe would write in his *Acts and Monuments,* the cardinal "did exceed so far all measure of a good subject, that he became more like a prince than a priest."[39] With an anti-Catholic sentiment typical of post-Reformation accounts of Wolsey, Foxe specifically decries how Wolsey's statesmanship and magnificence violated his clerical identity. But for Wolsey's contemporaries, an equal if not greater outrage consisted in just how far the cardinal had risen above his humble rank as the son of an Ipswich trader, supposedly a butcher. Thus the anonymous author of "Of the Cardnall Wolse" proclaims that "To se A Churle, A Bochers Curre, / To Rayne & Rule in soche honour. / hyt ys to hye, with-owte mesure."[40] The identification in the poem of Wolsey as a "churl" born to a butcher may well be imprecise, as recent scholarship has demonstrated. Whatever his trade actually was (the possibilities include innkeeper, grazier, and butcher), Wolsey's father Robert enjoyed some financial success and was linked by marriage to the most powerful family in his prosperous trading town of Ipswich, Suffolk.[41] Still, as T. W. Cameron acknowledged over a century ago, if Wolsey's father was not indigent, he "doubtless . . . was poor when his circumstances are compared with the height of splendour to which his son rose."[42] The author of "Of the Cardnall Wolse" certainly suggests as much, as do other contemporaneous observers. The Venetian ambassador Giustinian portrays Wolsey as a man "of low origin," and George Cavendish famously describes Wolsey as "an honest poore mans Sonne."[43] These and other accounts suggest that, if the cardinal did not begin life at the very bottom rung of the social ladder, from the perspective of his astounding social elevation he might as well have.

Even as a member of a successful merchant family, Wolsey was still a man of relatively modest roots that made his ambitions excessive or—to return to "Of the Cardnall Wolse"—"to hye, with-owte mesure." Such English censures of Wolsey's ascent to "soche honour" offer a personal version of the geographic critique we see in Colonna's dismissal of Wolsey's papal aims. In the case of the Roman Colonna, the baseness of the Englishman's homeland makes Wolsey's occupation of the papal seat absurd. For English satirists, the baseness of the cardinal's social origin renders his ascent to the cardinalate and English chancellorship abhorrent. A man challenged by both the geographic and social distances he sought to traverse, Thomas Wolsey was at once a social *arriviste,* and a member of an *arriviste* nation.

Those two constructions of Wolsey, as a man demonstrating a certain national rusticity and a merchant class vulgarity, did not merely parallel each other but also intersected in complex and contradictory ways during the cardinal's career. Wolsey's personal ambitions, characterized as they so often were by an appetitive quest for power within the clergy, signaled a Roman Catholic draining of England's resources that confirmed its status as a cultural wasteland. Thus "Of the Cardnall Wolse" proclaims that "As long as" the cardinal "Dothe Reyne & Rule, as ye do see, / so long in poverte þis Realme shalbe."[44] But, as we shall see, at times Wolsey's elevation was also tied to that of his isolated homeland, a project that the cardinal promoted, moreover, at the expense of Christendom's Roman capital. We can best begin to understand this fraught and volatile intersection of the geography of self and nation, by focusing on the local ramifications of Wolsey's assertions of individual power. Only after close inspection of the cardinal's performance of authority on English terrain can we gain an adequate sense of the depth and complexity of Wolsey's engagement with English isolation.

Like his efforts to occupy the papal seat at Rome, Wolsey's English rise entailed his traversing of physical space. Namely, the "honour" whose attainment Wolsey's critics deemed excessive, was exhibited through extravagant processions. Originating from the Latin *processio, processionis*—meaning the marching onward or advance of the imperial army—the procession was a traveling and highly theatrical assertion of power that was fundamental to Renaissance rhetorics of identity. Thus, as Edward Muir points out, the notably dramatic Venetian ducal processions not only "reinforced the ideology of Venice" but also offered nothing less than "the narrative outline for the myth of Venetian republicanism."[45] Scholars of Renaissance Rome similarly assert the fundamental role that the procession—largely in the form of the Roman stations of the Cross— "would serve as a means to restore the paleo-Christian conception of Rome's sacredness."[46] That English authorities shared with their European counterparts such an investment in the procession has been well proven by the wealth of critical analyses of Tudor and Stuart processions and progresses by Steven Mullaney and other scholars.[47]

Given their overall emphasis during the Renaissance, it is no surprise that the processions led by Wolsey loom large in accounts of his magnificence. Thus it is none other than the "pyllers, pollaxis, & crosse[s]" featured in Wolsey's train that the anonymous political ballad "An Impeachment of Wolsey" enjoins the cardinal to "ley downe."[48] The most detailed of all such contemporary allusions to his histrionic processions appears in the biography by Cavendish (1500–ca. 1562), which offers the following account of Wolsey's journey to Westminster Hall from his Privy Chamber:

> beyng advertised of the furnyture of his chambers without with noble men and gentilmen / with other persons [Wolsey] wold issue owt in to theme apparelled in all red in the habytt of a Cardynall whiche was other of fynne skarlett or elles of crymmosyn Satten / Taffeta Dammaske / or Caffa / the best that he could gett for mony / and vppon hys hed a round pyllion with a nekke [fol. 15v] of blake velvett set to the same in

the Inner side / he had also a tippett of fynne Sables a bought his nekke / . . . / There was also borne byfore hyme first the great Seale of Englond / And than his Cardynalles hatt by a noble man or some worthy Gentilman right Solemply barehedyd / And as Sone as he was entered in to hys chamber of presence where was attendyng his Commyng to awayt vppon hyme to westminster hall as welle noble men and other worthy gentilmen / as noble men & gentilmen of his owen famely / thus passyng forthe with two great Crossis of Syluer borne byfore hyme with also two great pillers of syluer / And his seriaunt at Armez with a great mase of syluer gylt / Than his gentilmen vsshers cried and sayd / on my lordes & maysters / make way for my lordes grace / thus passed he down frome his chambers thoroughe the hall / And whan he came to the hall doore ther was attendaunt for hyme his mewle trapped all to gether in Crymmosyn velvett and gylt Stirroppes / whan he was mounted / with his crosse berers / and Piller berers also / vppon great horsis trapped with red skarlett Than marched he forward with his trayn & furnyture in maner as I haue declared / hauyng abought hyme four footmen with gylt pollaxes in ther handes / And thus he went vntill he came to westminster hall doore / And there lighted and went after this maner. (23–24)

Like parades and other similarly territorialized displays of power, Wolsey's histrionic procession works through what we might term, following Gilles Deleuze, a "dynamic geography" of movement, since it offers up for visual consumption the ritualized and grand journey of a public official from one place to another.[49] Hence the many verbs of motion used by Cavendish, who describes how Wolsey's procession issues out, enters, passes forth, and marches onward. That last verb is particularly salient, since it points to the status of the procession as a spatial performance of power. To invoke Michel de Certeau's idea that "space is a practiced place," Wolsey's train transforms the place between the Privy Chamber and Westminster into a space socially dominated by the cardinal.[50] Indeed, with its inclusion of "gentilmen vsshers [who] cried and sayd . . . make way for my lordes grace," Wolsey's procession commands the territory previously occupied by its audience. Further evidence of the aggressive and even militaristic aspects of Wolsey's train emerges in the martial nature of two of its featured objects, maces and pole-axes.[51] Both items, of course, are only ornamental versions of weapons of war. Yet, as Georg Simmel has taught us, such decorative objects, by dint of their very splendor, powerfully assert themselves into space.[52] As spectacular objects composed of crimson satin, red and black velvet, rich sable, and gleaming silver, Wolsey's elaborate costume and manifold props engage in a silent version of the territorial domination voiced by Wolsey's ushers, with their call that onlookers "make way" for the cardinal.

But above all, what Cavendish manifests in his account of Wolsey's procession is its sheer size. Devoting a good deal of textual territory to enumerating the components of Wolsey's train, Cavendish makes clear just how much space Wolsey occupied in his processions, with their numerous footmen, mules, guards, and bearers of his many accoutrements: the national seal, his cardinal's hat, two crosses, two pillars, and four pole-axes. That stress on the great expanse of Wolsey's train in Cavendish's text would find a visual counterpart in an illustrated Elizabeth version of the biography. One of the images

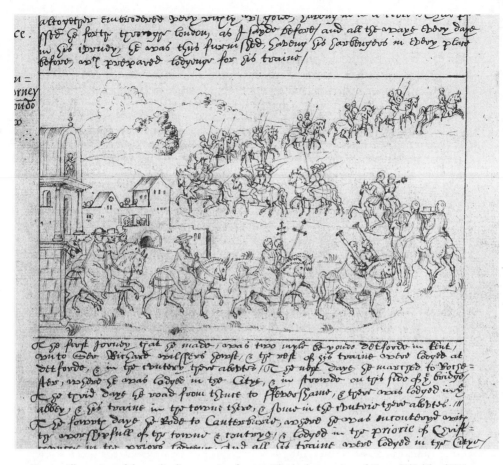

**Fig. 20.** Illustration of the cardinal's procession from an Elizabethan version of Cavendish's life of Wolsey. Oxford, Bodleian Library, MS. Douce 363, fol. 58. By permission of the Bodleian Library, University of Oxford.

that appear in the edition depicts Wolsey's train as a seemingly endless procession that extends beyond the horizon of the image (fig. 20). In a similar vein, in their satire *Rede Me and Be Nott Wrothe,* Jerome Barlow and William Roye emphasize the extensive length of Wolsey's procession, by expending some twenty lines delineating how Wolsey "dayly procedeth" with mules, priests, crosses, maces, pillars, and pole-axes, and other "worldly pompe incredible."[53] For all its detail, the satirists imply, their description cannot do justice to Wolsey's train; the character Jeffrey in *Rede Me* prefaces his description of the procession with the qualification that Wolsey travels "with so shamfull pryde, / That to tell it is not possible."[54]

We might dismiss Jeffrey's *occupatio* as mere rhetorical convention, but Wolsey's processions in fact were unusually grand in scale. The cardinal not only took advantage of all the ceremonial honor which he was due but also embellished upon it, by having borne before him, in addition to the silver mace of the cardinal, two silver gilt pillars.

And, as Italian historian Polydore Vergil notes with disdain, Wolsey "was also not satis-fied with the one cross which he had used in his capacity as archbishop of York, but would have another carried before him by two elegantly proportioned priests riding on great horses, who solemnly advanced bare-headed at all times of the year."[55]

Wolsey, then, was a man who exceeded social boundaries not only in his rise from merchant's son to cardinal and lord chancellor, but also in the unusually extravagant processions through which he performed his new identity. To be sure, at times the car-dinal revealed an anxiety to conform precisely to the standards of his new roles. He wrote, for example, to Silvestro Gigli in Rome for hoods and silks such as those "used by Cardinals there [in Rome]" for their habits.[56] Wolsey's request to Gigli suggests an intense investment in Rome as a site whose cultural authenticity both the parvenu car-dinal and his frontier homeland desperately need. Through the duplication of such signs of Roman cultural authority, Wolsey sought to overcome his own personal lack as well as England's status as the kind of heathenish cultural wasteland that Pompeo Colonna derided during the 1523 papal election. But in his processions Wolsey went beyond the limits of both Holy Roman and English ceremonial decorum. Their excess partly sug-gests the status of Wolsey's processions as a kind of bad theater—a sign of the cardinal's failure to transcend his social roots. As Norbert Elias and others have stressed, the loos-ening of traditional social rankings and the consequent reordering of individuals cre-ated an acute anxiety during the Renaissance over what constituted appropriate behavior and good taste.[57] Wolsey strives to conduct himself in keeping with his newfound au-thority through his processions, with their display of accurate and seemingly authentic cultural signs of power, but he goes too far. While Erasmus would stress in his 1530 ci-vility book how "modesty, above all, befits" the truly noble, Wolsey's professions are pompous and overblown.[58] Breaching propriety, the processions seem to expose Wolsey as a man who doesn't know the rules of the elite society he has entered.

Yet there is more to the story. For all the social inadequacy and class anxiety they may suggest, the cardinal's processions also carry with them a certain menace to the privi-leged social circle he has entered. As scholarship on the outsider status of Elizabethan writers such as the "prodigals" studied by Richard Helgerson and the courtiers analyzed by Frank Whigham has shown, the sentiments of the newcomer tend toward contra-diction.[59] Wolsey surely did view his modest and distinctly non-aristocratic status as a problem he needed to overcome, but he also certainly felt smug about his accomplish-ments. Not every Englishman can achieve the position of cardinal and lord chancellor. Conversely, at the same time that a social aspirant such as Wolsey esteems the elite aris-tocratic society he has entered, he also may resent the concept of hereditary privilege altogether. Such resentment emerges in Wolsey's strident enforcement of laws of livery and maintenance, a "check" on "the 'pretension' of the nobility" that led to the swift im-prisonment of an earl and questioning of several other aristocrats.[60]

Taken as signs not of anxiety but of arrogance, not of respect but of resentment, the cardinal's processions emerge as something altogether different from a failed attempt to compensate for his rude origins. Rather, the processions indicate Wolsey's status as a successful master of ceremonies. Displaying less his ignorance of social protocol than his skill at manipulating and even parodying it, Wolsey dramatically displays his shockingly massive personal mobility. Far from attempting to suppress the affront that constituted his social rise, Wolsey uses his theater of excess to stage the tremendous distance between his personal roots as the child of an Ipswich trader and his new identity as cardinal and English chancellor. The gap between Wolsey's processions and respectable processions—between bad taste and good taste—cannot help but indicate the gulf between the merchant class and the power elite. Exposing the fact that aristocrats have no monopoly on privilege, Wolsey, in effect, makes a spectacle of his status as a social outsider who has nevertheless appropriated the authority traditionally accorded the elite. That histrionic flaunting of the social power attained by the modest newcomer reflects the kind of English imperial pride we saw at work in his letter to Henry regarding the Calais mission. In that document Wolsey celebrates the astounding capacity of the ruler of a mere "angle of the worlde" determining how "the gretest parte of Crystendame, shalbe rulyd and governyd"; and in his processions Wolsey celebrates his own remarkable journey from the margins of English society into its most elite circle. For both the low-born Wolsey and his backwater nation, their seeming inconsequence is worth highlighting, insofar as it renders their newly gained powers all the more marvelous. While the notion of an aristocrat from the world's Roman center such as Pompeo Colonna possessing great power hardly surprises, the might attained by a commoner from the English world border astounds and amazes.

## Flying beyond England in *Speke, Parott*

Such links between transcending the limits of national and personal territories were not lost on John Skelton (ca. 1465–1529), the priest and sometime court poet, sometime prison-dweller who wrote a series of political poems attacking Wolsey during the early 1520s. Critics have long regarded Skelton as a man deeply invested in the maintenance of boundaries. In particular, scholars have noted his tendency to promote a respect for the sacred space of sanctuary, a move that reflects his own conservative priestly impulses and perhaps even his habitation at Westminster Abbey from 1518 onward. Thus the satiric poems *Ware the Hauke* and *Phyllyp Sparowe* each decry a bird's presence within a church, angrily condemning "an act of profanation," as Richard Halpern puts it with respect to *Ware,* understood "primarily as the violation of a boundary or territory."[61] The first of Skelton's satires against Wolsey, *Speke Parott* (ca. 1521) contributes to this trend, by blaming Wolsey for "so myche sayntuary brekyng."[62] Yet, as we shall see, the boundaries defended by Skelton in *Speke Parott* encompass not only the religious limits of the church but also the more secular borders of the nation and its social customs.

Skelton's sensitivity to the ostentation of Wolsey's processions emerges in the key position in which he refers to them in *Speke Parott,* in a notably comprehensible sequence of a poem otherwise given to obscurity (difficult multilingual turns, arcane allusions, cryptic citations, and the like).[63] In the final, seemingly straightforward, section of

*Speke Parott,* the poet presents the reader with a long list of the excesses wrought by Wolsey, a man "so bold and so braggyng, and was so baselye borne" (507). After delineating Wolsey's abuse of everything from the provision of clergy ("so myche provision, and so lytell wytte at nede," 454) to his issuing of pardons ("So many bullys of pardon publysshed and shewyd," 515), Skelton ends his poem with the couplet, "Suche pollaxis and pyllers, suche mulys trapte with gold— / Sens Dewcalyons flodde, in no cronycle ys told" (517–18). Skelton's list, in other words, culminates in a reference to three of the famed elements in Wolsey's processions, the mules on which he rode and the pole-axes and pillars borne before him. That a poet seemingly bent on confusing the reader caps a frank list of abuses by alluding to the cardinal's sartorial accessories suggests that, for Skelton, Wolsey's processions are so offensive as to merit clear and unmitigated censure.[64] If, as critics such as A. R. Heiserman attest and even Skelton himself suggests, the poet deployed his difficult style to mask biting political critique, these processions offended him so much as to warrant forsaking obscurity in favor of a lucid indictment of Wolsey's regrettable excesses.[65]

Long before Skelton cites Wolsey for his inordinate pageantry in *Speke Parott,* the poet binds the cardinal's violation of social limitations to his efforts to exceed the physical borders of his island home. In the second envoy of the poem, Skelton censures Wolsey for his papal ambitions (or, as Skelton has it, Wolsey's "Popering") during the 1521 Calais convention.[66] Sending his titular protagonist, Parrot, "ovyr the salte fome" of the English Channel to address himself "lyke a sadde messengere" to Wolsey in Calais, Skelton endeavors "Home to resorte Jerobesethe [Wolsey] perswade" (302, 279). Wolsey "cum home," Skelton writes, asserting the impropriety of both the prospective Holy Roman destination that motivates the Calais mission and the cardinal's pseudo-diplomatic journey from England to the continent (304). Not only does Skelton enjoin Wolsey to return to the English mainland, he maps out that journey. Asking Parrot to "desire hym [Wolsey] to cum home, / Makyng hys pylgrimage by *Nostre Dame de Crome,*" Skelton imagines Wolsey returning to England by way of the remote Church of St. Mary the Virgin in Hill Croome, located in southern Worcestershire, near the Gloucestershire border (304–5). Robert Kinsman has offered us one way of making sense of this curious geographic detail, pointing out in his edition of Skelton's poetry how this "round-about and obscure" journey asked of Wolsey by Parrot responds to "the circuitous and ignominious negotiations he has concluded" at Calais.[67] Yet Wolsey's out-of-the-way and hidden return to England also responds to the very public journeys for which, as we have seen, the cardinal was infamous. Given the emphasis Wolsey's pole-axes and pillars receive at the end of the poem, Skelton's image of the cardinal's hidden return from Calais can't be read as anything other than the poet's effort to counter Wolsey's notoriously grand processions. Addressing the violation of boundaries as geographic as they are social, Skelton admonishes Wolsey not only to come home, but also to return to England as a withdrawn and modest pilgrim.

In exhorting Wolsey to respect his homeland's boundaries and return to English territory, Skelton specifically asserts the cardinal's status as a violator of his nation's isolated geographic identity. In other words, Skelton, not unlike Pompeo Colonna, constructs the English as a people who belong "home," that is, well within the confines of their far-flung homeland. Calais was in a sense "home" to Wolsey; the coastal town had "stood upon English ground" since 1347.[68] Wolsey, moreover, lived in Calais in 1503–7 as chaplain to the deputy of the English stronghold. But by advising Wolsey to "cum home" "From Calys to Dovyr, to Caunterbury in Kente," the anti-expansionist Skelton suggests that for an Englishman, "home" can never be anything but the island west of the channel (340). In stark contrast to Wolsey's own epistolary celebration of the English "angle of the worlde" extending its dominion outward into "the gretest parte of Crystendame," Skelton disdains the idea of the otherworldly English straying into the world, even to their own continental stronghold.[69]

Skelton was acutely aware of England's classical status as an isolated realm. The poet's investment in English geographic marginality emerged early in his career with his decision, sometime between 1485 and 1490, to "English" Poggio Bracciolini's ca. 1449 Latin translation of Diodorus of Sicily's *Library of History* (ca. 36 BC).[70] One of only two English translations of world geographies to be made in the fifteenth century, Skelton's *Diodorus* offers the usual image of English isolation found in classical literature. "The ile-land of Brutaigne" appears in the *Diodorus* as marginalized territory, lumped with other world borders such as the "coostes and regions which lyeth toward the pole artike," the "coostes of Arabye," or the Red Sea.[71] Among these frontier territories Britain figures as the most alien, located in a "portion of the worlde" about which, the Sicilian writer tells his readers, "there be but few that haue any parfight knowleige."[72] That Skelton highly regarded the status of England as a strange land emerges in the literary act of self-promotion he would write in 1523, the *Garlande or Chapelet of Laurell*. In the lengthy recitation of his own literary works that appears in the dream vision, Skelton refers to the *Library* as a text whose value resides in its "Recountyng commoditis of many a straunge nacyon" (1500). Within a work made interesting, for Skelton, by its representation of "straunge nacyon[s]," Britain looms as the strangest and thus most fascinating of nations.

Skelton would put that territorial knowledge to good use in *Speke Parott*. Reflecting not only his source Ovid's emphasis on geography in his *Amores,* but also the world geography offered in his version of the *Diodorus,* Skelton begins the poem by emphasizing Parrot's own travels across the world: "My name ys Parott, a byrde of Paradyse, / By Nature devysed of a wonderowus kynde, / Deyntely dyetyd with dyvers delycate spyce, / Tyll Eufrates, that flodde, dryvythe me into Ynde, / Where men of that contre by fortune me fynde, / And send me to great ladyes of estate" (1–7). "Removed," as Stanley Fish writes, "from paradise to sixteenth-century England," Parrot undergoes a journey that leads him from one end of the world to its English opposite.[73] That Parrot's global journey begins and ends in a borderland suggests the bird's own identification with world borders. Long considered to have been "created in the earthly paradise," parrots also appear in Skelton's *Diodorus* in "Ynde" (which often occupies the eastern world edge), "the Rede Se" (which occupies the southeastern corner of the world), "Ethiop, and a part of Liby" (both of which typically extend to the southern shores of the world ocean), and "the farre contreis and coostes of Sirye" or Syria.[74] The long-

Fig. 21. The East in the Ebstorf world map, ca. 1235. From Birgit Hahn-Woernle, *Die Ebstorfer Weltkarte: Dem Kloster Ebstorf und seinen Konventualinnen gewidmet* (Ebstorf: Das Klosterf, 1987), 49. By permission of Birgit Hahn-Woernle.

standing identification of parrots with world borders emerges in mappae mundi as well; parrots, for example, appear in the far reaches of both the Orient in the Ebstorf map and Ethiopia in the Vercelli map (fig. 21).[75] Through its literary and cartographic identification with Old World borders, the parrot thus functions in much the same manner Britain does in texts such as the *Diodorus*. Just as Britain figures in the *Library* as an isolated region of which "there be but few that haue any parfight knowleige," the parrot was linked with distant and unknown regions. As Ovid phrases it in the *Amores*, Psittacus is "a gift from the ends of the earth" (*extremo mundos ab orbe datum*, II.6.38).[76] Indeed, by the time Skelton turned to writing *Speke Parott*, well after 1492, parrots had become the prime symbol of the newly discovered, and still largely unexplored, western territories. New World parrots impressed Portuguese explorers around the turn of the century so much so that they first referred to South America as *Terra de Papagaios* or the land of the parrot, a phrase that came to serve as the popular name for the area.[77] Cartographers would go on to identify that portion of the New World on maps through drawings of the South American macaws that proliferated there (plate 4).[78]

In the case of Skelton's poem, however, Parrot symbolizes not the new world in the West, but the English otherworld. Parrot's arrival in England at the start of the poem, like the arrival of Custance in England in the *Man of Law's Tale,* points to a special relationship between traveler and destination. And in the same way that Custance brought a kind of sublime geographic alterity to her new English home, so too does Parrot bring a privileged category of identity to England. As a bird from Paradise, Parrot represents the sublime meanings of geographic marginality.[79] As Skelton puts it in *Speke Parott,* "Above all other byrdis, set Parrot alone" (112). Like his hailing from Paradise, Parrot's ability to speak also suggests his privileged status, his occupation of a more elevated category of identity on the chain of being: not only is the parrot *auium gloria* or a "prince among birds" in Ovid (II.6.20), but also "There was no bird on earth which imitated speech more closely" (*non fuit in terris uocum simulantior ales,* II.6.23). Indeed, according to early modern thinking, the parrot's ability to speak made the bird nearer to man— and, by extension, God—than other birds and beasts. Skelton thus accords Parrot a saintlike incorruptibility: "When Parrot is ded, he dothe not putrefy" (213).[80] The spiritual status of the parrot was such that medieval writers describe how the bird (like the slave boys at the Forum) is "admired of the Pope."[81] About a century before Skelton wrote his poem, Pope Martin V went so far as to appoint a Keeper of Parrots at the Vatican; "half a century later, in 1462, Pope Pius II was still authorizing payments to a 'custodian of the parrot.'"[82]

Bringing that sublime geographic identity to the England of Skelton's poem, Parrot becomes a loyal subject, proclaiming "In Englysshe to God . . . 'Cryste save Kyng Herry the viiith, owur royall kyng, / The red rose in honour to flowrysshe and sprynge!'" (33–35). Doubly bounded by both the "cage curyowsly carven" from which he sings and the watery border separating England from the world, Parrot serves as an icon of insularity, a symbol of the sublime identity their remoteness accords the English. Notably, even when the bird does leave his cage to fly beyond England, it is only to bring Wolsey back to his insular homeland and impress upon the roaming cardinal the value of staying within one's proper national limits. In the geographic terms of *Speke Parott,* Thomas Wolsey has strayed too far beyond the limits of both his insular homeland and English social convention.

But we cannot always take Skelton at face value.[83] Belying his denigration of Wolsey is the fact that, only two years after *Speke Parott,* the poet would begin working in the cardinal's employ. In exchange for the promise of a clerical living for the poet and the publication of his poetry, Wolsey commissioned Skelton to write a piece of ribald anti-Scot propaganda in verse, a project in which the cardinal himself took part.[84] It appears that fueling Skelton's attack on Wolsey's excessive ambition was thus not simply conservatism but also envy over Wolsey's achievements, a careerism that eventually led the poet to the conclusion that his best chance at success lay in, as Greg Walker notes, "aligning himself with his erstwhile target."[85]

For all his proclaimed opposition to Wolsey, Skelton actually resembles the cardinal in certain respects. In terms of the social and physical geography of *Speke Parott,* at the same time that Skelton expresses disgust at Wolsey's transgression of social and physical boundaries, the poet also indulges in such spatial violations. After all, though Skelton may charge Parrot with the job of reining in an overly mobile Wolsey, that task of retrieval does allow the bird, however briefly, to leave his caged isolation.[86] Parrot's journey, in turn, gives Skelton the vicarious means to imagine his own breakout from the Westminster sanctuary-cum-prison in which he lived, the marginal positioning he occasionally occupied at court, and the confines of his remote homeland. In Parrot's journey beyond cage and England we witness Skelton's suppressed desire to burst, Wolsey-like, from his own social isolation onto the center of the national and international political stage. A more overt version of that ambition appears in the *Garlande or Chapelet of Laurell*, which imagines that Skelton's literary accomplishments so impress the poets laureate that of their "trumpettis and clariouns the noyse went to Rome" (1507).[87] Imagining his poetic fame spreading as far as Rome, Skelton displays a literary version of the political and religious ambition evinced by what the poet disparagingly calls Wolsey's "popering" (70). Invested primarily in neither the outright violation nor the maintenance of borders, both Skelton and Wolsey assume toward boundaries a flexible and manipulative stance that hinges on the poet's and cardinal's respective aspirations. Providing a crucial space through which they play out their ambitions, the border is not esteemed in and of itself by Skelton and Wolsey, but used and manipulated by both men as a political tool.

## Wolsey and the English *Lapis Angularis*

One of the best indicators of the paradoxes of Wolsey's own engagement with English boundedness appears in the greatest Roman office he would in fact acquire: that of papal legate *a latere*. Papal legates were emissaries of the pope who "exercise[d] papal jurisdiction" and represented the pope's authority in regions outside Rome.[88] There were two kinds of legates during the Tudor period, *natus* and *latere,* with the latter enjoying precedence over the former kind of emissary and, "outside the city of Rome," as Franz Wasner points out, "over all other cardinals as well."[89] Thus when Wolsey obtained in 1518 a temporary appointment as papal legate *a latere* that he eventually parlayed into a grant for life, he garnered for himself the most ecclesiastical authority—except for that of the pope himself—a man of the cloth could have. Normally, the power accorded the legate *a latere* stemmed from his presumably Roman geographical origins. While the papal legate *natus* was an agent of Rome who nevertheless was a native of the region in which he resided and therefore was subject to that land's sovereign, the legate *a latere* typically served as a bona fide papal ambassador sent to a particular country from Rome. Sent *a latere* or "from the side" of the Roman pontiff, the legate possessed an authority that had everything to do with the idea of his physical proximity to the pope in Rome, a spatial intimacy that signified his status as the pope's virtual alter ego.[90]

Wolsey, however, did not come from the pope's side, as Edward Hall's account in his chronicle (1548) of Wolsey's first commission demonstrates. In a commission shared by Wolsey and fellow legate Lorenzo Campeggio, these twoo Cardinalles as legates, toke their barges & came to Grenewiche, eche of them had beside their crosses two pillers of siluer, two litle axes gilte, and two cloke bagges embroudered, and the Cardinalles hattes borne before them. And when they came to the kynges hall, the Cardinall of Yorke went on the right hande: and there the king Royally appareled and accompaignied, met them euen as though bothe had come from Rome, and so brought them bothe vp into his chamber of presence . . . and after dinner they toke their leaue of the kyng and came to London and rode through the citee together, in great pompe and glory, to their lodgynges.[91]

The king greets Wolsey and his comrade "euen as though bothe had come from Rome." "*Euen as though,*" for while Campeggio had indeed journeyed from the Papal See to England, Wolsey had not. Traveling upon on the Thames in a barge with Campeggio, loaded with the signs of his ecclesiastical authority, Wolsey behaves *as if* he has, like his Italian companion, "come from Rome." But the cardinal, unlike other legates *a latere,* did not live in Rome and would in fact never travel to the seat of Christendom.[92] As John Palsgrave would put it in his sardonic list of Wolsey's national "achievements," the cardinal established "the precedent how one may be *legatus a latere,* and not be sent from Rome."[93] Each time he served as the pope's emissary, Wolsey engaged in a geographical farce in which he feigned his completion of a journey he would never undergo, and pretended to have arrived from a place he would never visit. That fundamental spatial irony entailed by the grand entries Wolsey staged for himself as legate *a latere* adds a new, crucial wrinkle to our understanding of the geography of his Holy Roman ambitions.[94] While—as the Calais mission confirms—movement abroad on the continent was at times part and parcel of the cardinal's desire to gain Roman authority, the greatest Roman office Wolsey gained ironically involved only a fictional departure from his homeland.

The territorial paradox entailed by Wolsey's legatine entries also complicates our understanding of the politics of his processions. Even as the cardinal's train manifests a bundle of contradictory attitudes toward his own rude origins, so too does it express the ambiguities of English geographic marginality. The processions, in other words, enable the condensation of multiple fantasies of class and national identity. The fact that he never did go to Rome may have troubled Wolsey, and thus intensified the compensatory function of his excessive train. Hoping to offset his failure to journey to Rome, Wolsey over-asserts himself locally into English space via his massive train of richly arrayed men, mules, pole-axes, crosses, and the like, thus exposing his spatial inadequacy. But as we have seen, Wolsey's processions attest to his aggression and resentment as much as they suggest his anxiety. Just as his excessive train constitutes an affront to the English estate system, it also can be seen as an assault on Rome. That Wolsey felt a certain disregard for Rome is clear. Indeed, the extent to which the cardinal "failed . . . conspicuously to ingratiate himself with the Curia" has led most historians to dismiss the seriousness of both Wolsey's motto "Ubi Petrus, ibi Anglia" and his repeated papal bids.[95] Most notable for us is the territorial form that Wolsey's neglect of Rome assumed. For example, during the years encompassing his acquisition of his legateship, the English did not have an ambassador resident at Rome.[96] That English absence indicates Wolsey's repudiation of Rome's contemporary status as the diplomatic center of Christendom, a dismissal that seems to be of a piece with the cardinal's legateship. After all, Wolsey's curious status as Roman legate flaunts the fact that an Englishman need not ever leave his far-flung country to have what the Romans have. Wolsey, to be sure, admired Rome for its magnificence and power, as Cavendish indicates when he recounts the cardinal telling the duke of Norfolk that in his "dignyte legantyn . . . consisted all my highe honour" (116). But forasmuch as Wolsey was drawn to Roman power, he was also bound to English soil. During a time when Rome was "the place to be," Wolsey implies the value of English territory.

Wolsey's entries as papal legate, then, were as much about staging the nation as they were about staging the self. At the same time that the cardinal's processions attacked the supposed monopoly on privilege possessed by English aristocrats, they also denied Rome its status as privileged center. If Wolsey was guilty of fashioning himself—as Skelton suggests—to the detriment of England, his histrionic performances also at times intersected with a fashioning of England to the detriment of Rome. That for Wolsey, the isolated English, among all Christian peoples, were entitled to engage in such a disregard for Rome emerges in an earlier communication with the Curia. In a letter responding to a 1516 missive from Leo X lamenting that he rarely heard news from England, Wolsey points out England's global isolation. "We are from the very ends of the earth" ("nos esse in extrema orbis parte"), he wrote to Leo.[97] Due to the great distance between England and Rome, Wolsey explained, he receives many *fabulas* or false tales and thus cannot write meaningfully to the pope unless he knows his real intentions. On the face of it, Wolsey's letter appears to placate the pope (Wolsey does concede to ordering a daily report from his private secretary Andreas Ammonius). But, fundamentally, the letter is, in Joycelyne G. Russell's words, "a masterpiece of verbose contempt" that uses English otherworldliness to license political antagonism toward Rome.[98] A similar logic implicitly informs the entries from Rome Wolsey so ostentatiously staged, whereby the cardinal's status as a legate from the English world border legitimates his failure to pay his respects to the Roman Curia by visiting it. The pope cannot expect to know what happens in England in the manner that he knows of goings on elsewhere in Christendom, and cannot expect Wolsey to behave in the manner of other papal legates *a latere,* because England is a special case. As a supreme world outpost, England should enjoy special latitude in terms of its relationship with Rome.

Wolsey did more than set England apart as a nation whose geographic isolation entitled it to unique exemptions within Christendom. At the time he initially garnered his legateship, his appointment comprised part of a far grander strategy of "stealing Rome's thunder" to elevate England in terms at once geographic, political, religious, and cultural.[99] The cardinal became a legate when Leo X was in the process of sending Campeggio to England to preside over what became known as the universal peace, an alliance among the major European powers in order to set up a crusade against the Turks. Leo's brainchild, the universal peace was to play a crucial role in that Medici pope's neoclassical empowerment of himself and Rome. Under Leo, humanism had become merged with Catholic ceremony in an unprecedented manner; as Marga Cottino Jones writes, "Cultural magnificence was apotheosized especially at the court of the Medici pope."[100] That neoclassical project had everything to do with the notion that Leo's papacy would witness the return of a Golden Age, an era of which, as Charles Stinger notes, "peace was a hallmark."[101] Leo's engineering of a universal peace was intended to mark the culmination of his neoclassical achievement, the restoration of Rome's ancient standing as world center and Eternal City.

Campeggio's legation to England geographically manifested Rome's claim to sempiternity. The isolated English setting of the universal peace suggested how the renewed beneficence—and renewed dominance—of *Roma aeterna* extended to the very ends of Christendom. Wolsey, however, had other things in mind. When he learned of Campeggio's journey to execute this commission, Wolsey promptly informed Leo that "the King will in no wise allow Campeggio to enter England" unless "Wolsey be joined with Campeggio in equal authority by papal mandate."[102] Preventing Campeggio's crossing of the English Channel, Wolsey forces the legate to wait for permission to enter England. Exacerbating what was already one of the longest European journeys a legate could take, Wolsey shores up the Curia's lack of control over English territory. Once Campeggio did arrive in England, Wolsey would, moreover, transform his homeland from the stage for the performance of a Roman-authorized alliance into the setting of an English diplomatic triumph. On October 3, 1518, in St. Paul's Cathedral in London, Wolsey proclaimed a universal peace, signed first by England and France and eventually by all the major European powers.[103] Thus, according to Scarisbrick, "What had begun as a plan for a five-year truce under papal auspices, to be followed by a crusade, had ended as a multilateral treaty of universal peace organized by a cardinal and concluded in London, with peace in Christendom as its objective."[104] For the English, the treaty indisputably was a national triumph. When Wolsey appropriated the Pope's conciliatory function, he made London, in Anglo's words, "the focal point of European diplomacy."[105]

Surrounding the treaty were a variety of grand ceremonies from processions, banquets, masses, and joustings to various pageants and other court entertainments. The massive English expenditure entailed by such celebrations emerges in the fact that, as Anglo notes, "the personal expenses of the King for October 1518 were over three times as much as for the previous October."[106] Many of those festivities and rituals were led by Wolsey who, for example, sang a mass that was, according to Italian ambassador Sebastian Giustinian, possessed of "so many pontifical ceremonies and such unusual splendour, as to defy exaggeration" (224). As Giustinian's account suggests, for some viewers those ceremonies were as excessive as Wolsey's notorious processions. The "sumptuous supper" Wolsey hosted after the mass at Hampton Court thus even surpassed those of "Cleopatra or Caligula; the whole banqueting hall being so decorated with huge vases of gold and silver, that I [Giustinian] fancied myself in the tower of Chosroes, where that monarch caused divine honours to be paid him" (225). Drawing a critical comparison of Wolsey to history's most greedy and proud personages, Giustinian registers his umbrage at the proceedings as a manifestation of Wolsey's ambition. In the ambassador's opinion, "one cannot please him [Wolsey] more than to style him the arbitrator of the affairs of Christendom" (258).[107] But as an Italian ecclesiastical official, Giustinian was also offended by the manner in which the universal peace and its attending rituals praised England to the detriment of Rome. With some disdain, the Venetian ambassador notes how even the pope had "lavished every possible expression of honour upon him [Henry VIII], somewhat to the disparagement and degradation, perhaps, of the Apostolic chair" (257).

That ceremonial elevation of England would culminate on October 7th, when the universal peace was commemorated by a banquet and court entertainment.[108] The latter festivity entailed a pageant whose featured performer Hall describes in his chronicle as "a flyeng horse with wynges & fete of gold called Pegasus."[109] Playing the role of narrator, the horse began its performance via a long address whose beginning an Italian observer summarizes as: "I am the horse Pegasus, who, having heard of this peace . . . flew to announce it to the whole world, and about this the whole world is singing."[110] Anglo has queried the presence of Pegasus here, identifying the winged horse as "the strangest character" in a court entertainment whose imagery "was, in the main, very simple."[111] Compared to Skelton's Parrot, however, Pegasus may not appear so odd. Like the winged protagonist of Skelton's poem, Pegasus traverses the space of the entire world only to alight upon its English edge. Both the bird and the horse arrive in England as animals especially tied to world borders; the winged horse is identified in classical mythology alternately as the animal that transports Perseus to the global border home of the Gorgons or the being that issues forth on that isolated region from Medusa's neck. Like Parrot as well, Pegasus merges territorial isolation with a privileged category of identity, for the animal is no ordinary horse but a fabulous creature that can fly and speak. And, above all, as a winged creature like Parrot, Pegasus manifests a characteristically English tension over geographic boundaries. An animal linked especially to English space but also able to soar beyond England's territorial limits, Pegasus distinguishes the English world margin as sublime and spreads the authority of England beyond its borders. Pegasus arrives in England only after establishing its global fame, whereby the universal peace secured by the English is made known throughout the "whole world and about this the whole world is singing."

The renown of England's lord chancellor and cardinal would sweep throughout Christendom as well. As Anglo puts it, "the prestige of England in general, and of Wolsey in particular, were at their highest level."[112] Even Wolsey's erstwhile enemies appreciated the cardinal's achievement. Henry's longtime counselor Foxe, a man who "had opposed Wolsey's adventures," praised the cardinal by describing the universal peace to Wolsey as "the best deed that ever was done for England; and, next to the King, the praise of it is due to you."[113] And, for all his disgust, the Venetian Giustinian also appreciated the magnitude of Wolsey's triumph. Upon first learning of Wolsey's pacific aims, Giustinian told the cardinal that "he could do nothing more glorious in the world, or that could add greater splendour to his eminent qualities, than in the midst of such great strife amongst princes to prove himself that *lapis angularis* which joined the two detached walls of the temple" (177). Giustinian's response invokes the biblical image of the cornerstone to praise Wolsey, suggesting how the cardinal's unification of Europe's leaders would make him a type of Christ, whom Paul identifies as the "chief cornerstone" of the church in Ephesians 2. Moreover, insofar as *lapis angularis* puns on *Anglia* and the long-standing status of England as an *angulus orbis* or angle of the world, Giustinian's likening of Wolsey to a cornerstone conflates the cardinal with his nation. The "glorious" peace garnered by Wolsey recalls the splendid unifying power of the cornerstone, whether that metaphorical rock joining God's temple, or the English angle binding Christendom.[114]

Giustinian would not be the only European to admire Wolsey along such geographic lines. A French performance honoring the papal legate similarly represents Wolsey as a man whose accomplishments distinguish his isolated nation. That entertainment would be produced in 1527, well after Wolsey's supervision of the universal peace treaty. The 1518 treaty, for all the acclaim it immediately generated, turned out to be relatively short-lived. Wolsey would continue to play the part of European mediator into the early 1520s, most famously during the spectacular Field of Cloth of Gold of 1520, and the 1521 Calais conference. But from 1522 on, warfare would tear through Europe, in particular, through Italy. Not until those upheavals culminated, in 1527, would Wolsey resume the role of world diplomat and again usurp Rome's glory. Namely, when on May 6 the imperial troops of Charles V invaded and sacked Rome, Wolsey found the ultimate chance to reverse the traditional power asymmetry between the Roman center and English margin of the world. The fortnight of looting, pillaging, rape, murder, and overall devastation entailed by the sack amounted to an "unparalleled humiliation of city, papacy, and *italianità*" that enabled a unusually grand staging of Wolsey as none other than Rome's deliverer.[115] As Anglo tells us, "the way was open for the exploitation of the idea that the Cardinal was the potential saviour of the violated Church, and Wolsey appeared as the hero of plays and pageants both in England and in France."[116]

The occasion for the French pageants was Wolsey's diplomatic meeting with Francis I, to whom Henry had dispatched the cardinal to discuss matters including an Anglo-French response to Rome's sack. Arriving in French towns from England, traveling as a legate sent from the side not of the pope but of Henry VIII, Wolsey in his very itinerary evoked England's usurpation of Rome's erstwhile territorial prominence. That heightening of English geopolitical power would be made manifest in the most elaborate performance hailing Wolsey's legatine entry into a French city, five spectacles produced at Amiens. The first of those spectacles would repeat the very architectural pun used by Giustinian some ten years earlier to praise Wolsey. The pageant depicted a temple whose walls, inscriptions in Latin and French explained, would not meet until they were linked together with a stone, "the cornerstone that made both one [lapis angularis qui fecit utraque unum]."[117] While Christ was prophesied as the true cornerstone ("Christ fut prévu vraie pierre angulaire") "ce seigneur"—that is, a figure representing Wolsey—is Christ's type ("est à son exemplaire"). Identifying Wolsey again as a figure of the scriptural *lapis angularis,* the pageant demonstrates the renewed pertinence of the English world angle after Rome's sack. With the Roman center of Christendom now plagued by an unprecedented degree of disorder, barbarity, and waste, now more than ever did the unifying power of Christendom's English edge—and its religious leader, Wolsey—merit emphasis.

As if to remind audience members of England's geographic positioning in the world, the final spectacle at Amiens portrayed an ocean and a model of the world. The fifth pageant placed Wolsey in the heavens, issuing forth from a star whose light will reestablish, an inscription explained, peace ("par qui paix nous sera rendue"). Imagining Wolsey as a heavenly body, the pageant recalls the flight fantasies represented in the figures of Parrot and Pegasus. Moreover, the notion of Wolsey as star suggests the more exalted meanings of English identity, a message that the fourth pageant at Amiens also affirmed. That spectacle depicted Wolsey as a red-cloaked cherub taking his place by Holy Church. The image of Wolsey as an angel contributes to the cumulative force of the Amiens entertainment's hailing of the cardinal in terms that also imply the sublimity and power of England. Taken together, the depiction of the world and world ocean, as well as the representation of Wolsey as both *lapis angularis* and *angelus* from *Anglia,* all signaled the cardinal's status as a man whose actions had shored up the best implications of England's geographic isolation. With Rome in ruins and the Englishman Wolsey as her savior, a virtual inversion of the usual relationship between Christendom's center and its "barbaric" border had taken place. Wolsey had imaginatively reterritorialized Europe as a place no longer revolving around its powerful Roman center but now resting upon its mighty English cornerstone.

## Wolsey, the English Reformation, and Its "Progress"

The 1527 zenith of Wolsey's fame nearly coincided with the beginning of the cardinal's great downfall, a decline that exposed the limits of just how far Rome could be manipulated for English ends.[118] With Anne Boleyn having supplanted Wolsey as the king's prime confidante and advisor, the cardinal's continued favor with Henry depended on securing the annulment of his marriage to Catherine of Aragon.[119] Wolsey's potential resolution of the king's "great matter" emerged in two failed projects. In the fall of 1528, the cardinal sought to grant Henry his divorce (however slim the grounds upon which it rested) by determining the case himself at his legatine court in England.[120] While Wolsey got his decretal commission, the project proved unsuccessful due to Clement VII's submission to the will of both Catherine and above all the Holy Roman emperor, whom the pope feared more than he did Henry. Then, in February 1529, when news arrived in England of Clement's death, the old idea of Wolsey's election to the papacy again arose. English ambassadors at Rome were informed: "The king desires . . . to use every means to advance Wolsey's election, as that on which depends the making or marring of the King's cause."[121] Toward that end, the diplomats were to address the territorial threat that Wolsey's papal elevation doubtless portended: the stripping of Rome's status as the capital of western Christendom. "The Cardinals need not fear," Henry wrote, "that Wolsey would reside at Avignon or other place away from Rome; for, first, he would resign all his dignities, and have no convenient habitation except Rome."[122]

Henry had ample reason to address the issue of where Wolsey would base his papacy. A papal legate who never bothered to travel to Rome, Wolsey was a man whose career notoriously opposed the geography of Roman privilege. As pope, Wolsey very well might "reside at Avignon" (likely due to a recent France-England alliance) "or other place," possibly the very English terrain where he tried to bring his legatine authority to bear on Henry's divorce case. Insofar as it speaks to the prospect of an English capital of Christendom, Henry's letter suggests the status of the cardinal's famous motto *ubi Petrus, ibi Anglia* as a cover, whereby Wolsey wants not to have England follow Rome, but to make the Petrine church follow England.

Henry's eager resumption of Wolsey's candidature was doomed, however, as Pope Clement VII had not died. Unable to give Henry what he wanted from Rome, the overweening Wolsey became vulnerable to his enemies as never before. Those adversaries were vast: the common lawyers whose jurisdiction Wolsey had overridden, the upper clergymen whose rights Wolsey had seized, the lower clergymen Wolsey had taxed, the nobility Wolsey's arrogance had offended, and others. In November 1529, having, as Christopher Haigh notes, "alienated all possible support," Wolsey died a man arrested for treason, indicted under the medieval statute of praemunire (which restricted papal jurisdiction in England), and stripped of nearly all his privileges.[123]

Not long after his famous decline there occurred a still more familiar fall, the end of the authority of the Roman church itself over the English. In retrospect, Wolsey's death may seem to foreshadow the demise of Roman authority in England. Certainly from the perspective offered by the earliest protestant historians of England, Wolsey represents the Papist church, a domineering and unjust religious authority opposed to everything for which the English Reformation stands. And in traditional post-Reformation scholarship as well, Wolsey figures as a man who, in the final analysis, was more Roman than English. Ultimately bound to the pope, Wolsey, so the story goes, opposed the aims of an English state that would break with Rome in 1534.[124] That story, of course, is part of a larger drive in Reformation scholarship to divide events and persons into Roman Catholics and English Protestants. Yet recent critical work urges against such divisions. According to Peter Marshall and Alec Ryrie, during the Henrician era, "religious reform was a many-headed monster . . . Subsequent confessional clarity should not be allowed to obscure the kaleidoscopic diversity of the early years of the Reformation, or the messy complexity of the processes by which those possibilities were resolved into the Protestantism which we know."[125] That "messy complexity" is such that many scholars, following the lead of Haigh, have come to speak not of the reformation in the singular but of the multiple *reformations* of England. With his own paradoxical combining of Roman religious authority and English identity, Wolsey embodies a version of the complexity and indefiniteness stressed by Marshall, Ryrie, Haigh, and other scholars. That Henry, at least initially, enlisted Wolsey in his divorce effort reveals how the very messy England-Rome dynamic the cardinal represents spilled into and informed a key event in Reformation history. And the geographical aspects of that dynamic would continue to complicate the pre- and post-Reformation culture that emerged after Wolsey's demise.

Consider the degree to which a version of Wolsey's medieval geographic rhetoric figured in the king's approach to the Rome problem. A year after the cardinal's death, Henry ordered the transcription for the Royal Library of the anonymous *Cosmographia,* a world chorography that, in Taylor's words, "follows the traditional medieval pattern, and is borrowed from the usual medley of classical and medieval writers."[126] In particular, the *Cosmographia* draws heavily from Higden's *Polychronicon* to describe England as not merely a corner of the world but also a *fertilis angulus orbis* or fertile angle of the world that "does not need the entire world" (toto non eget orbe).[127] The coincidence of the transcription with Henry's great matter suggests that the king had the document copied because the medieval notion of a remote yet potent English otherworld stressed by Higden and manipulated by Wolsey could aid his divorce case. Medieval geography also informed the arguments of the crown's polemicists, who were endeavoring to overturn the papal demand that Henry plead his divorce case in Rome. In a variety of documents, through moves that reiterated Wolsey's own strategic deployment of England's status as an "angle of the worlde" the king's defenders (and maybe even the king himself) strategically invoked the great distance between England and the Curia: because of "the more than one thousand miles separating Rome and England," due to "overmuche farrenes," Henry "could not go *ad loca tam remota* as Rome" to have his case heard.[128] "Had it been to [the more proximate] Avignon the matter would have been different."[129]

Perhaps the most significant use of that geographic rhetoric appears in the legislation banning all appeals to the pope that Parliament ratified in 1533. A key document in English Reformation history coauthored by Wolsey's protégé Thomas Cromwell, the Act in Restraint of Appeals employs medieval geography as the pivotal, final rationale for its claim that the appeal of English cases to Rome has blocked their "trewe and spedy determynacion": "And forasmoche as the greate distaunce of waye is so farr out of this Realme, so that the necessarie proves nor the true knowlege of the cause can nether there be so well knowen ne the Witnesses there so well examined as within this Realme."[130] With its claim that the swift and proper administration of justice for the king's case can only be found in England, the act recalls the national alignment of due process with national territory in Magna Carta. But while the idea of the law of the land ("per legem terrae") is used against the crown in Magna Carta, the 1532 Act in Restraint of Appeals uses English geography on behalf of the king. Because Rome is "so farr out of" England, it physically cannot obtain the information necessary for the proper and just determination of English cases. Reversing the traditional phraseology of English isolation, the act stresses not England's distance from Rome, but vice versa. Like earlier propaganda that bestowed the status of remote on Rome, the act constructs that city as a kind of "desert" of juridical knowledge. By implication, then, the act gives England the position of center—a foreshadowing of its imminent claims for spiritual autonomy. With their reconfiguration of the Roman center of Christendom as a lawless wasteland, and the English world margin as the only place where Henry can receive justice, the king's polemicists recall Wolsey's own efforts to use world geography to license English disregard of Rome.

For all its construction by the English as a kind of desert, however, Rome still had some cachet in England, even after 1534. While Henry VIII and his supporters did reject Rome as privileged center, the king was nevertheless attracted to Roman pretension and ritual as a means of authorizing his new religious identity and newly autonomous nation. Thus an orthodox English verse decrying the Henrician Reformation begins, "When Rome remeueth Into England."[131] By using the verb "remove," the poem describes Henry's break with the papacy in medieval geographic terms: as an offensive transportation of Roman power westward to the English edge of Christendom, an act through which, the poem claims, "Moche Care & Sorough shalbe brought Into England."[132] Complicating our perception of Henry's Act of Supremacy as an edict through which, to cite Scarisbrick, "the umbilical cord uniting English Catholicism to Rome was cut," the idea that Henry removed Rome to England suggests how we might better understand one of the earliest formulations of England's reformations as an aggressive *translatio imperii*.[133]

Thus, unlike so many other emergent protestant denominations such as the Lutherans or Zwinglians, the *ecclesia anglicana* that Henry headed seemed to constitute a far-western translation of Roman religious practice and ritual. Above all, Henry was vehemently orthodox when it came to that sacrament at the heart of Roman Catholic religious culture, the mass.[134] As the religious conservative John Worth wrote to Arthur Lisle in a 1539 letter, "his Grace every Sunday doth receive holy bread and holy water, and doth daily use all other laudable ceremonies, and in all London no man upon pain of death to speak against them."[135] Most important for our purposes, Henry's orthodoxy manifested itself in spectacular displays reminiscent of Wolsey's deployments of Roman ceremony. Five years after declaring himself Supreme Head of the Church of England, the king celebrated Ascension Day with what Eamon Duffy has described as "an extravagant display of old-fashioned piety."[136] That show of traditional religion began on the eve of the holy day, when, as Worth wrote to Lisle:

> the King's Grace took his barge at Whitehall, and so rowed up to Lambeth, and had his drums and fifes playing; and so rowed up and down the Thames an hour in the evening after evensong. And on Holy Thursday his Grace went a procession about the Court at Westminster in the Whitehall; and my Lord Cobham bare the sword before the King's Grace, with all other nobles a great multitude. And the high altar in the chapel was garnished with all the apostles upon the altar, and mass by note, and the organs playing, with as much honour to God as might be devised to be done.[137]

Henry's hour-long cruise along the Thames to music, his procession at Westminster, and his attendance at an elaborate sung mass make clear that with the king's rejection of Rome came a certain desire for Roman ritual. Like the performances of his erstwhile lord chancellor and cardinal, Henry's continued use of Roman ceremony after 1534 was at once an affront and a homage to Rome and its traditional geography of privilege. In the face of the long-standing and persistent notion of Rome's sacral centricity, the king demonstrated the radical mobility of Rome. Henry's use of church ceremony for the grand performance of his new national identity aggressively exposed how the dramatic signs of Roman majesty can travel, can even "remeueth Into England." At the same time, however, Henry's religious performances suggest an anxiety over the long-standing linkage of English isolation with barbarity. More isolated than ever from Christendom, the fledgling English nation can establish itself only by poaching from Rome its theatrical trappings of power. What better precedent did Henry have for that fraught use of Roman ritual to legitimate a newly sovereign England, than in the superb precedent set by the king's erstwhile lord chancellor and fellow newcomer, Wolsey, with his own spectacular and charged manipulation of medieval world geography?

To argue that one of the pivotal events of Renaissance English history depended on— indeed, repeatedly invoked—a medieval geographic rhetoric is not to deny the force of one of the great revolutions of modern English history. Rather, it is to acknowledge how the seeds of such transformation are multiple and are planted in much earlier times and, above all, in various *locations*. By attending, that is, to the global geography of Wolsey's performances, we find that the historical instability his theatricality embodies has a spatial counterpart. At the same time that Wolsey's dramatic self-fashioning made the medieval cardinal also a modern prototype, the cardinal's "modern" embrace of the English angle of the world complicated his "medieval" veneration for Rome.

Space and place, in other words, play a more important role than we typically imagine in the rethinking of period and periodicity. Space as a metaphor, to be sure, has long proved helpful in articulating historical relations. Thus Burckhardt evoked his notion of the Renaissance by referring to its resting upon a unique "foundation" (*Basis*) and its development from "rich soil" (*mächtigste Grund*); and the editors of an important 1992 volume rethinking periodization take as its title *Redrawing the Boundaries*.[138] But more than an effective figure of speech, space is mutually constitutive with time. At stake in the fraught territoriality of Wolsey's staging of power is the undermining of the border traditionally thought to divide the Middle Ages and Renaissance. Moreover, insofar as its contradictory geography epitomizes a long-standing trend, Wolsey's self-fashioning troubles more than the limit marking the end of the medieval and the beginning of the modern. His deployment of a medieval dynamic extending back to the tenth century, when English mapmakers and writers first wrestled with the problems and potentials of their isolation, demonstrates how even the earliest English cultural practices resist our easy categorization as "medieval." In this light, the advent of English history marks the beginning of no steady and easily tracked temporal trajectory, but a persistent crisscrossing between formations at once geographic and historical.

# NOTES

## Introduction

1. Henri Lefebvre, *The Production of Space,* trans. Donald Nicholson-Smith (Oxford: Blackwell, 1991), 280.

2. Christopher North (John Wilson), *Noctes Ambrosianae* no. 42, *Blackwood's Magazine,* April 1829.

3. On cartography and English imperialism see: Terry Cook, "A Reconstruction of the World: George R. Parkin's British Empire Map of 1893," *Cartographica* 21.4 (1984): 53–65; Matthew H. Edney, *Mapping an Empire: The Geographical Construction of British India, 1765–1843* (Chicago: University of Chicago Press, 1990); Anne Godlewska and Neil Smith, eds., *Geography and Empire* (Oxford: Blackwell, 1994); Jeremy Black, *Maps and Politics* (Chicago: University of Chicago Press, 1997); Teresa Ploszajska, *Geographical Education: Empire and Citizenship: Geographical Teaching and Learning in English Schools, 1870–1944* (Bristol: Historical Geography Research Group, 1999); and J. B. Harley, *The New Nature of Maps: Essays in the History of Cartography* (Baltimore: Johns Hopkins University Press, 2001).

4. On wall maps, see Cook, "Reconstruction." On schoolbooks, see Ploszajska, *Geographical Education.*

5. P. H. Kerr and A. C. Kerr, *The Growth of the British Empire* (London: Longmans, Green, 1911). On the Kerr volume and its designation for children in the Transvaal, see J. R. M. Butler, *Lord Lothian (Philip Kerr), 1882–1940* (London: Macmillan, 1960), 42. Two additional examples appear in Margaret Drabble, *For Queen and Country: Britain in the Victorian Age* (London: Deutsch, 1978), color plate 5; and Cook, "Reconstruction."

6. Kerr and Kerr, *Growth,* 2.

7. Ibid.

8. David Harvey, *The Condition of Postmodernity: An Enquiry into the Origins of Cultural Change* (Oxford: Blackwell, 1989), 203.

9. E. H. Gombrich, *The Sense of Order: A Study in the Psychology of Decorative Art* (Ithaca: Cornell University Press, 1979), 155–56. A system of representing the entire globe in two-dimensional rectangular space (i.e., a sheet of paper), the Mercator projection also makes lands farther from the equator look larger than they really are, thus contributing to the vastness of English territories. On the Mercator projection see also Black, *Maps,* and Harley, *New Nature,* 66.

10. Greenwich was deemed the international prime meridian in 1884. See Derek Howse, *Greenwich Time and the Discovery of the Longitude* (Oxford: Oxford University Press, 1980).

11. On medieval *mappae mundi,* see David Woodward, "Medieval *Mappaemundi,*" in *HC,* 286–370; P. D. A. Harvey, *Medieval Maps* (Toronto: University of Toronto Press, 1991); and *MTS.*

12. As P. D. A. Harvey puts it, "well over a thousand survive from the seventh century onwards, far more than all other medieval maps put together" (*Medieval Maps,* 19), and, as Woodward points out, nine thousand of those maps are found in manuscript books ("*Mappaemundi,*" in *HC,* 286; 324).

13. The other prime category of mappa mundi was the zonal, hemispheric, or Macrobian map. For tables depicting the absolute and relative numbers of extant tripartite, tripartite variants, and zonal maps from the eighth to fifteenth centuries, see figs. 18.8 and 18.9 in Woodward, "*Mappaemundi,*" in *HC,* 298.

14. Mappae mundi orient themselves in all directions, but they typically orient themselves toward the East (hence the origin of the term "orient"). North and South followed next in terms of popularity. See Woodward, "*Mappaemundi,*" in *HC,* 336–37. On the meaning of *oikoumené,* which is first found in Herodotus, see James S. Romm, *The Edges of the Earth in Ancient Thought: Geography, Exploration, and Fiction* (Princeton: Princeton University Press, 1992), 37.

15. The Beatus map also includes a fourth continent—the Antipodes. See Woodward, "*Mappaemundi,*" in *HC,* 303–4.

16. As with modern world maps, the center typically constitutes the site of greatest privilege in mappae mundi. It is there, especially in maps produced during and after the Crusades, where Jerusalem appears, the city "set among the nations, with the other countries around her" in Ezekiel 5:5. Yet we tend to overemphasize the centrality of Jerusalem. As David Woodward points out, "Jerusalem was not shown as the center of most medieval *mappaemundi*" (*HC,* 340). In addition to Rome, other key classical sites such as Delos, as well as other biblical sites such as Mt. Sinai and key biblical personages such as Christ, appear at the center of mappae mundi.

17. For Solinus, see Theodor Mommsen, ed., *C. Iulii Solini Collectanea Rerum Memorabilium* (Berlin: Raabe, 1895), 101–2; trans. Arthur Golding in *The Excellent and Pleasant Worke. Collectanea Rerum Memorabilium* (1587), facsimile reproduction by George Kish (Gainesville: Scholars' Facsimiles and Reprints, 1955), chap. 34. Solinus's likening of Britain to another world may well reflect the fact that Britain was first identified by classical writers as not an island but another *orbis* (a huge continent). See Romm, *Edges,* 140–41. Other classical references to British geographic marginality appear in Claudian, Hegesippus, and Servius. See Josephine Waters Bennett, "Britain among the Fortunate Isles," *Studies in Philology* 53 (1956): 114–40; and Carl Erdmann, *Forschungen zur politischen Ideenwelt des Frühmittelalters; aus dem Nachlass des Verfassers* (Berlin: Akademie-Verlag, 1951), 8–9, 38–43.

18. Isidore of Seville, *Isidori Hispalensis Episcopi Etymologiarum sive Originum libri XX,* ed. W. M. Lindsay (London: Oxford University Press, 1985), XIV.vi. On medieval knowledge of Virgil, Horace, and Claudian, see L. D. Reynolds and N. G. Wilson, *Scribes and Scholars: A Guide to the Transmission of Greek and Latin Literature,* 3rd ed. (Oxford: Clarendon, 1991). On the classics in the medieval classroom, see Aldo Scaglione, "The Classics in Medieval Education," in *The Classics in the Middle Ages,* ed. Aldo S. Bernardo and Saul Levin (Binghamton: Center for Medieval and Early Renaissance Studies, 1990), 343–62.

19. We should bear in mind Woodward's caveat that "we do not even know how far a publicly displayed *mappa mundi* such as the Hereford world map may have been actually used (as is often implied) to instruct the peasants and pilgrims who may have stood before it" ("*Mappaemundi,*" 508). Typically, only a diagrammatic, tripartite globe appeared in medieval churches. Such an orb would lie in the hand of a sovereign or Christ, as depicted in stained glass windows. See, for example, Penny Hebgin-Barnes, *Corpus vitrearum medii aevi,* Great Britain, Summary Catalogue 3, Lincolnshire (Oxford: Oxford University Press, 1996), color plates 13a and 23b. Stained glass representations of the creation, the sons of Noah, and the Last Judgment could also offer such an iconic image of the world, as well as more detailed mappae mundi.

20. Cf. S. McArthur, *McArthur's Universal Corrective Map of the World* (Norwood, Australia: MMA, 1979), an Australian world map that situates Australia at the top and the center of the world. The most famous alternative to the Mercator projection is Arno Peters, *The New Cartography,* trans. Ward Kaiser, D. G. Smith, and Heim Wohlers (New York: Friendship Press, 1983).

21. Harvey, *Medieval Maps,* 25.

22. See appendix 18.2 in *HC.*

23. "Mansitque haec in ecclesiis Christi quae erant in Brittania pax usque ad tempora arrianae uaesaniae, quae corrupto orbe toto hanc etiam insulam extra orbem tam longe remotam ueneno sui infecit erroris." *EH,* 34–37; J. R. R. Tolkien and E. V. Gordon, eds., *Sir Gawain and the Green Knight,* rev. Norman Davis (Oxford: Clarendon, 1967), 1.

24. The benefits of bringing together visual and literary artifacts have been made increasingly clear to us by medievalists from D. W. Robertson (*A Preface to Chaucer: Studies in Medieval Perspectives* [Princeton: Princeton University Press, 1963]) to V. A. Kolve (*Chaucer and the Imagery of Narrative: The First Five Canterbury Tales* [Stanford: Stanford University Press, 1984]) and Michael Camille (*Image on the Edge: The Margins of Medieval Art* [London: Reaktion, 1992]). More recently, medieval studies has brought together issues of literature and geography. See Mary B. Campbell, *The Witness and the Other World: Exotic European Travel Writing, 400–1600* (Ithaca: Cornell University Press, 1988); Scott D. Westrem, ed., *Discovering New Worlds: Essays on Medieval Exploration and Imagination* (New York: Garland, 1991); Paul Zumthor, *La mesure du monde: Représentation de l'espace au Moyen Age* (Paris: Seuil, 1993); Iain Macleod Higgens, *Writing East: The "Travels" of Sir John Mandeville* (Philadelphia: University of Pennsylvania Press, 1997); and Sylvia Tomasch and Sealy Gilles, eds., *Text and Territory: Geographical Information in the European Middle Ages* (Philadelphia: University of Pennsylvania Press, 1998).

25. *Rotuli parliamentorum III*, 415, cited by Charles Plummer in his edition of Sir John Fortescue's *The Governance of England* (Westport, CT: Hyperion, 1979), 287. Arundel puns on the English angle of the world in order to make a jibe at Richard II and the newly deceased monarch's advisers.

26. Meditation upon "the extraordinary disparity between [Britain's] relative geographical size and political (or commercial or cultural) power" was typical of imperialist geographic rhetoric. See Ploszajska, *Geographical Readers,* 143–44.

27. Arundel's comment looks toward the lines Shakespeare attributes to his ally John of Gaunt. Gaunt's celebration of fourteenth-century England as an "other Eden" and "little World" in *Richard II* reflects how Renaissance writers were also well aware of the classical identification of England as an otherworldly island. On the manner in which the rediscovery of the classics in the Renaissance gave new life to the notion of an otherworldly England, see Bennett, "Fortunate Isles"; and Jeffrey Knapp, *An Empire Nowhere: England, America, and Literature from* Utopia *to* The Tempest (Berkeley: University of California Press, 1992). In his important and illuminating book, Knapp articulates an ambivalence toward otherworldliness on the part of early modern writers similar to that which I identify in medieval and pre-Reformation texts. For Knapp, English writers such as Thomas More generally "cannot conceive of modern England as other-worldly in any positive sense" (21). I argue for a more optimistic stance on the part of medieval writers toward their island's isolation, and as well provide a more geographic context for our understanding of English literary texts. In a study that came to my attention shortly before submitting the manuscript to press, Daniel Birkholz traces links between English world maps to thirteenth-century royalist concerns. While the issue of English global marginality plays no role in Birkholz's study, he shares with me an interest in seeing certain English interests at work (namely those of royal policy and governmental practice). See *The King's Two Maps: Cartography and Culture in Thirteenth-Century England* (New York: Routledge, 2004).

28. Geraldine Heng, *Empire of Magic: Medieval Romance and the Politics of Cultural Fantasy* (New York: Columbia University Press, 2003), 99. A well-established body of work on nationalism in the Middle Ages includes: G. G. Coulton, "Nationalism in the Middle Ages," *Cambridge Historical Journal* 4 (1935): 15–40; Joseph Strayer, "The Laicization of French and English Society in the Thirteenth Century," *Speculum* 15 (1940): 76–86; Johan Huizinga, *Men and Ideas: History, the Middle Ages, the Renaissance,* trans. James S. Holmes and Hans van Marle (New York: Meridian, 1959 [1940]); Gaines Post, "'Blessed Lady Spain': Vincentius Hispanus and Spanish National Imperialism in the Thirteenth Century," *Speculum* 19 (1954): 198–209; Vivian Galbraith, "Nationality and Language in Medieval England," *Transactions of the Royal Historical Society* 23 (1941): 113–29; Ernst Kantorowicz, *The King's Two Bodies: A Study in Mediaeval Political Theology* (Princeton: Princeton University Press, 1957), 249–58; Marc Bloch, *Feudal Society,* 2 vols., trans. L. A. Manyon (Chicago: University of Chicago Press, 1964); Hugh Seton-Watson, "Language and National Consciousness," *Proceedings of the British Academy* 67 (1981): 1–18; and Susan Reynolds, *Kingdoms and Communities in Western Europe, 900–1300* (Oxford: Clarendon Press, 1984). More recent work on nationalism and medieval England includes: Lee Patterson, "Making Identities in Fifteenth-Century England: Henry V and John Lydgate," in *New Historical Literary Study: Essays on Reproducing Texts, Representing History,* ed. Jeffrey N. Cox and Larry J. Reynolds (Princeton: Princeton University Press, 1993); Claus Bjørn, Alexander Grant, and Keith J. Stringer, eds., *Nations, Nationalism, and Patriotism in the European Past* (Copenhagen: Academic Press, 1994); 69–107; Lynn Staley, "The English Nation," in Margery Kempe's *Dissenting Fictions* (University Park: Pennsylvania State University Press, 1994), 127–70; Simon Forde, Lesley Johnson, and Alan V. Murray, eds., *Concepts of National Identity in the Middle Ages* (Leeds: University of Leeds Printing Services, 1995); *EN;* Adrian Hastings, *The Construction of Nationhood: Ethnicity, Religion, and Nationalism*

(Cambridge: Cambridge University Press, 1997); Kathleen Davis, "National Writing in the Ninth Century: A Reminder for Postcolonial Thinking about the Nation," *Journal of Medieval and Early Modern Studies* 28 (1998): 611–37; Patricia Claire Ingham, *Sovereign Fantasies* (Philadelphia: University of Pennsylvania Press, 2001); Derek Pearsall, "The Idea of Englishness in the Fifteenth Century," in *Nation, Court, and Culture: New Essays on Fifteenth-Century English Poetry,* ed. Helen Cooney (Dublin: Four Courts Press, 2001), 15–27; and Kathy Lavezzo, ed., *Imagining a Medieval English Nation* (Minneapolis: University of Minnesota Press, 2003).

29. See Hans Kohn, *The Idea of Nationalism: A Study of Its Origins and Background* (New York: Macmillan, 1944), 79. On the doctrine of universal siblinghood throughout Christian history, see Marc Shell, *Children of the Earth: Literature, Politics, Nationhood* (New York: Oxford University Press, 1993).

30. On Bede's reference to the "historia nostrae nationis" in his preface to the *Ecclesiastical History,* which he addressed to King Ceolwulf of Northumbria, see Hastings, *Construction of Nationhood,* 38. On the introduction of the term *Angelcynn* in the Anglo-Saxon Chronicle, see Smyth, "Emergence of English Identity," 39–40; and J. M. Bately, ed., *Anglo-Saxon England: MSA* (Cambridge: Cambridge University Press, 1983), 59.

31. See Hastings, *Construction of Nationhood,* 39; Smyth, "Emergence of English Identity," 42–43.

32. *ER,* 181.

33. Hastings, *Construction of Nationhood,* 37; but see also Smyth, "Emergence of English Identity," 42–43.

34. *ER,* 2–3.

35. Ibid., 8. See also Alan Harding, *The Law Courts of Medieval England* (London: Allen & Unwin, 1973); G. L. Harris, *King, Parliament, and Public Finance in Medieval England to 1369* (Oxford: Clarendon, 1975); R. H. Britnell, *The Commercialisation of English Society, 1000–1500* (Cambridge: Cambridge University Press, 1993); and Barnaby Keeney, "Military Service and the Development of Nationalism in England, 1272–1327," *Speculum* 22 (1947): 534–49.

36. See William Pfaff, *The Wrath of Nations: Civilization and the Furies of Nationalism* (New York: Simon and Schuster, 1993). For one critique of such celebrations of the democratic nation-state, see Will Kymlicka, "Misunderstanding Nationalism," in *Theorizing Nationalism,* ed. Ronald Beiner (Albany: State University of New York Press, 1999), 131–40.

37. John Smith Roskell, *Parliament and Politics in Late Medieval England* (London: Hambledon Press, 1981).

38. Scholarship claiming that the state is not primary to the nation includes Liah Greenfeld, *Nationalism: Five Roads to Modernity* (Cambridge: Harvard University Press, 1992); Partha Chatterjee, "Whose Imagined Community?" in *Mapping the Nation,* ed. Gopal Balakrishnan (London: Verso, 1996), 214–25; and Hastings, *Construction of Nationhood.* But see also John Breuilly, *Nationalism and the State* (Manchester: Manchester University Press, 1982); and Eric J. Hobsbawm, *Nations and Nationalism since 1780: Programme, Myth, Reality* (Cambridge: Cambridge University Press, 1990).

39. Philip G. Kreyenbroek and Stefan Sperl, eds., *The Kurds: A Contemporary Overview* (London: Routledge, 1992).

40. Ingham, *Sovereign Fantasies,* 8.

41. Work on nationalism and fantasy is vast. A partial list could include: *IC;* Ernest Gellner, *Nations and Nationalism* (Oxford: Blackwell, 1983); Homi K. Bhabha, *The Location of Culture* (London: Routledge, 1990), 139–70; Lauren Berlant, *The Anatomy of National Fantasy: Hawthorne, Utopia, and Everyday Life* (Chicago: University of Chicago Press, 1991); Richard Helgerson, *Forms of Nationhood: The Elizabethan Writing of England* (Chicago: University of Chicago Press, 1992); Andrew Hadfield, *Literature, Politics, and National Identity: Reformation to Renaissance* (Cambridge: Cambridge University Press, 1994); Michael Moon and Cathy N. Davidson, eds., *Subjects and Citizens: Nation, Race, and Gender from Oroonoko to Anita Hill* (Durham: Duke University Press, 1995); Chatterjee, "Whose Imagined Community?"; and Phillip E. Wegner, *Imaginary Communities: Utopia, the Nation, and the Spatial Histories of Modernity* (Berkeley: University of California Press, 2002).

42. My thinking here reflects the understanding of art as an imaginative resolution to historical events articulated both by Fredric Jameson in *The Political Unconscious: Narrative as a Socially Symbolic Act* (Ithaca: Cornell University Press, 1981) and by Kenneth Burke in *The Philosophy of Literary Form: Studies in Symbolic Action,* 2nd ed. (Baton Rouge: Louisiana State University Press, 1967); and the theorization of the reality and historical agency of fantasy in Louise O. Fradenburg and Carla Freccero, "Introduction: Caxton, Foucault,

and the Pleasures of History," in *Premodern Sexualities in Europe,* ed. Fradenburg and Freccero (New York: Routledge, 1996).

43. For a theory of how England's actual (not perceived) physical remoteness from world centers contributed to nationalism during the period, see William H. McNeill, *Polyethnicity and National Unity in World History* (Toronto: University of Toronto Press, 1985). While McNeill contends that the polyethnicity that characterized classical Mediterranean society persisted in the main centers of Latin Christendom, he does point to certain exceptions to the rule of polyethnicity: areas that were geographically remote or marginal to the urban centers of the West and East. Spatial separation, that is, went hand-in-hand with a decrease in "the ethnic intermingling and complexity of human groupings" and a rise in autonomy (17). Macedon and especially Japan epitomize McNeill's exception to the rule of polyethnicity. Yet England also appears in the historian's account as a locale whose physical remoteness from urban centers such as Rome and Byzantium contributed to the rise of a "national state" after 900 AD. Given his emphasis on polyethnicity, McNeill provides us with a particularly striking claim for the importance of assuming a global stance when engaging with the question of geography and English nationalism. For it is only the geographic marginality of a people to the civilized world that spurs a rare acknowledgment by this historian of the presence of medieval nationalism.

44. *EN;* Ingham, *Sovereign Fantasies;* Michelle Warren, *History on the Edge: Excaliber and the Borders of Britain, 1100–1300* (Minneapolis: University of Minnesota Press, 2000); Heng, *Empire.* See also Daniel Birkholz, "The Vernacular Map: Re-Charting English Literary History," *New Medieval Literatures* 6 (2004): 11–78.

45. *IC,* 7.

46. *EN,* 2.

47. See for example Harvey, *Condition;* Doreen Massey, "Politics and Space/Time," *New Left Review* 196 (1992): 65–84; Edward Soja, *Postmodern Geographies: The Reassertion of Space in Critical Social Theory* (London: Verso, 1989); Peter Jackson, *Maps of Meaning: An Introduction to Cultural Geography* (London: Unwin Hyman, 1989). On Sauer, see Jackson, 10–24.

48. A sampling of the diverse theoretical works with which cultural geographers engage could include: Gaston Bachelard, *The Poetics of Space* (New York: Orion, 1964); Michel Foucault, *The Archaeology of Knowledge,* trans. A. M. Sheridan Smith (New York: Pantheon, 1972); Raymond Williams, *The Country and the City* (Oxford: Oxford University Press, 1973); Michel Foucault, "Nietzsche, Genealogy, History," in *Language, Counter-Memory, Practice: Selected Essays and Interviews,* ed. Donald F. Bouchard (Ithaca: Cornell University Press, 1977), 139–64; Michel de Certeau, *The Practice of Everyday Life* (Berkeley: University of California Press, 1984), and *Heterologies: Discourse on the Other,* trans. Brian Massumi (Minneapolis: University of Minnesota Press, 1986); and Lefebvre, *Production.*

49. Harvey, *Condition,* 203.

50. Sara Blair, "Cultural Geography and the Place of the Literary," *American Literary History* 10 (1998): 547. Recent cultural geographic work by medievalists includes Jesse A. Gelrich, *The Idea of the Book in the Middle Ages* (Ithaca: Cornell University Press, 1985), 51–93; Tomasch and Gilles, eds., *Text and Territory;* and Barbara A. Hanawalt and Michal Kobialka, eds., *Medieval Practices of Space* (Minneapolis: University of Minnesota Press, 2000).

51. For example, in *The Condition of Postmodernity,* Harvey notes how, insofar as they emphasize "the sensuous rather than the rational and objective qualities of spatial order," "mediaeval art and cartography, interestingly, seem to match the sensibility portrayed in de Certeau's 'spatial stories'" (241–42; see de Certeau, *Practice,* 242). Granted, this moment is rather unusual in Harvey and appears in the midst of his lengthy account of changes—not of continuities—in spatial perceptions from the Middle Ages to postmodernity. Nevertheless, Harvey diverges here from the general tendency of post-Enlightenment western intellectuals to invest all aspects of their culture with modernity (that is, with newness). Given that most theorists of postmodernity are compelled to construct a premodern time when thinking modern and postmodern forms was impossible, Harvey's citation of medieval correspondences with de Certeau's pedestrian rhetoric is noteworthy, as are similar impulses on the part of other cultural geographers. See Lefebvre, *Production,* 231, 262ff., 369; Harley, *New Nature,* 66; and William E. Phipps, "Cultural Commitments and World Maps," *Focus* 41 (1991): 7–9.

52. While they at times served as repositories of geographic data for practical use by travelers such as pilgrims, mappae mundi were largely didactic artifacts that provided the viewer with all sorts of information in graphic form. See Woodward, "*Mappaemundi,*" in *HC,* 334–42.

53. W. L. Bevan and H. W. Phillott, *Mediaeval Geography: An Essay in Illustration of the Hereford Mappa Mundi* (Amsterdam: Meridian, 1969), xxii; John Kirkland Wright, *The Geographic Lore of the Time of the Crusades: A Study in the History of Medieval Science and Tradition in Western Europe,* 1925 rev. ed. (New York: Dover, 1965), 43–44; W. W. Jervis, *The World in Maps: A Study in Map Evolution* (New York: Oxford University Press, 1937), 74. Kirkland's contrast of fanciful medieval cartography with the more scientific map productions of another age typifies the tendency of scholars comparing medieval and modern maps. See George H. T. Kimble, *Geography in the Middle Ages* (London: Methuen, 1938), 181ff. C. Raymond Beazely as well employs a mythic/scientific binary (though he locates some scientific advances in the Middle Ages) in his *The Dawn of Modern Geography,* 3 vols. (New York: Peter Smith, 1949).

54. See Harley, *New Nature;* Denis Wood, *The Power of Maps* (New York: Guilford, 1992), 68–69; Black, *Maps;* and Mark S. Monmonier, *How to Lie with Maps* (Chicago: University of Chicago Press, 1996).

55. Harley, *New Nature,* 46, 66; see also 53, 153–58.

56. See especially Bruno Latour, *We Have Never Been Modern,* trans. Catherine Porter (Cambridge: Harvard University Press, 1993). See also Harley, *New Nature,* 66; Edney, *Mapping,* 301; and Kathleen Biddick, "The ABC of Ptolemy: Mapping the World with the Alphabet," in *Text and Territory,* ed. Tomasch and Gilles, 268–93. Scholarly work offering a revisionist history that counters the problematic characterization of the Middle Ages as "other" to the "modern" historical period it precedes includes: Lee Patterson, *Negotiating the Past: The Historical Understanding of Medieval Literature* (Madison: University of Wisconsin Press, 1987); Louise O. Fradenburg, "'Voice Memorial': Loss and Reparation in Chaucer's Poetry," *Exemplaria* 7 (1995): 41–54; Fradenburg and Freccero, "Caxton"; R. Howard Bloch and Steven Nichols, eds., *Medievalism and the Modernist Temper* (Baltimore: Johns Hopkins University Press, 1996); Kathleen Biddick, *The Shock of Medievalism* (Durham: Duke University Press, 1998); and Paul Freedman and Gabrielle M. Spiegel, "Medievalisms Old and New: The Rediscovery of Alterity in North American Medieval Studies," *American Historical Review* 103 (1998): 677–704.

57. Harvey, *Condition,* 205.

58. Patricia Yaeger, "Introduction: Narrating Space," in *The Geography of Identity,* ed. Yaeger (Ann Arbor: University of Michigan Press, 1996), 15.

59. The variety of work on nationalism and alterity encompasses: Edward Said, *Orientalism* (New York: Pantheon, 1978); Abdul R. JanMohamed, *Manichean Aesthetics: The Politics of Literature in Colonial Africa* (Amherst: University of Massachusetts Press, 1983); Bhabha, *The Location of Culture;* Paul Gilroy, *There Ain't No Black in the Union Jack* (London: Hutchinson, 1987); Slavoj Žižek, "Eastern Europe's Republics of Gilead," *New Left Review* 183 (1990), 50–62; Gyan Prakash, "The Modern Nation's Return in the Archaic," *Critical Inquiry* 23 (1997): 536–56; and Dipesh Chakrabarty, *Provincializing Europe: Postcolonial Thought and Historical Difference* (Princeton: Princeton University Press, 2000).

60. On gender asymmetry, see Gayle Rubin's landmark essay "The Traffic in Women: Notes on the Political Economy of Sex," in *Toward an Anthropology of Women,* ed. Rayna R. Reiter (New York: Monthly Review Press, 1975), 157, 210.

61. Žižek, "Eastern Europe's Republics," 53.

62. Julia Kristeva, *Strangers to Ourselves,* trans. Leon S. Roudiez (New York: Columbia University Press, 1991), 1.

63. Sigmund Freud, "The Uncanny," *The Standard Edition of the Complete Psychological Works of Sigmund Freud,* 17:220, cited and discussed in Kristeva, *Strangers,* 183.

64. *IC,* 6.

65. Žižek, "Eastern Europe's Republics," 53, 54. Žižek is citing G. W. F. Hegel, *The Science of Logic* (Oxford: Oxford University Press), 402.

66. Bhabha, *The Location of Culture,* 139–70.

67. For a representative sampling of scholarship on medieval Orientalism and medieval Occidentalism, see: *MR;* Campbell, *Witness;* Iain Macleod Higgins, *Writing East: The "Travels" of Sir John Mandeville* (Philadelphia: University of Pennsylvania Press, 1997); Kathryn Lynch, "East Meets West in Chaucer's Squire's and Franklin's Tales," *Speculum* 70 (1995): 530–51; Susan Schibanoff, "Worlds Apart: Orientalism, Antifeminism, and Heresy in Chaucer's Man of Law's Tale," *Exemplaria* 8 (1996): 59–96; Biddick, *The Shock of Medievalism;* Heng, *Empire;* Christine Chism, "Too Close for Comfort: Dis-Orienting Chivalry in the Wars of Alexander," in *Text and Territory,* ed. Tomasch and Gilles, 116–42; Lucy K. Pick, ed., *Edward Said: Orientalism in the Middle Ages, Medieval Encounters* 5 (1999): 265–357; Sharon Kinoshita, "'Pagans Are Wrong and

Christians Are Right': Alterity, Gender, and Nation in the *Chanson de Roland*," *Journal of Medieval and Early Modern Studies* 31 (2001): 79–111; and Jeffrey Jerome Cohen, ed., *The Postcolonial Middle Ages* (New York: Palgrave, 2001).

68. Cultural geographers have at times stressed the differences between the terms "space" and "place." Following the work of Yaeger and other critics, my analysis generally allows for some slippage between the two. On the different ways in which theorists conceive of the terms, see Yaeger, "Introduction," note 5.

69. The medieval Irish also linked their marginality (indeed, a marginality even more intense than that of the English) with a special national status, as I discuss in chapter 2. Later, in the eighteenth and nineteenth centuries, Gothic and Romantic discourse also could entail national European identifications with the strange and foreign. See, for example, Cannon Schmidt, *Alien Nation: Nineteenth-Century Gothic Fictions and English Nationalism* (Philadelphia: University of Pennsylvania Press, 1997). The national discourse of Puritan America seized upon the notion of wilderness as means of engaging with the problems and potentials of American identity. See Sacvan Bercovitch, *The American Jeremiad* (Madison: University of Wisconsin Press, 1978).

70. The Jews were expelled from England in 1290. See Patricia Skinner, ed., *The Jews in Medieval Britain: History, Literary, and Archaeological Perspectives* (Woodbridge, UK: Boydell Press, 2003).

71. That problem of terminology of course would persist through the Renaissance to the present day. See Helgerson, *Forms,* 8, and Bernard Crick, "The English and the British," in *National Identities,* ed. Crick (London: Blackwell, 1991), 90–104.

72. *MR,* 46.

73. George H. Williams, *Wilderness and Paradise in Christian Thought: The Biblical Experience of the Desert in the History of Christianity and the Paradise Theme in the Theological Idea of the University* (New York: Harper, 1962), 12–14. My discussion of the wilderness in Christianity owes much to Williams and Alison Goddard Elliott, *Roads to Paradise: Reading the Lives of the Early Saints* (Hanover: University Press of New England, 1987), esp. 83–180; and *MI,* esp. 47–59.

74. Antoine Guillaumont, "La conception du désert chez les moines d'Egypte," *Revue de l'Histoire des Religions* 188 (1975): 11, trans. and cited in Elliott, *Roads,* 106.

75. Robert Pogue Harrison, *Forests: The Shadow of Civilization* (Chicago: University of Chicago Press, 1992), 23.

76. Ibid.

77. Romm, *Edges,* 15–26.

78. Williams, *Wilderness,* 5, 15–19; Elliott, *Roads,* 105–16. The central role of the desert in Judeo-Christian discourse results in the rather paradoxical location of the mount of the Sinai desert at the center of the world in some mappae mundi.

79. While the dual function of the wilderness persisted in the New Testament (particularly in the gospel of Mark), it is in the discourse of late classical and early medieval Christianity, in the *vitae* of the desert "fathers," that the ambiguous role of the wilderness as at once a dangerous and a beneficial place first flourishes in Christianity (Williams, *Wilderness,* 24).

80. Romm, *Edges,* 45–48; *MR,* 163–77.

81. Bevan and Phillott, *Mediaeval Geography,* 56.

82. Hans Kurath, ed., *Middle English Dictionary* (Ann Arbor: University of Michigan Press, 1954–), s.v. "straunge." On the ambiguity of alterity in the Middle Ages, see also F. R. P. Akehurst and Stephanie Cain Van D'Elden, eds., *The Stranger in Medieval Society* (Minneapolis: University of Minnesota Press, 1997).

83. The term "intellectual" is fraught, and the scholarship on intellectuals is vast; two introductory volumes are George B. de Huszar, ed., *The Intellectual: A Controversial Portrait* (Glencoe: Free Press, 1960); and Bruce Robbins, *Intellectuals: Aesthetics, Politics, and Academics* (Minneapolis: University of Minnesota Press, 1990). On the medieval intellectual, see Jacques Le Goff, *Intellectuals in the Middle Ages,* trans. Teresa Lavender Fagan (Cambridge: Harvard University Press, 1993).

84. "Brute sub occasu solis trans gallica regna; Insula in occeano est habitata gigantibus olim. Nunc deserta quidem gentibus apta tuis . . . Hic de prole tua reges nascentur. & ipsis. Totius terrae subditus orbis erit." *HRB,* 239; *HKB,* 46–47.

85. On the map see Peter Barber, "The Evesham World Map: A Late Medieval English View of God and the World," *Imago Mundi* 47 (1995): 13–33.

86. Hence in the unusually imperialistic Evesham map, in contrast to the disproportionately large amount of space given English holdings, scant space is accorded Rome. Though geographically central,

Rome is portrayed by a tiny place icon eclipsed by the symbols for Calais and St. Denis. By minimizing the size of Rome, the mapmaker exposes its status as a threat requiring imaginative suppression, a move similar to the cartographer's reduction of France "to the size of an insignificant province" (Barber, "The Evesham World Map," 24).

87. Work on the notion of *translatio imperii* and empire in the Middle Ages includes: Charles T. Davis, *Dante and the Idea of Rome* (Oxford: Clarendon, 1957); Werner Goez, *Translatio Imperii* (Tübingen: Mohr, 1958); Marie-Dominique Chenu, *Nature, Man, and Society in the Twelfth Century,* trans. Jerome Taylor and Lester K. Little (Chicago: University of Chicago Press, 1968); and Robert Folz, *The Concept of Empire in Western Europe,* trans. S. A. Ogilvie (London: Edward Arnold, 1969).

88. Eusebius of Caesarea, *Theophania* 3, 2, trans. Samuel Lee in *Eusebius on the Theophania* (Cambridge: Duncan and Malcolm, 1853), 157. On the attitudes of Augustine, Eusebius, and other early Christians toward Rome, see R. A. Markus, *From Augustine to Gregory the Great: History and Christianity in the Middle Ages* (London: Variorum Reprints, 1983); and D. S. Wallace-Hadrill, *Eusebius of Caesarea* (Westminster, MD: Canterbury, 1961).

89. From 1309 to 1376, not Rome but Avignon enjoyed the universal obedience of the Christian West. And for nearly thirty years more, the Avignon papacy continued to be recognized within certain areas of Europe. Throughout both the Avignon papacy and the Great Schism of 1378–1409, England officially supported Rome, a move that was itself a sign of nationalism insofar as support for a Roman pope meant a rejection of England's French opponents during the Hundred Years' War. But a lingering investment in the idea of Rome—a lingering sense of the propriety of housing the universal church in the great classical capital—no doubt underlies that allegiance as well.

90. *IC,* 53–54.

91. Gregorius, *Narracio de Mirabilibus urbis Romae,* trans. John Osborne (Toronto: Pontifical Institute, 1987), 18.

92. Nicholas Brooks, "Canterbury, Rome, and the Construction of English Identity," in *Early Medieval Rome and the Christian West: Essays in Honour of Donald A. Bullough,* ed. Julia M. H. Smith (Leiden: Brill, 2000), 222.

93. Johan Huizinga, *Men and Ideas: History, the Middle Ages, the Renaissance,* trans. James S. Holmes and Hans van Marle (New York: Meridian, 1959), 108.

## 1. Another Country

1. Most variations in the different accounts of the legend stem from the differences between its two earliest extant versions, in Bede's *EH* (731) and in the Whitby writer's life of Gregory (ca. 704–14). Unlike Bede, the Whitby writer does not identify the men as slaves and renders them literate (i.e., readers or speakers of Latin); he also is unsure whether they are boys or men. While both Bede and the Whitby writer have Gregory pun on the boys' identity as "Angles" from "Dere" under king "Ælle," other versions limit Gregory's puns to merely one or two Anglo-Saxon words (typically "Angle" or "English," which Gregory puns with "angel"). Later in this chapter, I discuss in detail the differences between these and other Anglo-Saxon writers' versions of the story. By referring to the slave-boy story as an English legend, I mean to emphasize that the question of its historical veracity is not germane to my analysis. As an Anglo-Saxon narrative, the slave-boy story tells us much more about England's Gregory than Gregory's England.

2. John Boswell, *Christianity, Social Tolerance, and Homosexuality: Gay People in Western Europe from the Beginning of the Christian Era to the Fourteenth Century* (Chicago: University of Chicago Press, 1981), 143–44; Patrick Wormald, "Bede, the *Bretwaldas* and the Origins of the *gens Anglorum,*" in *Ideal and Reality in Frankish and Anglo-Saxon Society: Studies Presented to J. M. Wallace-Hadrill,* ed. Wormald et al. (Oxford: Blackwell, 1983), 129; Jonathan Culler, *On Puns: The Foundation of Letters* (Oxford: Blackwell, 1988), 15; Nicholas Howe, *Migration and Mythmaking in Anglo-Saxon England* (New Haven: Yale University Press, 1989), 119–20; Allen Frantzen, *Desire for Origins: New Language, Old English, and Teaching the Tradition* (New Brunswick: Rutgers University Press, 1990), 39; Ruth Mazo Karras, "Desire, Descendants, and Dominance: Slavery, the Exchange of Women, and Masculine Power," in *The Work of Work: Servitude, Slavery, and Labor in Medieval England,* ed. Allen J. Frantzen and Douglas Moffat (Glasgow: Cruithne, 1994), 26 n. 14; Allen J. Frantzen, *Before the Closet: Same-Sex Love from* Beowulf *to* Angels in America (Chicago: Univer-

sity of Chicago Press, 1998), 266–77; Nicholas Howe, "An Angle on This Earth: Sense of Place in Anglo-Saxon England," *Bulletin of the John Rylands University Library of Manchester* 82 (2000): 3–6; Stephen J. Harris, "Bede and Gregory's Allusive Angles," *Criticism* 44 (2002): 271–89.

3. Peter A. M. Clemoes, "The Chronology of Ælfric's Works," in *The Anglo-Saxons: Studies in Some Aspects of Their History and Culture Presented to Bruce Dickins,* ed. Clemoes (London: Bowes and Bowes, 1988), 212–47.

4. In *An Anglo-Saxon Dictionary* (Oxford: Clarendon, 1898), J. Bosworth and T. N. Toller list many significations for "þeod," among them: people, nation, tribe, country, "race," language, and fellowship (s.v. "þeod"). When it meant "nation," "þeod" did not refer to the modern sense of the nation-state, but to the notion of a distinct people living in a particular territory. For example, the term often referred to the particular tribal kingdoms within England, such as Northumbria or Mercia. But as we shall see, in Ælfric "þeod" refers to a single English people. When he has Gregory ask from what "þeod" the boys hail, Ælfric departs from his sources by linking the boys not with "Britain," but with "engla-londe." It is this sense of a bounded and distinct people, marked by their particular ethnic, "racial," and religious affiliations, that Ælfric seeks to establish in his text. Ælfric, *Catholic Homilies: Second Series,* ed. Malcolm Godden, EETS SS 5 (Oxford: Oxford University Press, 1979), 74. All subsequent page references to this text will be from Godden's edition and will be identified as *Catholic Homilies.* Unless otherwise specified, all translations are mine, in consultation with those offered by Benjamin Thorpe in *Sermones Catholici,* vol. 1 (1846; New York: Olms, 1983); subsequent references to Thorpe's edition will appear as *Sermones Catholici.* Cf. *EH,* 132; Paul the Deacon, *Gregor I der Grosse,* ed. Walter Stuhlfath (Heidelberg: Winter, 1913), 106; all subsequent references to this edition will appear as *Gregor;* Thomas Miller, ed., *The Old English Version of Bede's* Ecclesiastical History of the English People, EETS OS 95 (1890; London: Oxford University Press, 1959), 96.

5. *The Old English Orosius,* ed. Janet Bately, EETS SS 6 (London: Oxford University Press, 1980).

6. P. D. A. Harvey, *Medieval Maps* (Toronto: University of Toronto Press, 1991), 21. On the Cotton or Anglo-Saxon map, see also *MTS,* 16–19; Konrad Miller, *Mappaemundi: Die ältesten Weltkarten,* III (Stuttgart: J. Roth, 1895–98); and Patrick McGurk, D. N. Dumville, M. R. Godden, and Ann Knock, eds., *An Eleventh-Century Anglo-Saxon Illustrated Miscellany: British Library Cotton Tiberius B.V. Part I,* EEMF 21 (Copenhagen: Rosenkilde and Bagger, 1983), 79–87.

7. C. Raymond Beazely, *The Dawn of Modern Geography,* 3 vols. (New York: Peter Smith, 1949), 2:608.

8. On British Library Cotton MS. Tiberius B.V., see McGurk et al., *An Eleventh-Century Anglo-Saxon Illustrated Miscellany;* N. R. Ker, *A Catalogue of Manuscripts Containing Anglo-Saxon* (Oxford: Clarendon Press, 1957), 255–56; and Howe, "Angle," 12–16; *MTS,* 74–75.

9. The manuscript also lists Roman popes (fols. 19v–22r). On the *computus* tables, see *MTS.* On Sigeric's itinerary, see Veronica Ortenberg, "Archbishop Sigeric's Journey to Rome in 990," *Anglo-Saxon England* 19 (1990): 197–246.

10. "Brittannia insula in extremo ferme orbis limite circium occidentemque versus divina." *Gildas: The Ruin of Britain and Other Works,* ed. and trans. Michael Winterbottom (London: Phillimore, 1978), 89, 16.

11. On Isidore, see Helmut Gneuss, "A Preliminary List of Manuscripts Written or Owned in England up to 1100," *Anglo-Saxon England* 9 (1981): 1–60; and Nicholas Howe, *The Old English Catalogue Poems, Anglistica* 23 (Copenhagen: Rosenkilde and Bagger, 1985), 67–72. On Eadmer, see *The Life of St. Anselm, Archbishop of Canterbury,* ed. and trans. R. W. Southern (Oxford: Clarendon Press, 1962), 105.

12. "Sospes enim ueniens supremo ex orbe Britanni / Per uarias gentes, per freta perque uias, / Vrbem Romuleam uidit" (*EH,* 472–73).

13. Howe, "Angle," 11. See also idem, "Rome: Capital of Anglo-Saxon England," *Journal of Medieval and Early Modern Studies* 34 (2004): 147–72.

14. On exile in works such as *The Wanderer* and *Andreas,* see Robert Edwards, "Exile, Self, and Society," in *Exile in Literature,* ed. María-Inés Lagos Pope (Lewisburg: Bucknell University Press, 1988); and Stanley Greenfield, *Hero and Exile* (London: Hambledon, 1989).

15. "Þes eard nis eac ealles swa mægen-fæst / her on uteweardan þære eorðan brad nysse / swa swa heo is to-middes on mægen-fæstum eardum" (*Lives of Saints,* ed. Walter Skeat, EETS OS 82 [Oxford: Oxford University Press, 1966], 290–91).

16. G. P. Krapp, ed., *Andreas and the Fates of the Apostles* (Boston: Ginn, 1906); translated by R. K. Root in "The Legend of St. Andrew," *Yale Studies in English* 7 (1899). Anglo-Saxon isolation is also worth considering in relation to their ambivalence toward the monstrous races inhabiting the eastern and southern

margins of the world demonstrated in the group of Anglo-Saxon illustrated manuscripts on the marvels of the East (the items [*Beowulf, the Letter of Alexander, the Wonders of the East,* etc.] in Cotton Vitellius A.xv; Cotton Tiberius B.V.; Bodleian 614). In particular, what John Friedman has identified as the imaginative displacement of monsters traditionally affiliated with the eastern edges of the world to England in *Beowulf* may reflect the Anglo-Saxons' sense of how their own isolation parallels that of the monstrous races (*MR,* 103–7). On the exotica in the *Beowulf*-manuscript, see Andy Orchard, *Pride and Prodigies: Studies in the Monsters of the Beowulf-Manuscript* (Cambridge: Brewer, 1995); and Asa Simon Mittman, "Living at the Edge of the World: Marginality and Monstrosity in Anglo-Saxon Manuscripts and Beyond" (Ph.D. diss., Stanford University, 2003).

17. On Portolan maps, see Tony Campbell, "Portolan Charts from the Late Thirteenth Century to 1500," in *HC,* 371–463.

18. Oswald Cockayne, ed., *Leechdoms, Wortcunning, and Starcraft of Early England,* 2 vols., RS 35 (London: Kraus, 1965), 3:432–35.

19. For a full-length study of how the Anglo-Saxons likened themselves to the Israelites, see Howe, *Migration.*

20. Howe, *Migration,* 119–20.

21. The legend seems to have circulated as popular hagiography before being written down (*EH,* 132, 134; Bertram Colgrave, ed., *The Earliest Life of Gregory the Great by an Anonymous Monk of Whitby* [Lawrence, Kans.: University of Kansas Press, 1968], 90–91).

22. I follow the dating of the second series by Michael Lapidge in "Ælfric's *Sanctorale,*" in *Holy Men and Holy Women: Old English Prose Saints' Lives and Their Contexts,* ed. Paul E. Szarmach (Albany: State University of New York Press, 1996), 127 n. 13.

23. Mary Clayton, "Of Mice and Men: Ælfric's Second Homily for the Feast of a Confessor," *Leeds Studies in English* NS 24 (1993), 1–26; idem, "Homiliaries and Preaching in Anglo-Saxon England," *Peritia* 4 (1985): 207–4; Milton McGatch, *Preaching and Theology in Anglo-Saxon England: Ælfric and Wulfstan* (Toronto: University of Toronto Press, 1977), 27 and 119; M. R. Godden, "Experiments in Genre: The Saints' Lives in Ælfric's *Catholic Homilies,*" in *Holy Men,* ed. Szarmach, 261–88.

24. "manega hálige bec cyðað his drohtnunge and his halige líf. and eac historia anglorum, ða ðe Ælfred cyning of ledene on englisc awende. Seo bóc sprecð genoh swutelice be ðisum halgan were; Nu wylle we sum ðing scortlice eow be him gereccan for ðan ðe seo foresæde bóc nis eow eallum cuð þeah ðe heo on englisc awend sy" (Ælfric, *Catholic Homilies,* 72).

25. "ideoque nec obscura posuimus verba, sed simplicem Anglicam, quo facilius possit ad cor pervenire legentium vel audientium, ad utilitatem animarum suarum, quia alia lingua nesciunt erudiri, quam in qua nati sunt" (*Sermones Catholici,* 1; trans. S. Harvey Gem in *An Anglo-Saxon Abbot: Ælfric of Eynsham* [Edinburgh: Clark, 1912], 133).

26. *EN,* 11.

27. *Ælfric's Colloquy,* ed. George N. Garmonsway (Exeter: University of Exeter Press, 1978). *Ælfrics Grammatik und Glossar,* ed. Julius Zupitza (Berlin: Weidmann, 1966).

28. Ælfric offers this sort of reasoning in his letter to Archbishop Sigeric (*Sermones Catholici,* 1: 1). We should understand Ælfric's defense of English in relation to the grammarian's efforts at standardizing the language. See C. C. Eble, "Noun Inflection in Royal 7 C.xii, Ælfric's First Series of *Catholic Homilies*" (Ph.D. diss., University of North Carolina at Chapel Hill, 1970). On the self-conscious manner in which Ælfric fashions his orthodox vernacular writings, see Jon Wilcox, "Introduction," *Ælfric's Prefaces* (Durham: Durham Medieval Texts, 1994), 68–71.

29. "ac hì ne sind na ealle of godspellum genumene. ac sind forwel fela of godes halgena lífe oððe þrowunge gegaderode. þæra anra þe angelcynn mid freolsdagum wurðað" (*Catholic Homilies,* 2).

30. Nicholas Banton, "Monastic Reform and the Unification of Tenth-Century England," in *Religion and National Identity,* ed. Stuart Mews, Ecclesiastical History Society 18 (Oxford: Blackwell, 1982), 81.

31. For Ælfric's use of *Engla londe,* see *Catholic Homilies,* 74. On the rise of the term "England" in reference to a united Anglo-Saxon people, see Banton, "Monastic Reform"; Wormald, "Bede"; and Wormald, "*Engla Lond:* The Making of an Allegiance," *Journal of Historical Sociology* 7 (1994): 1–24. See also Sarah Foot, "The Making of *Angelcynn:* English Identity before the Norman Conquest," *Transactions of the Royal Historical Society,* 6th ser., 6 (1996): 25–49; Pauline Stafford, *Unification and Conquest: A Political and Social History of England in the Tenth and Eleventh Centuries* (London: Arnold, 1989); and James Campbell, "The Late Anglo-Saxon State: A Maximum View," *Proceedings of the British Academy* 87 (1995).

32. Stafford, *Unification.*

33. Dom Thomas Symons, ed. and trans., *Regularis Concordia Anglicae Nationis Monachorum Sancti-monialiumque* (London: Nelson, 1953), 6–7. On the English aspects of the reform, see Banton, "Monastic Reform"; and D. H. Farmer, "The Progress of the Monastic Revival," in *Tenth-Century Studies: Essays in Commemoration of the Millennium of the Council of Winchester and* Regularis Concordia, ed. David Parsons (London: Phillimore, 1975), 10–20.

34. David Knowles, *The Monastic Order in England* (Cambridge: Cambridge University Press, 1949), 697–700.

35. As a pupil and biographer of the bishop responsible for the *Regularis Concordia* (Æthelwold [ca. 909–984], one of the three original leaders of the revival), and as a monk possessed of many links with England's episcopal and secular leaders (as the dedications in his literary corpus to the thane Æthelmær; to Æthelmær's powerful father, Æthelweard; to Sigeric, the archbishop of Canterbury; and to Wulfstan, the archbishop of York, all testify), Ælfric was certainly one for whom the intimate relation of church and state in tenth-century England resonated.

36. *Liber Eliensis,* ed. E. O. Blake, Camden Series 92 (London: Royal Historical Society, 1962), qtd. in Stafford, *Unification,* 57.

37. Stafford, *Unification,* 57–68.

38. M. R. Godden, "Ælfric's Saints' Lives and the Problem of Miracles," *Leeds Studies in English* NS 16 (1985), 97.

39. Clayton, "Of Mice."

40. Godden, "Ælfric's Saints' Lives," 95.

41. The origins of all extant manuscripts from Ælfric's *Catholic Homilies* have not been located, and it is likely that the distribution was even wider than that indicated in M. R. Godden, "Ælfric and the Vernacular Prose Tradition," in *The Old English Homily and Its Backgrounds,* ed. Paul E. Szarmach and Bernard F. Huppé (Albany: State University of New York Press, 1978), 110; and Godden, "Introduction," in *Catholic Homilies,* lx–lxxviii.

42. Godden, "Introduction," in *Catholic Homilies,* lxv.

43. Moreover, following the insights on medieval textual communities offered in Seth Lerer, *Literacy and Power in Anglo-Saxon Literature* (Lincoln: University of Nebraska Press, 1991), and Brian Stock, *The Implications of Literacy: Written Language and Models of Interpretation in the Eleventh and Twelfth Centuries* (Princeton: Princeton University Press, 1983), we may speculate that national sentiments were produced within the readers of the *Catholic Homilies.*

44. *Catholic Homilies,* 72; George Herzfeld, ed., *An Old English Martyrology,* EETS OS 116 (London: Paul, Trench, Trubner, 1900).

45. Mechthild Gretsch, "Ælfric and Gregory the Great," in *Ælfric's Lives of Canonised Popes,* ed. Donald Scragg, *Old English Newsletter Subsidia,* 30 (2001): 11.

46. Gregory altogether disappears from Ælfric's narrative at one point, when Ælfric narrates the beginnings of Augustine of Canterbury's mission (*Catholic Homilies,* 77–79). The only detailed episode from Gregory's life that Ælfric relates that does not explicitly pertain to English interests is Gregory's sermon on the plague to the Roman people. However, we might interpret this sequence as Ælfric's own warning to his intended English readership of the need to repent during their own time of hardship due to the Viking invasions. Such a possibility seems even more probable given the fact that the mix of "ge preosthádes ge munuchádes menn. and ðaet læwede folc" that Ælfric claims constituted the multitude who heard Gregory's sermon virtually describes Ælfric's own intended audience (*Catholic Homilies,* 77). See also Godden, "Experiments," 276.

47. "Þa geseah he betwux ðam warum. cypecnihtas gesette. þa wæron hwites lichaman. and fægeres and-wlitan menn. and æðellice gefexode; Gregorius ða beheold þæra cnapena wlite. and befrán of hwilcere þeode hí gebrohte wæron. Þa sæde him man þæt hí of engla lande wæron. and þæt ðære ðeode mennisc swa wli-tig wære. Eft ða gregorius befrán. hwæðer þæs landes folc cristen wære. ðe hæðen; Him man sæde. þæt hí hæðene wæron" (*Catholic Homilies,* 74). The mystifying otherness of the English to Gregory is especially ev-ident in the Whitby writer's text (Colgrave, *Earliest Life,* 90).

48. Dorothy Whitelock, ed., *English Historical Documents: 500–1042* (London: Eyre and Spottiswoode, 1955), 791; cited in Howe, *Migration,* 118 n. 16.

49. Celtic missionaries began converting the Anglo-Saxons in Northumbria after the Augustine mission. See Peter Blair, *An Introduction to Anglo-Saxon England* (Cambridge: Cambridge University Press, 1977), 124–29.

50. On Ælfric's use of slavery as a metaphor for sin, see David Pelteret, *Slavery in Early Mediaeval England: From the Reign of Alfred until the Twelfth Century* (Woodbridge: Boydell Press, 1995), 61–62.

51. David Pelteret, "Slave Raiding and Slave Trading in Early England," *Anglo-Saxon England* 9 (1981): 99–114; and Pelteret, *Slavery*, 25. The youths' "noble hair" may reflect the fact that anyone, from any class background, could have been captured and sent into slavery. See Pelteret, "Slavery in Anglo-Saxon England," in *The Anglo-Saxons: Synthesis and Achievement*, ed. J. Douglas Woods and Pelteret (Waterloo, Ont.: Wilfrid Laurier University Press, 1986), 120.

52. See Blair, *Introduction*, 179.

53. Pelteret, *Slavery*, 70; Richard Hodges, *Dark Age Economics: The Origins of Towns and Trade, AD 600–1000* (London: Duckworth, 1989), 128; Alfred Smyth, *Scandinavian Kings in the British Isles* (Oxford: Oxford University Press, 1977), 157.

54. See Wulfstan's *Sermo ad Anglos*, as discussed in Pelteret, *Slavery*, 95–101.

55. Alexander Murray, *Reason and Society in the Middle Ages* (Oxford: Clarendon Press, 1978), 40–54; Pelteret, *Slavery*, 70–71; Richard Hodges and David Whitehouse, "Introduction," *Mohammed, Charlemagne, and the Origins of Europe* (Ithaca: Cornell University Press, 1983).

56. Maurice Lombard, *The Golden Age of Islam*, trans. Joan Spencer (Amsterdam: North-Holland, 1975), 201; Pelteret, *Slavery*, 74–76; Hodges, *Dark Age Economics*, 217; Murray, *Reason*, 41.

57. Murray, *Reason*, 41.

58. E. Ashtor, *A Social and Economic History of the Near East in the Middle Ages* (Berkeley: University of California Press, 1976), 71.

59. Lombard, *Golden Age*.

60. A monastic formulation of homoerotic desire would continue to inform the literary history of the legend. Consider Benedictine abbot Terence Snow's rendering of Bede's text in his Victorian life of Gregory: "Passing through the forum one day, he saw three youthful slaves exposed for sale. Loose tunics but partially concealed their lithe forms and shapely limbs; light flaxen hair hung down their shoulders, and their blue eyes, restless in their fresh, fair faces, glanced, half defiantly, half timidly, at the inquisitive crowd. Gregory drew near, and, struck with their beauty and grace, asked the dealer whence they came" (*St. Gregory the Great: His Work and Spirit* [London: Hodges, 1892], 41). Obviously, the liberties Snow takes in this near-pornographic retelling of the legend intensify its latent homoerotic tendencies. But while Snow's scopophilic vision of the slave boys heightens the homoerotic elements of earlier versions of the myth, it does not make them explicit, given the monk's own Catholic investments. And, of course, neither does Ælfric, as a member of a premodern church explicitly opposed to sodomy, overtly point to a male-male erotic attraction at work in his version of the legend.

61. On this topic, see Frantzen, *Before the Closet*; on the manner in which Ælfric addresses the problem of pederasty in the monastery and marshals the love of a boy for specifically national and racialist ends, see my "Gregory's Boys: The Homoerotic Production of English Whiteness," in *Sex and Sexuality in Anglo-Saxon England*, ed. Carol Braun Pasternack and Lisa Weston (Tempe: MRTS, 2005).

62. "Gregorius ða of innweardre heortan langsume siccetunge teah. and cwæð; Wá la wá. þæt swa fægeres híwes menn. sindon ðam sweartan deofle underðeodde" (*Catholic Homilies*, 74).

63. Richard Dyer, "White," in *The Matter of Images: Essays on Representation* (New York: Routledge, 1993), 141.

64. As Frantzen rightly observes, Gregory's "curious" preference for the boys "strongly suggests that the anecdote originates with an English author whose views Gregory is made to express" (*Before the Closet*, 268).

65. While the first definition of "hiwe" in Bosworth-Toller is "form, fashion, appearance," I would argue that it is the second definition of "hue, color" that signifies here, given the positioning of the phrase "fægeres hiwes menn" in opposition to "sweartan deofle," in which "sweartan" signifies "swart, black, gloomy" (Bosworth-Toller, *Dictionary*, s.v. "hiwe"; "sweart").

66. *Sermones Catholici*, 1:456–57, 466.

67. *Sermones Catholici*, 2:160–61. See also the representation of an "atelic sceadu, on sweartum hiwe" in *Sermones Catholici*, 2:508–9.

68. See also Winthrop Jordan, *White over Black: American Attitudes toward the Negro, 1550–1812* (Chapel Hill: University of North Carolina Press, 1968), 24, 93–94; and Thomas Hahn, ed., *Race and Ethnicity in the Middle Ages*, special issue of *JMEMS* 31 (2001).

69. Dyer, "White," 142. See also *MR*; Jeffrey Burton Russell, *Lucifer: The Devil in the Middle Ages* (Ithaca:

Cornell University Press, 1984); Peter Dendle, *Satan Unbound: The Devil in Old English Narrative Literature* (Toronto: University of Toronto Press, 2001).

70. Genesis B, line 487 (George Philip Krapp, ed., *The Junius Manuscript* [New York: Columbia University Press, 1931], 18); George Philip Krapp and Elliott Van Kirk Dobbie, eds., *The Exeter Book* (New York: Columbia University Press, 1936), 122; both references are cited by Pelteret in *Slavery,* 52 nn. 10 and 13. Mary Clayton and Hugh Magennis, eds., *The Old English Lives of St. Margaret* (Cambridge: Cambridge University Press, 1994), 162–63; see also 122–25. I would like to thank Carol Braun Pasternack for this reference.

71. Krapp and Elliott, *The Exeter Book,* 186; trans. W. S. Mackie in *The Exeter Book, Part II: Poems IX–XXXII* (London: K. Paul, Trench, Trubner, 1934), 101–3; cited and discussed in Pelteret, *Slavery,* 51–52.

72. "'Heu, pro dolor!' inquit quod tam lucidi uultus homines tenebrarum auctor possidet, tantaque gratia frontispicii mentem ab interna gratia uacuam gestat" (*EH,* 132–33).

73. *Gregor,* 106.

74. While Ælfric's sources employ a light-dark binary to describe the youths and Satan, whereby the latter's status as the author of darkness opposes the fair forms and bright faces of the slaves, Ælfric uses a racialist color polarity, in which the devil's swarthiness or blackness opposes the fair color of the Englishmen (*EH,* 132; Miller, *Old English,* 96; *Gregor,* 106). See also Pelteret, "Slave Raiding."

75. Henry Louis Gates Jr., *The Signifying Monkey: A Theory of Afro-American Literary Criticism* (New York: Oxford University Press, 1988), 237; Dyer, "White," 47.

76. Augustine of Hippo, *On Christian Doctrine,* trans. D. W. Robertson (New York: Bobbs-Merrill, 1958), bk. 2. On poststructuralism and Augustine's semiotics, see Eugene Vance, *Mervelous Signals: Poetics and Sign Theory in the Middle Ages* (Lincoln: University of Nebraska Press, 1986).

77. "Eft hé axode hu ðære ðeode nama wære. þe hí of comon; Him wæs geandwyrd. ðæt hí angle genemnode wæron; Þa cwæð he. rihtlice hí sind Angle gehátene. for ðan ðe hí engla wlite habbað. and swilcum gedafenað þæt hí on heofonum engla geferan beon; Gyt ða / Gregorius befrán. hu ðære scire nama wære. þe ða cnapan of alædde wæron; Him man sæde. þæt ða scírmen wæron dere gehatene; Gregorius andwyrde. Wel hi sind dere gehatene. for ðan ðe hi sind fram graman generode. and / to cristes mildheortnysse gecygede; Gyt ða he gefrán. Hu is ðære leode cyning gehaten? Him wæs geandsward þæt se cyning Ælle gehátten wære; Hwæt ða Gregorius gamenode mid his wordum to ðam naman. and cwæð; Hit gedafenað þæt alleluia sy gesungen on ðam lande. to lofe þæs ælmihtigan scyppendes" (*Catholic Homilies,* 74).

78. *Ibid.* As Wormald has suggested, Gregory actually may have been responsible for the construction of a unified "English" identity for the Angles, Saxons, and other peoples living in England: the pope did in his letters refer to his missionary objects in the whole of England to be a "gens Anglorum," despite the island's heterogeneous population (*Gregorii Registrum,* cited in Wormald, "Bede," 124 n. 109). If this is the case, Gregory's misrecognition of the English as such offers a remarkable instance of how the imperialistic conversion impulses of the Roman church inadvertently contributed to the production of national identity during the Anglo-Saxon period.

79. Karen Jolly, *Popular Religion in Late Saxon England: Elf Charms in Context* (Chapel Hill: University of North Carolina Press, 1996), 39–40; Farmer, "Progress." This is not to say that a wholesale turn to paganism had occurred in the north. A popular Christian piety existed side by side with pagan belief in those areas under Danelaw (see Jolly, *Popular Religion,* 39–40). See Banton, "Monastic Reform," on the possibility that the reform actually reached Northumbria.

80. Peter Clemoes, "Late Old English Literature," in *Tenth-Century Studies,* ed. Parsons, 105.

81. "Maran cyððe habbað englas to Gode þonne men" (*Sermones Catholici,* 1:10).

82. Massimo Cacciari, *The Necessary Angel,* trans. Miguel E. Vatter (Albany: State University of New York Press, 1994), 1.

83. Albert S. Cook, ed., *The Christ of Cynewulf* (Boston: Ginn, 1900), 39; trans. Charles W. Kennedy in *The Poems of Cynewulf* (New York: Peter Smith, 1949), 183.

84. "hí nabbað nænne lichaman, ac hí sindon ealle gastas swiðe strange and mihtige and wlitige, on micelre fægernysse gesceapene, to lofe and to wurðmynte heora Scyppende" (*Sermones Catholici,* 1:10–11).

85. Cook, ed., *Christ,* 39; trans. Kennedy, *Cynewulf,* 183. Bosworth-Toller (*Anglo-Saxon Dictionary,* s.v. "fægernes") defines "fægernes" as fairness or beauty.

86. British Library Cotton Vespasian A.viii fol. 2v, depicted in Richard Gameson, *The Role of Art in the Late Anglo-Saxon Church* (Oxford: Clarendon, 1995), plate 2a; Christopher D. Verey, T. Julian Brown, and Elizabeth Coatsworth, eds., *The Durham Gospels: Together with Fragments of a Gospel Book in Uncial, Durham, Cathedral Library MS A II.17* (Copenhagen: Rosenkilde and Bagger, 1980), plate II.

87. See C. R. Dodwell and Peter Clemoes, eds., *The Old English Illustrated Hexateuch: British Museum Cotton Claudius B. IV* (Copenhagen: Rosenkilde and Bagger, 1974), 17.

88. "engla and deofla . . . hwitra ond sweartra" (Cook, ed., *Christ,* 35; trans. Kennedy, *Cynewulf,* 180. Cited in Pelteret, *Slavery,* 52).

89. On puns in the Old English riddles, see the phonetic, syntactic, and semantic puns in the forty-fourth, fifty-eighth, and thirty-third Exeter riddles, respectively, in Nigel Barley, "Structural Aspects of the Anglo-Saxon Riddle," *Semiotica* 10.2 (1974): 171.

90. "Ða gelámp hit æt sumum sæle. swa swa gýt foroft deð" (*Catholic Homilies,* 74).

91. In contrast, Bede considerably downplays the story (Howe, *Migration,* 119 n. 3, and Wormald, "Bede," 124), as does Paul the Deacon to a lesser extent (*Gregor,* 106). While Bede's vernacular "translator" does qualify the legend as traditional, he allots it a more central role in his text (Miller, *Old English Bede,* 96). The important role played by the tale in both the Old English Bede and Ælfric's *Catholic Homilies* demonstrates how the monk's national and vernacular preoccupations reflect an investment in England and Englishness that originates with King Alfred's vernacular projects (see Clemoes, "Late Old English Literature," 104–5).

92. *Catholic Homilies,* 72; Cf. *Gregor,* 98.

93. Cf. *Catholic Homilies,* 73; *Gregor,* 99.

94. "Gregorious eode be ðære stræt to ðam engliscum mannum heora ðing *sceawigende*" (*Catholic Homilies,* 74, my emphasis). Cf. Miller, *Old English Bede,* 96; *Gregor,* 106; and *EH,* 132.

95. *Catholic Homilies,* 73.

96. "and hi on godes geleafan ðeonde ðurhwunodon. oð ðisum dægðerlicum dæge" (*Catholic Homilies,* 80).

97. *An English-Saxon Homily on the Birth-day of St. Gregory, Anciently used in the English-Saxon Church, Giving an Account of the Conversion of the English from Paganism to Christianity,* trans. and ed. Elizabeth Elstob (London: William Bowyer, 1709). See also Frantzen, *Desire,* 60.

98. Elstob, *Anglo-Saxon Homily,* xi–xiii.

99. See also the notes to Elstob's edition, where she writes that "sweartan deofle" is "word for word the *Black Devil,* the *Saxon* phrase for the Prince of Darkness" (ibid., 12).

## 2. Gerald de Barri and the Geography of Ireland's Conquest

1. See Catherine Delano-Smith and Roger J. P. Kain, *English Maps: A History* (London: British Library, 1999), 8–12.

2. "From the turn into the twelfth century," as Delano-Smith and Kain phrase it with regard to map production, "the situation changes radically" (ibid., 12). Of course, assessments of mapmaking based upon extant evidence are always uncertain; the possibility remains that maps continued to be made between the appearance of the Cotton and later maps on record.

3. The writer traditionally has been referred to as Gerald of Wales. On the manner in which the name "Gerald of Wales" misrepresents the variety of allegiances Gerald de Barri bore during his complicated and contradictory career, see John Gillingham, *The English in the Twelfth Century* (Woodbridge: Boydell, 2000), 154–55. On the Duchy of Cornwall fragment, see Graham Haslam, "The Duchy of Cornwall Map Fragment," in *Géographie du Monde au Moyen Age et à la Renaissance,* ed. Monique Pelletier (Paris: Editions du C.T.H.S., 1989,), 33–44; on the Sawley map, see P. D. A. Harvey, "The Sawley Map and Other World Maps in Twelfth-Century England," *Imago Mundi* 49 (1997): 33–42; on the Vercelli map, see Anna-Dorothee von Den Brincken, "Monumental Legends on Medieval Manuscript Maps: Notes on Designed Capital Letters on Maps of Large Size," *Imago Mundi* 42 (1990): 9–25; and Carlo Capello, *Il mappamondo medioevale di Vercelli, 1191–1218?* (Turin: Università di Torino, 1976); on the map at Lincoln Cathedral, see *GCO,* 7:165–71; and R. M. Thomson, *Catalogue of the Manuscripts of Lincoln Cathedral Chapter Library* (Cambridge: Brewer, 1988), plate 3; on the Durham Cathedral Priory map, see *Catalogi veteres librorum ecclesiae cathedralis Dunelm,* ed. Beriah Botfield, Surtees Society, vol. 7 (London, J. B. Nichols and Son, 1838) 118–19.

4. Additional thirteenth-century (and twelfth-century) English world maps are listed in the chronological list (appendix 18.2) in *HC.* On the links between thirteenth-century mappae mundi and the English monarchy, see Daniel Birkholz, *The King's Two Maps: Cartography and Culture in Thirteenth-Century England* (New York: Routledge, 2004).

5. Among the maps firmly placed in this group and those whose relation is more tenuous, are the Duchy

of Cornwall fragment, the Psalter map, and the maps of Hereford, Vercelli, Sawley, and Ebstorf. See Anna-Dorothee Von Den Brincken, "Mappamundi und Chronographia," *Deutsches Archiv für Erforschung des Mittelalters* 24 (1968): 161–74; David Woodward, "Medieval mappaemundi," in *HC,* 306–12; and P. D. A. Harvey, *Medieval Maps* (Toronto: University of Toronto Press, 1991), 19–37.

6. Robert Bartlett, *England under the Norman and Angevin Kings, 1075–1225* (Oxford: Clarendon Press, 2000), 102.

7. On the term "Angevin Empire" and its coining by Kate Norgate, see John Gillingham, *The Angevin Empire* (London: Arnold, 2001), 2–5.

8. Elizabeth Salter, *English and International Studies in the Literature, Art, and Patronage of Medieval England,* ed. Derek Pearsall and Nicolette Zeeman (Cambridge: Cambridge University Press, 1988), 18. On classical Greek cosmopolitanism and its practical limits, see Robert Fine and Robin Cohen, "Four Cosmopolitanism Moments," in *Conceiving Cosmopolitanism: Theory, Context, and Practice,* ed. Steven Vertovec and Robin Cohen (Oxford: Oxford University Press, 2002), 136–39.

9. *ER,* 124–25. On authorship and provenance, see Scott Westrem, *The Hereford Map: A Transcription and Translation of the Legends with Commentary* (Turnhout: Brepols, 2001), xviii–xxvii.

10. Salter, *English,* 8.

11. On Gervase's career and connection to the Ebstorf map, see *Otia Imperialia: Recreation for an Emperor,* ed. and trans. S. E. Banks and J. W. Binns (Oxford: Clarendon Press, 2002), xxv–xxxviii; and Jörg-Geerd Arentzen, *Imago Mundi Cartographica: Studien zur Bildlichkeit mittelalterlicher Weltund Ökumenekarten unter besonderer Berücksichtigung des Zusammenwirkens von Text und Bild* (Munich: Wilhelm Fink, 1984), 140.

12. Salter, *English,* 6–7.

13. Pliny the Elder, *Natural History,* ed. and trans. H. Rackham (Cambridge: Harvard University Press, 1938) 2:196–97.

14. Isidore of Seville, *Isidori Hispalensis Episcopi Etymologiarum sive Originum libri XX,* ed. W. M. Lindsay (London: Oxford University Press, 1985), XIV.vi.

15. *Pauli Orosii, Historiarvm adversvm paganos libri VII,* ed. Karl Friedrich Wilhelm Zangemeister (Lipsiae: In Aedibvs B. G. Tevbneri, 1889), 12; trans. Roy J. Deferrari in Paulus Orosius, *The Seven Books of History against the Pagans* (Washington: Catholic University of America Press, 1964), 16; Theodor Mommsen, ed., *C. Iulii Solini Collectanea Rerum Memorabilium* (Berlin: Raabe, 1895), 101–2; trans. Arthur Golding in *The Excellent and Pleasant Worke. Collectanea Rerum Memorabilium,* 1587, Facsimile reproduction by George Kish (Gainesville: Scholars' Facsimiles and Reprints, 1955), chap. 34; *EH,* 18–19.

16. Adrian Hastings, *The Construction of Nationhood: Ethnicity, Religion, and Nationalism* (Cambridge: Cambridge University Press, 1997), 44.

17. Salter, *English,* 6; Richard Southern, "Aspects of the European Tradition of Historical Writing: 4, The Sense of the Past," *TRHS,* 5th ser. 23 (1973): 243–63; Gillingham, *English,* 113–23.

18. Robert M. Stein, "Making History English: Cultural Identity and Historical Explanation in William of Malmesbury and Lagamon's *Brut,"* in *Text and Territory: Geographical Information in the European Middle Ages,* ed. Sylvia Tomasch and Sealy Gilles (Philadelphia: University of Pennsylvania Press, 1998), 97–115.

19. William of Malmesbury, *Gesta regum Anglorum: History of the Kings of England,* trans. R. A. B. Mynors, completed by R. M. Thompson and M. Winterbottom (Oxford: Clarendon Press, 1998–99), 386–87. Further page references to this edition will appear in the text.

20. *English Historical Documents, 1189–1327,* ed. H. Rothwell (London: Eyre & Spottiswoode, 1975), 998.

21. Salter, *English,* 6–7; *ER,* 173–75; Susan Reynolds, *Kingdoms and Communities in Western Europe, 900–1300,* 2nd ed. (Oxford: Clarendon Press, 1997), 267–70. See also Hastings, *Construction,* 44; and Gillingham, *English.*

22. Territories closer to home further undermined the singular geographic identity of the English. As the Sawley map attests, the very island occupied by the English also delimits the regions and nations of the Celtic fringe of *Scotia* (Scotland), *Walni* (Wales) and *Cornu* (Cornwall).

23. Textual sources such as Solinus and Adam of Bremen and, before them, Pliny, single Thule out as the most remote of islands. See Adam of Bremen, *History of the Archbishops of Hamburg-Bremen,* trans. Francis J. Tschan (New York: Columbia University Press, 1959), 4:xxxvi, 216–18; Pliny, *Natural History,* 4:198–99.

24. *Historiarum adversum paganos libri VII,* 12; *Seven Books,* 16.

25. Pliny, *Natural History,* 4:198–99.

26. On the dating and manuscript history of Gerald's Irish books, see Robert Bartlett, *Gerald of Wales, 1146–1223* (Oxford: Clarendon Press, 1982), 213–16.

27. Not only had his studies taken him as far east as Paris; his royal service had led him as far west as Ireland (Bartlett, *Gerald,* 11–12).

28. Ibid, 58.

29. Gillingham, *English,* xxi. Later in his career, which was marked by repeated efforts to restore metropolitan status to the church in Wales, Gerald would turn distinctly anti-English. For arguments that Gerald's Irish books are indeed anti-English or, more specifically, register Gerald's animosity toward Henry II, see Rhonda Knight, "Procreative Sodomy: Textuality and the Construction of Ethnicities in Gerald of Wales's *Descriptio Kambriae,*" *Exemplaria* 14.1 (2002): 57–58; and David Rollo, "Gerald of Wales' *Topographia Hibernica:* Sex and the Irish Nation," *Romanic Review* 86 (1995): 169–90. To be sure, as Robert Bartlett puts it, "Gerald's association with the Marchers of Wales and, especially those who invaded Ireland, had occasionally led to criticisms of royal policies," but as Bartlett also points out, during his years of royal service Gerald explicitly sought the favor of English kings (*Gerald,* 25, 58). It is this open support of English causes that makes Gerald appropriate for my analysis.

30. Harvey, "Sawley Map," 40.

31. " . . . in occiduis et extremis terrarum finibus natura reposuit. Quos ultra fines nec terra subsistit, nec hominum vel ferarum habitatio est ulla: sed trans omnem horizontem in infinitum per investigabiles et occultas vias solus oceanus circumfertur et evagatur." Gerald de Barri, *Topographia Hibernica,* in *GCO,* 5:20; trans. John O'Meara in *The History and Topography of Ireland* (London: Penguin, 1982), 31. Further citations of the *Topographia* appear in the text by distinction and chapter number of the Latin, followed by the page number in O'Meara's translation, which I employ with slight modifications.

32. Oxford, Bodleian MS Rawlinson B 512, fol. 97r.b 14–23; cited by Benjamin Hudson, in "Time Is Short: The Eschatology of the Early Gaelic Church," in *Last Things: Death and the Apocalypse in the Middle Ages,* ed. Caroline Walker Bynum and Paul Freedman (Philadelphia: University of Pennsylvania Press, 2000), 106. On medieval Irish nationhood, see James F. Lydon, "Nation and Race in Medieval Ireland," in *Concepts of National Identity in the Middle Ages,* ed. Simon Forde, Lesley Johnson, and Alan V. Murray (Leeds: University of Leeds Printing Services, 1995), 103–24; James Lydon, "The Middle Nation," in *The English in Medieval Ireland,* ed. idem (Dublin: Royal Irish Academy, 1984), 1–26; Hastings, *Construction,* 67; and Donnchadh Ó Corráin, "Nationality and Kingship in Pre-Norman Ireland," in *Nationality and the Pursuit of National Independence,* ed. T. W. Moody (Belfast: Appletree Press, 1978), 1–35.

33. Antonia Gransden, *Historical Writing in England, c.550 to c. 1307* (Ithaca: Cornell University Press, 1974), 68. On Bede's colossal influence, see also idem, "Prologues in the Historiography of Twelfth-Century England," in *England in the Twelfth Century,* ed. Daniel Williams (Woodbridge: Boydell, 1990), 55–81; and Nancy F. Partner, *Serious Entertainments: The Writing of History in Twelfth-Century England* (Chicago: University of Chicago Press, 1977), 5.

34. James S. Romm, *The Edges of the Earth in Ancient Thought: Geography, Exploration, and Fiction* (Princeton: Princeton University Press, 1992), 65.

35. "Hibernia autem et latitudine sui status et salubritate ac serenitate aerum multum Brittaniae praestat" (*EH,* 18–19).

36. On the Petrine ties of the early Irish church and Bede's representation of a "Celtic church" divergent from Rome, see Patrick Wormald, "The Venerable Bede and the 'Church of the English,'" in *The English Religious Tradition and the Genius of Anglicanism,* ed. Geoffrey Rowell (Nashville: Abingdon Press, 1992), 13–32.

37. "Misit idem papa Honorius litteras etiam genti Scottorum . . . sollerter exhortans ne paucitatem suam in extremis terrae finibus constitutam sapientiorem antiquis siue modernis, quae per orbem erant, Christi ecclesiis aestimarent, neue . . . aliud pascha celebrarent" (*EH,* 198–99).

38. Cf. the emphasis placed on Easter and the inclusion of mappae mundi in computus texts, one of the most influential of which was written by Bede. See *MTS.*

39. "utpote quibus longe ultra orbem positis nemo synodalia paschalis obseruantiae decreta porrexerat" (*EH,* 224–25).

40. "Nihil enim huius mundi quaerere, nil amare curabat. . . . Discurrere per cuncta et urbana et rustica loca non equorum dorso sed pedum" (*EH,* 226–27).

41. "Qui in insula Lindisfarnensi fecit ecclesiam episcopali sedi congruam, quam tamen more Scotto-

rum non de lapide sed de robore secto totam conposuit atque harundine texit" (*EH*, 294–95). *Scotti* in Bede (and in the work of later chroniclers) refers to the Irish people.

42. *MI*, 50.

43. The English saints Egbert and Chad spend their youth in Ireland "monachicam in orationibus et continentia et meditatione diuinarum scripturarum uitam sedulous agebat" (*EH*, 344–45).

44. ". . . Ecgberct, quem in Hibernia insula peregrinam ducere uitam pro adipiscenda in caelis patria retulimus . . ." (*EH*, 474–77). This is not to say that Bede was a proponent of the extremes to which the austerity of the Irish could lead. A member of the monastery at Jarrow founded by Benedict Biscop, Bede inherited a monastic lifestyle that emphasized ascetic moderation. Benedict Biscop evidently was determined, as Peter Hunter Blair points out, that Jarrow and his other "foundations in Northumbria should not be mere retreats for asceticism and the waging of holy warfare, but should also be seed beds for intellectual growth" (*The World of Bede* [New York: St. Martin's, 1970], 123). That said, Bede clearly appreciated the otherworldliness of his counterparts west of Britain. With his appreciative accounts of Irish saints such as Finan, Aidan, and Columba, "Bede has done more than anyone," as Patrick Wormald writes, "to make these 'Celtic' saints lovable" ("Venerable Bede," 16).

45. ". . . petens ut sibi mitteretur antistes, cuius doctrina ac ministerio gens quam regebat Anglorum dominicae fidei et dona disceret et susciperet sacramenta" (*EH*, 218–19).

46. "Exin coepere plures per dies de Scottorum regione uenire Brittaniam atque illis Anglorum prouinciis, quibus regnauit Osuald . . . Nam monachi errant maxime, qui ad praedicandum uenerant" (*EH*, 220–21).

47. "Huius igitur antistitis doctrina rex Osuald cum ea, cui praeerat, gente Anglorum institutus, non solum / incognita progenitoribus suis regna caelorum sperare didicit" (*EH*, 230–31).

48. Blair, *World*, 19–20; Gransden, *Historical Writing*, 19.

49. *EH*, 228–29. While the success of Aidan's mission qualifies the assessment of the first, failed evangelist regarding the English's intractability, it does not utterly undo the damage wrought by his assertion of it. The English whom Aidan encounters are still *barbarus* insofar as they are an *incredulos* (unbelieving) and *indoctos* (ignorant) people.

50. That Irish missionary expansionism was no thing of the past. The "dynamism within the Irish church" during the twelfth century was such that Irish religious were founding Christian congregations on the continent, first through a monastery at Regensburg and then at Würzburg, Erfurt, Nuremberg, Constance, Vienna and Eichstätt, Memmingen (in Bavaria), and Kiev. See F. X. Martin, "Diarmait Mac Murchada and the Coming of the Anglo-Normans," in *A New History of Ireland, II. Medieval Ireland, 1169–1534*, ed. Art Cosgrove (Oxford: Clarendon, 1987), 56.

51. "Hibernia insula sanctorum sanctis et mirabilibus perplurimis sullimiter plena habetur." John of Worcester, *The Chronicle of John of Worcester*, ed. R. R. Darlington and P. McGurk, trans. Jennifer Bray and P. McGurk (Oxford: Clarendon Press, 1995), 2:124–25. Worcester is citing the third book of the *Chronicon* of Marianus Scottus.

52. "mirabili igitur dono Deus hanc ditauit insulam, multitudinemque sanctorum ad eius tuitionem in ea constituit" (Henry, Archdeacon of Huntingdon, *Historia Anglorum: The History of the English People*, trans. Diana Greenway [Oxford: Clarendon Press, 1996], 28–29).

53. Malmesbury, 76–77. "Crescebat igitur fides monachisque uenientibus de Scotia feruenter docebatur" (*Historia*, 188–89).

54. On English representations of the Irish from the time of the conquest onward, see Elizabeth L. Rambo, *Colonial Ireland in Medieval English Literature* (Selinsgrove, PA: Susquehanna University Press, 1994).

55. "Huius igitur antistitis doctrina rex Osuald cum ea . . . regna terrarum plus quam ulli maiorum suorum ab eodem uno Deo, qui fecit caelum et terram, consecutus est; denique omnes nationes et prouincias Britanniae, quae in quattuor linguas, id est Brettonum Pictorum Scottorum et Anglorum diuisae sunt in dicione accepit" (*EH*, 230–31).

56. "Cum rex Oswaldus singulari potentia prouincias omnes Anglorum, Britonum, Pictorum, Scotorum in dicionem accepisset . . ." (*Historia*, 628–31; cf. 190–91).

57. Malmesbury, *Gesta*, 71; Roger of Wendover, *Flores Historiarum*, as found in vol. 1 of *Matthaei Parisiensis, Chronica Majora*, ed. Henry Richards Luard, RS 57 (London: Longman, 1872), 281.

58. "Quanti enim ualeret Hibernia si non annauigarent merces ex Anglia?" (*Gesta*, 738–39).

59. For a succinct and balanced account of the invasion and its medieval aftermath, see Seán Duffy, *Ireland in the Middle Ages* (New York: St. Martin's Press, 1997).

60. In Duffy's words, "The English invasion and long drawn-out conquest was, most scholars would argue, the most important development in Irish secular affairs during the Middle Ages" (ibid., 2).

61. Apologists of the conquest were by no means the first to describe the Irish as barbaric. See *Gildas, The Ruin of Britain,* secs. 14.1 and 16.1; cited in Rambo, *Colonial Ireland,* 27; and *Bernard of Clairvaux's Life of St Malachy of Armagh,* trans. and ed. H. J. Lawlor (London, 1920), 37, cited and discussed in Martin, "Diarmait Mac Murchada," 59–60.

62. "Per idem tempus rex Anglorum Henricus, nuncios solennes Romam mittens, rogavit Papam Adrianum, ut sibi liceret Hyberniae insulam hostiliter intrare, et terram subjugare, atque homines illos bestiales ad fidem et viam reducere veritatis, exstirpatis ibi plantariis vitiorum" (*Chronica Majora,* 2.210); Roger of Wendover, *Flowers of History,* trans. J. A. Gildes (London: Henry G. Bohn, 1849), 1:528.

63. Giraldus Cambrensis, *Expugnatio Hibernica: The Conquest of Ireland by Giraldus Cambrensis,* ed. and trans. A. B. Scott and F. X. Martin (Dublin: Royal Irish Academy, 1978), 22–23. Future page references to this edition will appear in the text. With slight variations, I employ Scott and Martin's translation.

64. See Bartlett, *Gerald,* 158–77; and Gillingham, *English,* 145–62.

65. Gillingham, *English,* 145.

66. Bartlett, *Gerald,* 177.

67. Gillingham, *English,* 158.

68. Jeffrey Jerome Cohen, "Hybrids, Monsters, Borderlands: The Bodies of Gerald of Wales," in *The Postcolonial Middle Ages,* ed. idem (New York: Palgrave, 2001), 87. Cohen refers here specifically to Gerald de Barri's construction of Wales as the object of English conquest.

69. Recent scholarship complicating the traditional view that England brought civilization to Ireland includes Duffy, *Ireland;* Keith D. Lilley, "'Non urbe, non vico, non castris': Territorial Control and the Colonization and Urbanization of Wales and Ireland under Anglo-Norman Lordship," *Journal of Historical Geography* 26 (2000): 517–31; and Anngret Simms, "Core and Periphery in Medieval Europe: The Irish Experience in a Wider Context," in *Common Ground: Essays on the Historical Geography of Ireland,* ed. William J. Smyth and Kevin Whelan (Cork: Cork University Press, 1988).

70. Bartlett, *Gerald,* 177.

71. *Topographia,* 1.28; *History,* 50; "sed hoc stupore dignum occurrit, quod nihil venenosum aliunde advectum unquam continere vel potuit vel potest" (*Topographia,* 1.29; *History,* 51).

72. "Aeris quoque clementia tanta est, ut nec nebula inficiens, nec spiritus hic pestilens, nec aura corrumpens" (*Topographia,* 1.33; *History,* 53).

73. "Fons venenorum ebullit in oriente. Quantoque remotius ab origine derivatur, tanto naturalis efficaciae vim minorem exercet. Per tot igitur tantaque locorum interstitia longa derivatione paulatim deficiens, in his tandem extremitatibus venenosus vigor prorsus evanuit. Sol quanto in remotiores a zodiaco partes radios mittit, minorem in subjecta vim caloris exercet" (*Topographia,* 1.39; *History,* 56).

74. Mary B. Campbell, *The Witness and the Other World: Exotic European Travel Writing, 400–1600* (Ithaca: Cornell University Press, 1988), 63 n 10.

75. Ibid.

76. *MR,* 35.

77. Pliny, *Natural History,* 1:320–23; cited in *MR,* 52.

78. *MR,* 53.

79. "omnia quidem elementa, licet ad usum hominum creata, miseris ibi mortalibus mortem interminando" (*Topographia,* 1.35; *History,* 54).

80. A graphic version of Gerald's production of the Irish border of the West as the utter opposite of an impure East would emerge in the Hereford map. With its representation of the most dangerous of serpents (i.e., dragons) on the southeastern border of the world in Sri Lanka (and hence the territory farthest from Ireland), the map visually supports the wholesome and untainted status of Ireland.

81. Tomaz Mastnak, *Crusading Peace: Christendom, the Muslim World, and Western Political Order* (Berkeley: University of California Press, 2002), 117.

82. Ibid., 127. See also Penny J. Cole, "'O God, the heathen have come into your inheritance' (Ps. 78.I): The Theme of Religious Pollution in Crusade Documents, 1095–1188," in *Crusaders and Muslims in Twelfth Century Syria,* ed. M. Shatzmiller (Leiden: E. J. Brill, 1993).

83. *MR,* 51.

84. Pliny, *Natural History,* 1:320–23; cited in *MR,* 52.

85. *Topographia,* 2.23–24; *History,* 75–76; *Topographia* 3.25, *History,* 110. See also *Topographia,* 2.21. The

interrelationship of sexuality, colonialism, and ethnicity in Gerald's works has received much attention of late. See Rollo, "Gerald"; Knight, "Procreative Sodomy"; and Rhonda Knight, "Werewolves, Monsters, and Miracles: Representing Colonial Fantasies in Gerald of Wales's *Topographia Hibernica*," *Studies in Iconography* 22 (2001): 55–86. For a look at the interplay of monstrous peoples, world geography, and the geography of the manuscripts of Gerald's *Topography,* see Asa Simon Mittman, "The Other Close at Hand: Gerald of Wales and the 'Marvels of the West,'" in *The Monstrous Middle Ages,* ed. Bettina Bildhauer and Robert Mills (Cardiff: University of Wales Press, 2003), 97–112. An essay that came to my attention after the completion of this chapter, Mittman's piece similarly points out Gerald's strategy of using Ireland to construct the centrality of Britain.

86. Homi K. Bhabha, *The Location of Culture* (London: Routledge, 1994), 82.

87. Ibid.

88. "Sanctus igitur Keivinus, quadragesimali quodam tempore hominum frequentiam ex consuetudine fugiens, solitudine quadam, tugurio modico, quo sole tantum et pluvia defenderetur" (*Topographia,* 2.28; *History,* 78); "abstinentiae quoque et parcimoniae civorum non mediocriter" (*Topographia,* 3.27; *History,* 112).

89. *Topographia,* 3.28; *History,* 112; *Topographia,* 3.30; *History,* 115. Gerald of course often criticized monks, usually owing to adverse personal experiences with them. However, a more communal slight partly motivates the representation of monasticism in the *Topographia,* namely a war of words Gerald engaged in on behalf of the clergymen who had entered Ireland under the auspices of its new English lord. See *De rebus a se gestis, GCO,* 2:13–16, trans. *The Autobiography of Giraldus Cambrensis,* ed. and trans. H. E. Butler (London: Cape, 1937), 91–96. Further citations of the *De rebus* appear in the text by page number in the Rolls Series edition followed by the page number in Butler's translation. At a gathering of the suffragans of the province of Dublin, the abbot of Baltinglass, Ailbe Ua Maelmuige, delivered a sermon on clerical incontinence. The Irish abbot asserts the cleanliness of the Irish clergy until their infection by a sexually illicit foreign religious, since "he who touches pitch shall be defiled thereby" (*De Rebus,* 13; *Autobiography,* 91). In this counter-narrative to the official English imperial discourse of the conquest, the supposedly superior invaders in fact corrupt the native inhabitants. In order to turn the tables on Albinus's elevation of the Irish over the new clergy, Gerald delivers a sermon on the Irish religious' "vices and excesses" (15, 96). It was shortly after this experience in Ireland that Gerald completed his *Topographia,* which applies the logic of purity and danger to the Irish laity and their land, and, as we will see, reinterprets Ireland's venerable monastic tradition as a key contributor to the filthy behaviors of the Irish people. That much of Gerald's account of the Irish clergy in the *Topographia* is taken from the sermon he delivered in Dublin shows how that text revises notions of Irish religious purity that not only had been memorialized by Bede and other writers but also had currency even after the conquest.

90. "Sed cum a convictu mores formentur, quoniam a communi terrarum orbe in his extremitatibus, tanquam in orbe quodam altero, sunt tam remoti, et a modestis et morigeratis populis tam segregati, solam nimirum barbariem in qua et nati sunt et nutriti sapiunt et assuescunt, et tanquam alteram naturam amplectuntur" (*Topographia,* 3.10; *History,* 102–3).

91. ". . . gens a primo pastoralis vitae vivendi modo non recedens. Cum enim a silvis ad agros, ab agris ad villas, civiumque convictus, humani generis ordo processerit, gens haec, agriculturae labores aspernans, et civiles gazas parum affectans, civiumque jura multum detrectans, in silvis et pascuis vitam quam hactenus assueverat nec desuescere novit nec descire" (*Topographia,* 3.10, *History,* 101–2).

92. "A monachorum malitia, libera nos, Domine." Gerald de Barri, *Symbolum electorum,* Epist. XXVIII; *De rebus,* 298; *Autobiography,* 143.

93. *MR,* 30.

94. *MR,* 30–31.

95. David Nicholas, *The Growth of the Medieval City: From Late Antiquity to the Early Fourteenth Century* (London: Longman, 1997), 90.

96. Ibid., 178.

97. Colleen McDannell and Bernhard Lang, *Heaven: A History* (New Haven: Yale University Press, 1988), 69–80.

98. Warren Hollister, *Medieval Europe: A Short History* (New York: John Wiley and Sons, 1982), 155.

99. As Barbara H. Rosenwein and Lester K. Little point out, "by 1200, not only the intellectual future lay in the towns but also the future of religious life, whose uncompromised goal remained a literal imitation of the life led by the Apostles." "Social Meaning in the Monastic and Mendicant Spiritualities," *Past and Present* 63 (1974): 27.

100. "Cum enim fere omnes Hiberniae praelati de monasteriis in clerum electi sint, quae monachi sunt

solicite complent omnia, quae vero clerici vel praelati fere praetermittunt universa. Sui enim tantum curam agentes, et tanquam sibi soliciti, pro grege commisso solicitari negligenter omittunt et postponunt" (*Topographia,* 3.29; *History,* 113).

101. Bipartiti ergo hujusmodi praelati quaedam contrahant ex monacho, et quaedam ex clerico. Ex monacho contrahant columbinam simplicitatem, ex clerico vero *serpentiam* prudentiam" (*Topographia,* 3.30; *History,* 114, my emphasis).

102. "Unde accidit ut nec verbum Domini populo praedicent, nec scelera eorum eis annuntient, nec in grege commisso vel extirpent vitia, vel inserant virtutes" (*Topographia,* 3.28; *History,* 113).

103. "Gens enim haec gens spurcissima, gens vitiis involuntissima, gens omnium gentium in fidei rudimentis incultissima" (*Topographia,* 3.19; *History,* 106).

104. "Ad haec autem, quamvis tanto jam tempore in terra ista fundata fides adoleverit, in nonnullis tamen ejusdem angulis multi adhuc sunt non baptizati, et ad quos ex pastorali negligentia fidei nunquam doctrina pervenit" (*Topographia,* 3.26; *History,* 110).

105. "Cumque ab ipsis quaereretur, an Christiani et baptizati fuissent, responderunt de Christo se nihil hactenus vel audisse vel scivisse" (*Topographia,* 3.26; *History,* 111).

106. Bartlett, *Gerald,* 169.

107. "Silente igitur insula in conspectu regis, et tranquilla iam pace gaudente ecclesie Dei decus, Christique cultum, in partibus illis magnificandi ampliori desiderio rex accensus, totius cleri Hibernie concilium apud Cassiliam convocavit" (*Conquest,* 96–97).

108. "Ubi, [at Cashel] requisitis et auditis publice terre illius et gentis tam enormitatibus quam spurciciis" (*Conquest,* 96–97); "Ipsi namque regi magnifico tam ecclesia quam regnum Hibernie debent quicquid de bono pacis et incremento religionis hactenus est assecuta. Nam ante ipsius adventum in Hiberniam, multimoda malorum genera a multis retro temporibus ibidem emerserant, quae ipsius potencia et munere in desuetudinem abiere" (*Conquest,* 100–101).

109. *English Historical Documents, 1140–1189,* ed. David C. Douglas and George W. Greenway (London: Eyre and Spottiswoode, 1953), 956–59.

110. Lucianus, monk of St. Werburgh's Abbey, *Extracts from the ms. Liber Luciani de laude Cestrie, Written about the Year 1195,* ed. Margerie Venables Taylor (Edinburgh: Record Society, 1912), 52. Indeed, the Roman church enjoyed unprecedented power during the twelfth century. See Robert Bartlett, *The Making of Europe: Conquest, Colonization, and Cultural Change, 950–1350* (London: Penguin, 1993), 243; and Richard Mortimer, *Angevin England, 1154–1258* (Oxford: Blackwell, 1994), 69.

111. Gransden, "Realistic Observation," 30.

112. *English Historical Documents,* ed. Douglas and Greenway, 959.

113. Bartlett, *Gerald,* 3.

114. On the derivation of the map from a mappa mundi see G. R. Crone, *Royal Geographical Society Reproductions of Early Maps VII: Early Maps of the British Isles, A.D. 1000–A.D. 1579* (London: Royal Geographical Society, 1961), 7; Harvey, "Sawley Map," 40; Thomas O'Loughlin, "An Early Thirteenth-Century Map in Dublin: A Window into the World of Giraldus Cambrensis," *Imago Mundi* 51 (1999): 31–32.

115. A. B. Scott, "Introduction," in *Conquest,* xlvi. Scott argues that such factors as the dating of the manuscript to Gerald's active scholarly period, the unique presence of both illustrations and maps in that manuscript, and the evidence of several "improvements and corrections" in it made by no less than three contemporary hands all demonstrate how "this was a manuscript lovingly executed for Giraldus' own pleasure, then subsequently used to enter later additions and alterations" (ibid., lv). More recently, Thomas O'Loughlin has made a forceful case that, with regard to the Europe map in particular, "we can ascribe to Giraldus a central role in its creation" ("An Early Thirteenth-Century Map," 26).

116. O'Loughlin also points to the fact that Gerald never refers to the map in his Irish books and the map's presence in only one copy of the *Topographia* ("An Early Thirteenth-Century Map," 26).

117. Among the 99 folios that make up the codex, the *Topography* occupies folios 1–47 and the *Conquest* takes up folios 49–99. With its placement on the recto of folio 48, the map in N.L.I. 700 appears nearly at the center of the manuscript, just after the *Topography* and before the *Conquest.* See O'Loughlin, "An Early Thirteenth-Century Map."

118. "Significasti siquidem nobis, fili in Christo carissime . . ."; ". . . gratum et acceptum habemus ut pro . . ." (*Conquest,* 144–45); "viciorum restringendo decursu, pro corrigendis moribus et virtutibus inserendis, pro Christiane religionis augmento" (*Conquest,* 146–47). On the authenticity of the "much controverted *Laudabiliter,*" see Martin, "Diarmait Mac Murchada," 57–58.

119. *Conquest,* 142 n. 5.6. Breakspear, who assumed the papal seat from 1154 to 1159, was elevated in response to his successful management of the geographically isolated Scandinavian kingdoms of Denmark, Norway, and Sweden.

120. A ca. 1148 booklist from Lincoln Cathedral refers to a mappa mundi. Lincoln Cathedral Library, MS 1, fol. 2r, printed in *GCO,* 7:165–71. And, as P. D. A. Harvey has pointed out, "a further record from Lincoln is a note of books that . . . shows that William of Avalon, brother of the bishop of Lincoln, borrowed a *mappa mundi*" ("Sawley Map," 40). Gerald went to Lincoln in 1196 (*Topographia,* liii n. 2).

121. L. Bevan and H. W. Phillott, *Mediaeval Geography: An Essay in Illustration of the Hereford Mappa Mundi* (Amsterdam: Meridian, 1969), 13.

122. O'Loughlin, "An Early Thirteenth-Century Map," 28.

123. Woodward, "Medieval *mappaemundi,*" in *HC,* 336.

124. As O'Loughlin has demonstrated, the map indeed appears based on Roman itineraries ("An Early Thirteenth-Century Map").

125. Gerald of course recalls here Bede's emphasis on Ireland's divergence from Roman doctrine. On the connections between Rome and Irish clerics, see Martin, "Diarmait Mac Murchada," 54.

126. J. B. Harley, *The New Nature of Maps: Essays in the History of Cartography* (Baltimore: Johns Hopkins University Press, 2001), 86, 85.

127. The topic of Becket and Gerald's Irish books is dense and rich, meriting more attention than the scope of this chapter allows. For example, even as Henry's involvement in Becket's murder undercut his status as a pillar of the church, Becket's martyrdom itself suggested the superior identity of England's religious over their Irish counterparts. In Gerald's critique of the Irish clergy in the *Topography,* he notes that "all the saints of this country are confessors and there is not martyr," because "there was found no one in those parts to cement the foundations of the growing church with the shedding of his blood" ("Mirum itaque quod ubi gens crudelissima et sanguinis sitibunda, fides ab antiquo fundata et semper tepidissima, pro Christi ecclesia corona martyrii nulla. Non igitur inventus est in partibus istis, qui ecclesiae surgentis fundamenta sanguinis effusione coementaret," *Topographia,* 3.28; *History,* 113).

128. On the manner in which not only the map in N.L.I. 700 but also the two maps in BL Arundel MS 14 and BL Additional MS 33991 render Britain "for all intents and purposes, the Mainland," see Mittman, "The Other Close at Hand," 106–7.

129. Along similar lines, Gerald writes of the Becket ordeal that when the king learned of the arrival of two papal legates in Normandy to investigate him, Henry is "grieved" (*dolet*) on the one hand that "he should be suspected of a crime for which he was guiltless" (*Conquest,* 104–5) but nevertheless "immediately appeared before the Roman cardinals at Coutances, showing a degree of piety praiseworthy when seen in a prince" (*Conquest,* 108–9). Henry emerges here as the ever-compliant subject of the church, a man poised to perform the Roman religious reform asked of him. This is not to say that Henry always is a pious and upstanding Christian in Gerald's Irish texts (cf. *Conquest,* 124–33). But, as the failing that most challenged his imperial authority over the Irish, Henry's part in Becket's murder is suppressed in the *Conquest.*

130. Froissart's account of the Anglo-Irish knight Henry Chrystede offers an illuminating example of the performative nature of English civility. See Claire Sponsler, "The Captivity of Henry Chrystede: Froissart's *Chroniques,* Ireland, and Fourteenth-Century Nationalism," in *Imagining a Medieval English Nation,* ed. Kathy Lavezzo (Minneapolis: University of Minnesota Press, 2003), 304–39.

131. The only Angevin holding not represented in the map is Toulouse.

132. O'Loughlin, "An Early Thirteenth-Century Map," 33.

133. "cum a Pirenaeis montibus usque in occiduos et extremos borealis oceani fines, Alexander noster occidentalis, brachium extendisti" (*Topographia,* 3.47; *History,* 124). Along similar lines, at the same time that Gerald suppresses Henry's role in Becket's murder and the Roman aggression it suggests, he discloses his own animosity toward the Roman legates who investigate the king, writing of the Cardinals Albert and Theodinus whom the pope dispatched to England, that they "were generally held to be good and just men, and had been chosen in good faith for this mission, *but for all that they were Romans.* They were sternly threatening to lay an interdict on his whole kingdom and all the lands subject to his jurisdiction, unless the king quickly came to meet them" (*Conquest,* 102–5, my emphasis). The legate's threat reflects how the twelfth century witnessed a reemergence within the high medieval church of the imperialism of ancient Rome. Namely, the aftermath of the investiture controversy of the eleventh century entailed the creation during the twelfth century of a papacy claiming supreme jurisdictional authority, a territorial supremacy the legate's interdict invokes.

134. Cf. William of Newburg's account of the conquest in his *History of the Kings of England* (1198), which stresses that it "is a singular fact with regard to" Ireland that while "Ireland (though the Romans had dominion even over the Orkney Isles), being difficult of access, and seldom and only slightly assailed by any nation in war, was never attacked and subdued, never subject to foreign control" until 1171, the year "of the reign of Henry II, king of England." William of Newburgh, *Historia Rerum Anglicarum,* in *Chronicles of the Reigns of Stephen, Henry II, and Richard I,* ed. Richard Howlett, RS 82 (London: Longman, 1884), 1:166; *The History of William of Newburgh,* trans. Joseph Stevenson (London: Seeleys, 1856), 481–82. As a territory that was "never disturbed," even by Caesar himself, Ireland emerges in William's chronicle as a jewel in Henry's imperial crown. By taking Ireland, Henry reaches an imperial height above even that of the Roman emperors.

135. In other words, not only did the Irish become—as M. T. Clanchy has noted—"scapegoats for Becket's murder," they also became scapegoats for the ancient British lawlessness that Henry's crime evoked (*ER,* 89).

136. Bartlett, *Gerald,* 25.

137. On Gerald's contradictory self-identifications, see Gillingham, *English,* 154–57; Bartlett, *Gerald,* 12–25; Cohen, "Hybrids," 85–104; and Knight, "Procreative Sodomy," 47–77. For a book-length analysis of high medieval border writing, see Michelle Warren, *History on the Edge: Excaliber and the Borders of Britain, 1100–1300* (Minneapolis: University of Minnesota Press, 2000).

### 3. Locating England in the *Polychronicon*

1. Some fifty years after the making of the Ramsey Abbey map, an anonymous cartographer would offer an even larger and more detailed representation of England in the Evesham mappa mundi, which I examine in the introduction.

2. The cities that appear in *Anglia* on the map are London, Durham, Lincoln, York, Nottingham, Worcester, Gloucester, Bristol, Cornub (?), Exeter, Winchester, Oxford, Northampton, Stanford (from the transcription of the Ramsey Abbey map by Konrad Miller in *Mappaemundi: Die ältesten Weltkarten* [Stuttgart: J. Roth, 1897], 3:98.)

3. On the use of color in mappae mundi, see David Woodward, "Medieval *Mappaemundi*," in *HC,* 326.

4. Like other English mappae mundi such as the thirteenth-century Psalter and Hereford maps, Ramsey Abbey uses red for the Arabian Sea, Red Sea, and Persian Gulf.

5. For a recent querying of Higden's direct links with the map, see Peter Barber, "The Evesham World Map: A Late Medieval English View of God and the World," *Imago Mundi* 47 (1995): 13–33.

6. Ibid., 14; John Taylor, *English Historical Literature in the Fourteenth Century* (Oxford: Clarendon, 1987), 95–96. See also John Taylor, *The Universal Chronicle of Ranulf Higden* (Oxford: Clarendon, 1966).

7. Andrew Galloway, "Latin England," in *Imagining a Medieval English Nation,* ed. Kathy Lavezo (Minneapolis: University of Minnesota Press, 2003), 41–95.

8. On national identity and the *Polychronicon,* see, in addition to Galloway, Peter Brown, "Higden's Britain," in *Medieval Europeans: Studies in Ethnic Identity and National Perspectives in Medieval Europe,* ed. Alfred P. Smyth (New York: St. Martin's Press, 1998), 103–18.

9. Ibid., 104.

10. Ranulf Higden, *Polychronicon Ranulphi Higden Monachi Cestrensis,* ed. Churchill Babington and J. R. Lumby, 9 vols., RS 41 (London: Longman, 1865–86), 1:28–29. References to the *Polychronicon* are by volume and page number in the Rolls Series edition. Unless otherwise indicated, translations are mine, in consultation with Trevisa and the anonymous translator.

11. That audience was immense. At least one hundred twenty manuscripts remain of the chronicle, a remarkably high number that renders Higden the closest thing that we have from the century to what we might loosely and anachronistically call a "public intellectual." Most *Polychronicon* manuscripts were possessed by the regular and secular clergy. See Taylor, *Universal Chronicle,* 16. Yet Higden's text certainly reached much of the English laity, either through translations by the clergy in public sermons, through the Middle English versions of the text made by Trevisa and his anonymous counterpart, or through the many vernacular texts that used the *Polychronicon* as a source.

12. 2:58–61. A. S. G. Edwards, "The Influence and Audience of the *Polychronicon:* Some Observations," *Proceedings of the Leeds Philosophical and Literary Society* 17 (1980): 113. For a reading of how moments in

Higden such as his diatribe on the state of the English language testify to an abiding and courageous criticism of things English in the *Polychronicon,* see Galloway, "Latin England."

13. On Trevisa's translation, see Ronald Waldron, "The Manuscripts of Trevisa's Translation of the *Polychronicon:* Towards a New Edition," *Modern Language Quarterly* 51 (1990): 281–318.

14. On the extant manuscripts of late medieval chronicles of England in Middle English, see Edward Donald Kennedy, "Chronicles and Other Historical Writing," in *A Manual of the Writings in Middle English, 1050–1500,* ed. Albert E. Hartung (New Haven, CT: Archon, 1989), 8:2617–74. One other Middle English chronicle, Robert of Gloucester's metrical chronicle, survives in the same number of manuscripts as does Trevisa's *Polychronicon* (ibid., 2617). The survival of fourteen manuscripts of Trevisa's text is remarkable given the expense of copying such a large work (Edwards, "Observations," 113).

15. Edwards, "Observations," 114. Richard Lavynham's *Litil Tretis on the seven deadly sins* as well alludes to Higden's chronicle (ibid.).

16. Ibid.

17. For example, Henry VIII's printer, Richard Pynson, issued an edition of the *Polychronicon* in 1510 (STC 9999).

18. Edwards, "Observations."

19. See A. S. G. Edwards, "Geography and Illustration and Higden's *Polychronicon,*" in *Art into Life: Collected Papers from the Kresge Art Museum Medieval Symposia,* ed. Carol Garrett Fisher and Kathleen L. Scott (East Lansing: Michigan State University Press, 1995), 96, and Thomas Middleton, *Hengist, King of Kent, or, The mayor of Queenborough,* ed. Grace Ioppolo (Oxford: Oxford University Press, 2003), 3.

20. Taylor, *Universal Chronicle,* 28. These chronicles include John of Reading's chronicle, Thomas Walsingham's chronicle, Adam of Usk's chronicle, John of Tynemouth's *Historia Aurea,* John of Brompton's chronicle, Sir Thomas Gray's *Scalacronica,* Henry Knighton's chronicle, and the *Eulogium Historiarum.* See ibid., 124–33; and Antonia Gransden, *Historical Writing in England* (London: Routledge and Kegan Paul, 1982), 2:56–57.

21. "sive, ut vult Isidorus, *Etymolog.,* quinto decimo, Anglia dicitur ab angulo orbis" (2:4–5); "Anglia Britannica alter orbis appellatur" (2:6); "Quod ideo fieri credo coelitus, ut natio extra orbem pene posita . . ." (2:28).

22. "urbs quidem in confinio Angliae ad prospectum Cambriae" (2:76–79).

23. Geoffrey Barraclough, *The Earldom and County Palatine of Chester* (Oxford: Blackwell, 1953), 22. Blundeville was the sixth Norman earl of Chester from 1181 to 1232.

24. On charges of cannibalism in England, see May McKisack, *The Fourteenth Century* (Oxford: Clarendon, 1959), 49.

25. Barraclough, *Chester,* 17.

26. Ibid., 23–24, 29.

27. The general uprising was directed against the justices in Eyre and led to an inquisition of Trailbaston led by the Black Prince. Rupert H. Morris, *Chester in the Plantagenet and Tudor Reigns* (Chester: Griffith, 1893).

28. Barraclough, *Chester,* 24. "In 1301 the justice of Chester was among those ordered to choose 'Welsh footmen' from the county and its surroundings for service in Scotland," and commissions of array continued to be issued later in the century (B. E. Harris, "The Palatinate 1301–1547," in *A History of the County of Chester,* ed. idem [Oxford: Oxford University Press, 1980], 2:32).

29. Cheshiremen such as Higden would not only have experienced in their county a version of the unruliness that characterized England as a whole, but also would have witnessed directly the very troubles of their nation. For example, as Higden notes in the *Polychronicon,* it was in Chester that Edward met with the exiled Gaveston (8:304–5).

30. Adam Usk, *The Chronicle of Adam of Usk: AD 1377–1421,* ed. Edward Maunde Thompson (Felinfach: Llanetch, 1990), 175–76, cited in Harris, *History,* 2:31.

31. The involvement of the abbey in Chester life resulted from its extensive holdings of churches, chapels, salt houses, manors, city tenements, and lands throughout the country; its role as a caregiver to the poor and sick; the extensive jurisdiction in the city claimed by the abbey, and its status as a site of worship for many of the inhabitants of Chester. See Ann Kettle, "Religious Houses," in *History,* ed. Harris, 3:132–38.

32. *Register of the Black Prince,* III, 1351–65, 18, cited in R. V. H. Burne, *The Monks of Chester: The History of St. Werbugh's Abbey* (London: SPCK, 1962), 79.

33. Burne, *Monks,* 85.

34. "Ibi postmodum constructum est monasterium satis locuples, si illi quorum interest non nebulonibus sed Dei servis impartirent, sed omnia nostro sub tempore ita in Anglia immutavit ambitio, ut res quas antiqui liberaliter contulerunt monasteriis magis dispergantur possessorum ingluviis quam indigentium aut hospitum famulentur vitae" (6:344–47).

35. "cum omnibus cronicis vestris et que sunt in custodia vestra ad loquendum et tractandum cum dicto consilio nostro super aliquibus que vobis tunc exponentur ex parte nostra" (trans. Beryl Smalley, cited in J. G. Edwards, "Ranulf, Monk of Chester," *EHR* 47 [1932]: 94).

36. On the links between world mapmaking and the English monarchy in the century before Higden wrote his chronicle, see Daniel Birkholz, *The King's Two Maps: Cartography and Culture in Thirteenth-Century England* (New York: Routledge, 2004).

37. Gérard Genette, *Paratexts: Thresholds of Interpretation,* trans. Jane E. Lewin (Cambridge: Cambridge University Press, 1997).

38. Philippe Lejeune, *Le Pacte autobiographique* (Paris: Seuil, 1975), 45, cited by Genette ibid., 2. Hence, like the geographically marginal site of England, the preface is double-edged; it is at once a site of subordination and privilege.

39. The ethical value of history is an ancient notion, as Henry of Huntington observes (*Historia Anglorum: The History of the English People,* trans. Diana Greenway [Oxford: Clarendon Press, 1996], 1–5). On the *laudatio historiae* in classical historiography, see Tore Janson, *Latin Prose Prefaces: Studies in Literary Conventions* (Stockholm: Almquist and Wiksell, 1964), 66–67.

40. Paulus Orosius, *Seven Books of History against the Pagans,* trans. and ed. Irving Woodworth Raymond (New York: Columbia University Press, 1936), 29–31.

41. *EH,* 2–3.

42. "ac sic tractatum aliquem, ex variis auctorum decerptum laboribus, de statu insulae Britannicae ad notitiam cudere futurorum" (1:6–7).

43. In the dedication of the *Historia,* Geoffrey, like Higden, links the telling of British history with the relation of praiseworthy deeds when he writes that "the deeds of" the Britons "were such that they deserve to be praised for all time" (*HKB,* 51).

44. "sibi invicem ita obedientiant fratres scentes per hanc obedientiae viam se ituros ad Deum" (D. Oswald Hunter Blair, ed. and trans., *The Rule of St. Benedict* [Fort Augustus, Scotland: Abbey Press, 1906], 71, 188–89). See also chapter five of the *Rule,* on obedience.

45. Burne, *Monks of Chester,* 61–66.

46. Cf. the preface to the *Rhetorica ad Herennium* (I.I), cited and discussed by Kevin Dunn in *Pretexts of Authority: The Rhetoric of Authorship in the Renaissance Preface* (Stanford: Stanford University Press, 1994), 4–5.

47. Ernst Robert Curtius, *European Literature and the Latin Middle Ages,* trans. Willard R. Trask (London: Routledge, 1953), 83.

48. "post tantos tubicines, cum sterili eloquio 'rancidulum quiddam balba de nare' proferre" (1:8–9). Higden is citing Persius, *Satura* I.33, perhaps via Walter of Châtillon, *Carmen* VI.

49. "Quis enim non rideat, seu potius irrideat, si post Herculeos labores, si post Olympicos agones plene consummatos, pygmaeus se praeparet ad conflictum?" (1:10–11).

50. Dunn, *Pretexts,* 7.

51. See also 1:52–53.

52. "ubi et Hercules posuit columnas mirabiles et memorabiles, tanquam in orbis extremo" (1:302–3).

53. The eastern location of the Pygmies is supported by Higden (1:52–53). On the location of the Pygmies in Africa, see *MR,* 18. Classical writers describe Hercules laughing off an attack of African pygmies, some of whom he took to his uncle Eurystheus.

54. *MR,* 30.

55. Albertus Magnus, *De Animalibus,* 2.13; cited in *MR,* 193.

56. Johannes Fabian, *Time and the Other: How Anthropology Makes Its Object* (New York: Columbia University Press, 1983).

57. Orosius, *Seven Books,* 418.

58. Vincent of Beauvais, *Bibliotheca Mundi* (Duaci: Baltazaris Belleri, 1624), 24–35.

59. Henri Lefebvre, *The Production of Space,* trans. Donald Nicholson-Smith (Oxford: Blackwell, 1991), 152–53.

60. Edward Soja, *Postmodern Geographies: The Reassertion of Space in Critical Social Theory* (London: Verso, 1989), 130.

61. For a description of this tradition, see Georges Edelen's introduction to his edition of William Harrison's *The Description of England* (Ithaca: Cornell University Press, 1968), xvi–xviii.

62. *HKB*, 53.

63. Henry of Huntington, *Chronicle,* 2–7.

64. Soja, *Postmodern Geographies,* 130.

65. Cf. Richard Helgerson, *Forms of Nationhood: The Elizabethan Writing of England* (Chicago: University of Chicago Press, 1992), 132.

66. Henry of Huntington, *Chronicle,* 7.

67. "Brittania oceani insula interfuso mari toto orbe divisa" (Vincent of Beauvais, *Bibliotheca Mundi,* 29).

68. "In primo tamen hujus operis libro, more divisi generis in species, mappa mundi describitur. Deinde, orbis in suas partes principaliores dividitur. Tertio, provincia quaeque partialis percurritur, donec perveniatur ad omnium novissimam Britanniam, tanquam ad speciem specialissimam, cujus gratia tota praesens lucubrata est historia" (1:26–27).

69. Beryl Smalley, *English Friars and Antiquity in the Early Fourteenth Century* (New York: Barnes and Noble, 1960), 61, cited in Taylor, *Universal Chronicle,* 76. See also Edwards, "Ranulf," 94. On the role of the Benedictine scriptorium in preserving the Latin classics during the Middle Ages, see Theodore Maynard, *St. Benedict and His Monks* (London: Styles, 1956), 186.

70. Lewis and Short, ed., *Harper's Latin Dictionary,* s.v. "*novus.*"

71. Ibid., s.v. "*percurro*"; "*pervenio.*"

72. "Sight" is hardly the only definition of *species* here; "kind," for example, would also work well in this sentence. Yet Higden may well have intended the primary visual meanings of *species* ("sight, look, view, appearance"), not only because of the visual metaphor that attends the entirety of his literary map of the world, but also because of the extent to which the production of English identity in the *Polychronicon* is a matter of considering England from without. The expansion of scope from the national to the universal enables Higden's English readers to adopt the vantage point of the rest of the "world" (i.e., the Roman classical world) upon England as an otherworldly place (ibid., s.v. "*species, ae*").

73. As a result of the connotations of *specialissimus, gratia,* and *lucubrata,* Higden's British exceptionalism intertwines with love for his nation. Britain constitutes a kind of nocturnal paramour for the monk, who writes during the night (*lucubrare*) his chronicle out of love (*gratia*) for the place that is *specialissimus* or "most intimate" to him.

74. Brown, "Higden's Britain," 107.

75. BL MS Harley, 4011; ed. Carl Horstmann in "Mappula Angliae, von Osbern Bokenham," *Englische Studien* 10 (1887): 1–34; William Caxton, *The discripcion of Britayne* (Westminster: William Caxton, 1480) (STC 13440a).

76. Edwards, "Geography," 99.

77. STC 13440b.

78. See chapter 5.

79. On Harrison's patriotism, see Edelen, *Description,* xxv–xxviii. In addition, William Lambarde used Higden's chorography for his topographical dictionary of England (ca. 1560–70); Sir Walter Raleigh owned a copy of the *Polychronicon;* John Dee and William Cecil, Lord Burghley each owned several copies of the chronicle (Edwards, "Geography," 99–100).

80. Galloway, "Latin England," 60–61.

81. "Civitatum nomina haec erant: Caerlud, id est, Londonia . . . Caerthleon, sive Caerlegion, id est, Urbs Legionum, que post Legecestria dicebatur, sed modo Cestria dicitur; . . . Caerpaladour, id est, Septonia, que hodie vocatur Shaftesbury" (2:52–55).

82. "De Britannia Majori jam Anglia dicta" (2:1–2).

83. Galloway delineates how even the focus upon English *varietas* contributes to certain national ends, insofar as "Higden's intense and self-consciously textual debate about England keeps and deepens the focus on England" ("Latin England," 62).

84. "Primitus haec insula vocabatur Albion ab albis rupibus circa littora maris a longe apparentibus; tandem a Bruto eam acquirente dicta est Britannia. Deinde a Saxonibus sive Anglis eam conquirentibus vocata est Anglia; sive ab Angela regina, clarissimi ducis Saxonum filia, quae post multa tempora eam possedit, sive, ut vult Ididorus, Etymolg., quinto decimo, Anglia dicitur ab angulo orbis; vel secundum Bedam, libro primo, beatus Gregorius videns Anglorum pueros Romae venales, alludens patriae vocabulo ait: Vere Angli, quia

vultu nitent ut angeli. Nam terrae nobilitas in vultibus puerorum relucebat. Alfridus. Anglia Britannica alter orbis appellatur; quam olim Carolus Magnus prae omnium bonorum copia cameram suam vocavit. Solinus. Ora Gallici littoris finis foret orbis, nisi Britannia insula nomen pene alterius orbis mereretur" (2:4–6).

85. "Anglia terra ferax et fertilis angulus orbis, / Anglia plena jocis, gens libera digna jocari / Libera gens, cui libera mens et libera lingua, / Sed lingua melior liberiorque manus / Anglia, terrarum decus et flos finitimarum, / Est contenta sui fertilitate boni. / Externas gentes consumptis rebus egentes, / Quando fames laedit, recreat et reficit. / Commoda terra satis mirandae fertilitatis / Prosperitate viget, cum bona pacis habet / Anglorum portus occasus novit et ortus, / Anglica classis habet quod loca multa juvet; / Et cibus et census magis hic communis habetur, / . . . Illa quidem longe celebri splendore beata / Glebis, lacte, favis supereminet insula cunctis. / Insula praedives, quae toto non eget orbe, / Et cujus totus indiget orbis ope; / Insula praedives, cujus miretur et optet / Delicias Salomon, Octavianus opes" (2:18–21).

86. *IC*, 17.

87. "The element that holds together a given community cannot be reduced to the point of symbolic identification: the bond linking its members always implies a shared relationship toward a Thing, toward Enjoyment incarnated" (Slavoj Žižek, "Eastern Europe's Republics of Gilead," *New Left Review* 183 [1990]: 52).

88. Ibid., 54–57. On how the reputed wealth of England "served as a strong inducement to conquerors and adventures," see *ER*, 25–30.

89. On Higden's extraordinary interest in things Roman, see Taylor, *Universal Chronicle*, 75–79.

90. Frederic Jameson, *The Political Unconscious: Narrative as a Socially Symbolic Act* (Ithaca: Cornell University Press, 1981); Hayden White, *The Content of the Form: Narrative Discourse and Historical Representation* (Baltimore: Johns Hopkins University Press, 1987), 56; Tzvetan Todorov, *The Morals of History* (Minneapolis: University of Minnesota Press, 1995).

91. R. A. Markus, *From Augustine to Gregory the Great: History and Christianity in the Middle Ages* (London: Variorum Reprints, 1983), 343. Eusebius, *The History of the Church from Christ to Constantine*, trans. G. A. Williamson (New York: New York University Press, 1966), 48. Cf. Genesis 17:4–6.

92. Markus, *From Augustine*, 345.

93. Ernst Breisach, *Historiography: Ancient, Medieval, and Modern* (Chicago: University of Chicago Press, 1994), 86.

94. Ibid., 87–88.

95. "Concerning Caesar, Higden's chronicle reflected the two sides of medieval thought, which saw Caesar on some occasions as a tyrant and on others as a just man" (Taylor, *Universal Chronicle*, 43; see *Polychronicon*, 4:204–14). On Higden's praise of Caesar, see 4:212–14, trans. in Taylor, *Universal Chronicle*, 41–42.

96. "Eutropius: Auxit urbem Romam aedificiis iste, glorians dicto, 'Urbem lateritiam reperi, relinquo nunc marmoream'"; "Suetonius: Videntes Romani hunc esse tantae pulchritudinis, deificare voluerunt, qui renuens inducias postulavit" (4:296–98).

97. The English appropriation of Roman glory evinced by the overall structure of books two through seven of the *Polychronicon* recalls earlier images of appropriation that appear in the first preface. After registering his feelings of unworthiness before his great scholarly predecessors, Higden recollects the words of either Virgil or Homer (he is not sure which), who, when accused of being "a gatherer of old writers, responded 'It were well a great feat to wrest a mace from the hand of Hercules'" ("Magnarum esse virium clavam de manu Herculis extorquere," 1:10–13). Taking succor from those words, Higden determines that he legitimately may, "as a dwarf sitting on a giant's neck, somehow increase the work of authorities, so that the young and the old who are ignorant of the greater volumes may learn from this treatise" ("quippiam adjiciam laboribus auctorum, nanus residens in humeris giganteis, unde non solum minores ad rudimentum sed et majores ad exercitium provocentur," 1:14–15). Both the words of Virgil (or Homer) and the image of the dwarf obviously apply to Higden's status as a compiler, "wresting" citations from medieval and classical texts. In addition, the physical image of a diminutive man resting on the neck of a vastly larger figure is not unlike that of England as an island posited on the edge of the world. The image of the dwarf on a giant's shoulders (originally conceived of by Bernard of Chartres and which Higden may have learned of through John of Salisbury or Alexander Neckam) also parallels the relationship between England and Rome that Higden establishes in his chronicle. Just as the dwarfish Higden sits upon the giant of classical scholarship, so too does the English past *rest* upon the past of Herculean Rome and "*wrest*" from it some of its imperial glory.

98. Robert Hanning, *The Vision of History in Early Britain: From Gildas to Geoffrey of Monmouth* (New York: Columbia University Press, 1966), 146–47; cf. *HKB*, 46–47.

99. The Constantinian climax of book four echoes that of the first Christian universal historiographer, Eusebius, whose "imperial theology" singled out this first Christian emperor as the divinely chosen instigator of a new kind of Christian *imperium.*

100. On Higden's criticism of the Arthurian legend, see also Brown, "Higden's Britain."

101. "Sed fortassis mos est cuique nationi aliquem de suis laudibus attollere excessivis ut quemadmodum Graeci suum Alexandrum, Romani suum Octavianum, Angli suum Ricardum, Franci suum Karolum sic Britones suum Arthurum praeconantur. Quod saepe contingit, sicut dicit Josephus, aut propter historiae decorem, aut propter legentium delectiationem, aut ad proprii sanguinis exaltationem" (5:336–37).

102. John E. Housman, "Higden, Trevisa, Caxton, and the Beginnings of Arthurian Criticism," *Review of English Studies* 23 (1947): 212.

103. See Ronald Waldron, "Trevisa's Celtic Complex Revisited," *Notes and Queries* 36 (1989): 303–7.

104. Taylor, *Universal Chronicle,* 16.

105. Ibid., 38–39.

106. Timothy Brennan, *At Home in the World: Cosmopolitanism Now* (Cambridge: Harvard University Press, 1997).

107. Saskia Sassen, *Globalization and Its Discontents* (New York: New Press, 1998).

## 4. Beyond Rome

1. William Godwin, *Life of Chaucer* (London: Richard Phillips, 1803), 2:151–52.

2. Godwin's celebration of Chaucer's alterity reflects the interest in difference that inspired Romanticism's medieval revival. The romantic nationalism exhibited in the *Life,* which praises Chaucer for rescuing the English language from Anglo-Norman, reveals how Godwin had retreated from the radical, pro-French stance he assumed ten years earlier. Thanks belong to Julie Carlson for this point.

3. On Chaucer as the inventor of literary English, see Christopher Cannon, *The Making of Chaucer's English: A Study of Words* (Cambridge: Cambridge University Press, 1998). On nationalism in Chaucer, see Donald R. Howard, *Chaucer: His Life, His Works, His World* (New York: Dutton, 1987), 406–9; David Wallace, *Chaucerian Polity: Absolutist Lineages and Associational Forms in England and Italy* (Stanford: Stanford University Press, 1997); Kathleen Davis, "Time behind the Veil: The Media, the Middle Ages, and Orientalism Now," in *The Postcolonial Middle Ages,* ed. Jeffrey Jerome Cohen (New York: St. Martin's, 2000), 105–22; Sylvia Tomasch, "Postcolonial Chaucer and the Virtual Jew," in ibid, 243–60; Peggy A. Knapp, "Chaucer Imagines England (in English)," in *Imagining a Medieval English Nation,* ed. Kathy Lavezzo (Minneapolis: University of Minnesota Press, 2003), 131–60; Kathleen Davis, "Hymeneal Alogic: Debating Political Community in *The Parliament of Fowls,*" in ibid, 161–190; and Geraldine Heng, *Empire of Magic: Medieval Romance and the Politics of Cultural Fantasy* (New York: Columbia University Press, 2003).

4. All quotations are from *The Canterbury Tales,* ed. Larry D. Benson (Boston: Houghton Mifflin, 2000), with fragment and line references in parentheses. While Chaucer's description of Becket's national following distinguishes Canterbury from the "straunge" and "ferne" destinations of medieval palmers, his introduction of Canterbury so closely on the heels of those sites also suggests that the Becket shrine also carries with it the cachet of difference. On the medieval pilgrim's interest in things strange, see Christian K. Zacher, *Curiosity and Pilgrimage: The Literature of Discovery in Fourteenth-Century England* (Baltimore: Johns Hopkins University Press, 1976).

5. David Raybin, "Custance and History: Woman as Outsider in Chaucer's *Man of Law's Tale,*" *SAC* 12 (1990): 69–70.

6. Ibid., 84.

7. Morton Bloomfield, "*The Man of Law's Tale:* A Tragedy of Victimization and a Christian Comedy," *PMLA* 87 (1972): 384–89. On Custance's isolation from her culture see Winthrop Wetherbee, "Constance and the World in Chaucer and Gower," in *John Gower: Recent Readings,* ed. R. F. Yeager (Kalamazoo: Medieval Institute, 1989), 65–93.

8. Susan Schibanoff, "Worlds Apart: Orientalism, Antifeminism, and Heresy in Chaucer's *Man of Law's Tale,*" *Exemplaria* 8 (1996): 59–96; Kathryn L. Lynch, "Storytelling, Exchange, and Constancy: East and West in Chaucer's *Man of Law's Tale,*" *Chaucer Review* 33.3 (1999): 409–22; Heng, *Empire,* 181–238. See also Christopher Bracken, "Constance and the Silkweavers: Working Woman and Colonial Fantasy in Chaucer's *The Man of Law's Tale,*" *Critical Matrix* 8 (1994): 13–39; Nicholas Birns, "Christian Islamic Rela-

tions in Dante and Chaucer: Reflections on Recent Criticism," in *Proceedings: Northeast Regional Meeting of the Conference on Christianity and Literature,* ed. Joan F. Hallisey and Mary Anne Vetterling (Weston, MA: Regis College, 1996), 19–24; Davis, "Time behind the Veil"; and Brenda Deen Schildgen, *Pagans, Tartars, Moslems, and Jews in Chaucer's* Canterbury Tales (Gainesville: University Press of Florida, 2001).

9. Heng, *Empire,* 193.

10. Schibanoff, "Worlds Apart," 61.

11. Nicholas Trevet, excerpt from *Les Chroniques ecrites pour Marie d'Angleterre, fille d'Edward I,* ed. Margaret Schlauch, in *Sources and Analogues of Chaucer's Canterbury Tales,* ed. W. F. Bryan and Germaine Dempster (New York: Humanities, 1958), 168. John Gower, *The Complete Works of John Gower: The English Works,* ed. G. C. Macaulay (Oxford: Clarendon Press, 1901), 2:714–17. Page citations of Trevet and book and line citations of Gower appear in the text. The lawyer's emphasis on geography qualifies Edward A. Block's claim that Chaucer is "less definite" than Trevet on such matters ("Originality, Controlling Purpose, and Craftsmanship in Chaucer's *Man of Law's Tale,*" *PMLA* 68 [1953]: 580).

12. V. A. Kolve, *Chaucer and the Imagery of Narrative: The First Five Canterbury Tales* (Stanford: Stanford University Press, 1984), 319.

13. R. A. Skelton, "A Contract for World Maps at Barcelona, 1399–1400," *Imago Mundi* 22 (1968): 107–13.

14. Peter Barber and Michelle P. Brown, "The Aslake World Map," *Imago Mundi* 44 (1992): 24–44; Peter Barber, "The Evesham World Map: A Late Medieval English View of God and the World," *Imago Mundi* 47 (1995): 13–33.

15. Sylvia Tomasch, "*Mappae mundi* and the 'Knight's Tale': The Geography of Power, the Cartography of Control," in *Literature and Technology,* ed. Lance Schachterle and Mark Greenberg (Lehigh, PA: Associated University Presses, 1992), 66–98.

16. Alfred David, "The Man of Law versus Chaucer: A Case in Poetics," *PMLA* 82 (1967): 217–25; A. S. G. Edwards, "Critical Approaches to the *Man of Law's Tale,*" in *Chaucer's Religious Tales,* ed. C. David Benson and Elizabeth Robertson (Cambridge: Brewer, 1990), 85–94; Kolve, *Chaucer;* Wallace, *Chaucerian Polity;* John A. Yunck, "Religious Elements in Chaucer's 'Man of Law's Tale,'" *ELH* 27 (1960): 249–61.

17. Wallace, *Chaucerian Polity,* 182; Kolve, *Chaucer,* 350.

18. References to both the English language and England by the Man of Law are matched in frequency only in the *General Prologue.* See *Glossarial Concordance to the Riverside Chaucer,* vol. 1, ed. Larry D. Benson (New York: Garland, 1993), s.v. "Engelond" and "English."

19. John M. Manly and Edith Rickert, *The Text of the Canterbury Tales* (Chicago: University of Chicago Press, 1940), 1:126–29.

20. Cf. especially Lydgate's legend of Saint Edmund, which repeatedly invokes the image of a quadripartite earth and its (English and other) edges, and deploys a pious Roman woman ("a parfit lady, ful holy of leuyng," line 301) to exalt the English border of the world. See Carl Horstmann, ed., *Altenglische Lengenden* (Heilbronn: Henninger, 1881).

21. On the more personal investments in the land exhibited by lawyers like the Man of Law (cf. 1.318), see Jill Mann, *Chaucer and Medieval Estates Satire: The Literature of Social Classes and the* General Prologue *to the* Canterbury Tales (Cambridge: Cambridge University Press, 1973), 87–88. Many critics have demonstrated the suitability of the tale to a lawyer. See, for example: Joseph E. Grennen, "Chaucer's Man of Law and the Constancy of Justice," *JEGP* 84 (1985): 511–12; Paul E. Beichner, "Chaucer's Man of Law and *disparitas cultus,*" *Speculum* 23 (1948): 70–75; Marie Hamilton, "The Dramatic Suitability of the *Man of Law's Tale,*" in *Studies in Language and Literature in Honor of Margaret Schlauch* (New York: Russell and Russell, 1971), 153–63; Walter Scheps, "Chaucer's Man of Law and the Tale of Constance," *PMLA* 89 (1974): 285–95; Joseph Allen Hornsby, *Chaucer and the Law* (Norman, OK: Pilgrim, 1988), 145–48; Carolyn Dinshaw, *Chaucer's Sexual Poetics* (Madison: University of Wisconsin Press, 1989), 88–112; Patricia J. Eberle, "Crime and Justice in the Middle Ages: Cases from the *Canterbury Tales* of Geoffrey Chaucer," in *Rough Justice: Essays on Crime in Literature,* ed. M. L. Friedland (Toronto: University of Toronto Press, 1991), 19–51; James Landman, "Proving Constant: Torture and the *Man of Law's Tale,*" *SAC* 20 (1998): 1–40; and Maura Nolan, "'Acquiteth Yow Now': Textual Contradiction and Legal Discourse in the Man of Law's Introduction," in *The Letter of the Law: Legal Practice and Literary Production in Medieval England, ed.* Emily Steiner and Candace Barrington (Ithaca: Cornell University Press, 2002), 136–53.

22. Alan Harding, *The Law Courts of Medieval England* (London: Allen and Unwin, 1973), 122.

23. For a book-length study of "the child's vulnerability in the body of the nurse/mother" (6), see Janet

Adelman, *Suffocating Mothers: Fantasies of Maternal Origin in Shakespeare's Plays*, Hamlet *to* The Tempest (New York: Routledge, 1992).

24. Feminist Chaucerians have long acknowledged that, in Schibanoff's words, together "these female figures define the full range of woman in medieval antifeminist thought" ("Worlds Apart," 91). Criticism on the misogyny at work in the Man of Law's depictions of Custance, Donegild, and the Sultaness includes: Dinshaw, *Chaucer's Sexual Poetics;* Sheila Delaney, *Writing Woman* (New York: Schocken Books, 1983), 36–46; and Priscilla Martin, *Chaucer's Women: Nuns, Wives, and Amazons* (Iowa City: University of Iowa Press, 1990), 131–42.

25. Cf. Margaret Homans, *Bearing the Word: Language and Female Experience in Nineteenth-Century Women's Writing* (Chicago: University of Chicago Press, 1986).

26. Frederick Pollock and Frederick William Maitland, *The History of English Law before the Time of Edward I,* 2nd ed. (Cambridge: Cambridge University Press, 1968), 1:113. Pollock and Maitland's assessment has been affirmed by R. H. Helmholz, *The Spirit of Classical Canon Law* (Athens: University of Georgia Press, 1996); and James A. Brundage, *Medieval Canon Law* (London: Longman, 1995). On the transmittal of canon law to the laity, see H. A. Kelly, *Love and Marriage in the Age of Chaucer* (Ithaca: Cornell University Press: 1975), 163–201.

27. Brundage, *Medieval Canon Law,* 70, 3.

28. "Unde cum omnia quae divinae providentiae subduntur a lege aeterna regulentur et mensurentur, ut ex dictis patet, manifestum est quod omnia participant aliqualiter legem aeternam"; "Et secundum hoc lex aeterna nihil aliud est quam ratio divinae sapientiae, secundum quod est directiva omnium actuum et motionum" (Thomas Aquinas, *Summa Theologiae. Volume 28: Law and Political Theory [1a2ae. 90–97],* ed. and trans. Thomas Gilby [Cambridge: Blackfriars, 1966], 1a2ae.91, 2; 1a2ae.93, 1).

29. "omnes comites et barones quotquot fuerunt una voce responderunt quod noluerunt leges Angliae mutare quae usque ad tempus illud usitatae fuerunt et approbatae" (Bracton, *De legibus* IV, 296, quoted in J. A. Watt, "Spiritual and Temporal Powers," in *The Cambridge History of Medieval Political Thought, c. 350–c. 1450,* ed. J. H. Burns [Cambridge: Cambridge University Press, 1988], 389).

30. G. O. Sayles, "Introduction," *Select Cases in the Court of King's Bench under Richard II, Henry IV, and Henry V,* ed. idem, Selden Society (London: Quaritch, 1971), 7:xxviii–xl.

31. William Searle Holdsworth, *A History of English Law* (London: Methuen, 1956), 2:305–6.

32. W. R. Jones, "Relations of the Two Jurisdictions: Conflict and Cooperation in England during the 13th and 14th Centuries," *Studies in Medieval and Renaissance History* OS 7 (1970): 210.

33. On the relation of this legislation to issues of English law, as well as its complex and contradictory relation to royal policy on the Curia, see Watt, "Spiritual and Temporal Powers," 367–423.

34. See Anne Hudson, "Lollardy: The English Heresy?" in *Religion and National Identity: Papers Read at the Nineteenth Summer Meeting and the Twentieth Winter Meeting of the Ecclesiastical History Society,* ed. Stuart Mews, *Studies in Church History* 18 (Oxford: Blackwell, 1982), 264; Edith C. Tatnall, "John Wyclif and *Ecclesia Anglicana*," *Journal of Ecclesiastical History* 20 (1969): 1, 24–31; and Pollock and Maitland, *History,* 50–53.

35. John Wyclif, *De Ecclesia;* cited in Tatnall, "John Wyclif," 28.

36. Tatnall, "John Wyclif," 27–31. See also a parliamentary petition for lay officers by "all the earls, barons, and commons of England" that intimates the distance of ecclesiastics from justice: "the government of the realm has for a long time been administered by people of Holy Church *who are never amenable to justice in any case*" (*Rot. Parl.* II, 304, cited in *English Historical Documents, c. 500–1042,* ed. Dorothy Whitelock [London: Eyre and Spottiswoode, 1955], 444, my emphasis). On divine justice in the *Man of Law's Tale,* see also Eberle, "Crime."

37. See Margaret Harvey, *Solutions to the Schism: A Study of Some English Attitudes, 1378–1409* (St. Ottilien, Germany: EOS Verlag, 1983), and John Holland Smith, *The Great Schism, 1378* (New York: Weybright and Talley, 1970).

38. Harvey, *Solutions,* 31.

39. Marcel Mauss, *The Gift: Forms and Functions of Exchange in Archaic Societies,* trans. Ian Cunnison (London: Cohen and West, 1954), 72. In light of gift theory, those English slaves at the Forum, by inspiring the Gregorian mission, effected the juridical "enslavement" of English lawyers to Roman canon law. Thus, for all his official condemnation of the Sultaness, the Man of Law may well have concurred with the Syrian queen mother's characterization of Rome's conversion mission as a project leading to "thraldom" (2.338).

40. That we can be certain that King Alla is the same historical figure cited in the slave-boy myth ob-

tains in Chaucer's primary source, Trevet's *Chronique.* Beginning his version of the Constance story not with Costance herself, but with her son Maurice, Trevet stresses his status as the child of an Englishman—"Alle, auant nome, que estoit le secund rei de Northumbre" (165). Trevet's reference to "Alle auant nome" directs the reader precisely to the slave-boy story, whose account of Gregory's claim that "lez suges le rey alle fusent apris de chanter Alleluija" appears in the *Chronique* proximate to Constance's life (Oxford, Magdalen College MS 45, fol. 51r).

41. Another key element of the lawyer's use of Celtic Christianity in his revisionist national history is his reworking of a famous aspect of Bede's *Ecclesiastical History.* While in Bede the miraculous cure of a blind Englishman stands at the center of Augustine of Canterbury's quarrel with Celtic Christians *uninterested* in the religious fate of the Anglo-Saxons, a blind Christian Briton enables Custance's conversion of her pagan host (2.547–74). And a "Britoun book, written with Evaungiles" or a Celtic Bible plays a central role in the trial that culminates in King Alla's conversion (2.666). Thus while native Celtic Christians in Bede often hinder English national welfare, they perform a more beneficial function in the *Man of Law's Tale.*

42. Raybin, "Custance."

43. On typology see Erich Auerbach, "Figura," in his *Scenes from the Drama of European Literature* (Minneapolis: University of Minnesota Press, 1984); and Cristelle L. Baskins, "Typology, Sexuality, and the Renaissance Esther," in *Sexuality and Gender in Early Modern Europe: Institutions, Texts, Images,* ed. James Grantham Turner (Cambridge: Cambridge University Press, 1993), 31–54.

44. This despite Custance's use of a "Latyn corrupt" (presumably Italian) in England (2.519). Insofar as Italian was perceived as a linguistic degradation that resulted from Roman imperialism (see Isidore, *Etymologiae* 9.1.6–7, cited in the explanatory notes to Benson's edition), the lawyer's characterization of it as corrupted may be a dig against Rome.

45. Wetherbee, "Constance," 85, 69.

46. John Capgrave, *The Chronicle of England,* ed. F. C. Hingeston, RS, vol. 1 (London: Longman, Brown, Green, Longmans, and Robert, 1858), line 2668.

47. On the identification of Mary with England, see Gail McMurray Gibson, *The Theater of Devotion* (Chicago: University of Chicago Press, 1989), 137–47 and 212–13 n. 3.

48. *HKB,* 217; J. R. R. Tolkien and E. V. Gordon, eds., *Sir Gawain and the Green Knight,* rev. Norman Davis (Oxford: Clarendon, 1967), 18; Mary Hamel, ed., *Morte Arthure: A Critical Edition* (New York: Garland, 1984), 206.

49. See John Lydgate, "Ave Regina Celorum," in *The Minor Poems of John Lydgate,* ed. Henry Noble MacCracken, EETS NS 107 (New York: Oxford University Press, 1911–34), 291–92.

50. *Registrum Johannis Trefnant, Episcopi Herefordensis,* ed. William W. Capes, Canterbury and York Series, vol. 20–21 (London: Canterbury and York Society, 1916), 294–95. On Brute's testimony, see Penn Szittya, "Domesday Bokes: The Apocalypse in Medieval English Literary Culture," in *The Apocalypse in the Middle Ages,* ed. Richard K. Emmerson and Bernard McGinn (Ithaca: Cornell University Press, 1992), 396–97; and Jeffrey Knapp, *An Empire Nowhere: England, America, and Literature from* Utopia *to* The Tempest (Berkeley: University of California Press, 1992), 66.

51. On the Lollards' role in rhetorics of English identity, see Tatnall, "John Wyclif"; Hudson, "Lollardy"; Jill Havens, "'As Englishe is comoun langage to oure puple': The Lollards and Their Imagined 'English,'" in *Imagining,* ed. Lavezzo, 96–130.

52. On the ambiguity of "trouthe" in this passage, see Richard Firth Green, *A Crisis of Truth: Literature and Law in Ricardian England* (Philadelphia: University of Pennsylvania Press, 1999), 29.

53. As Eberle puts it, Custance's trial displays how "often and how easily the practices of actual courts can lead to unjust convictions, when, as is more often the case, a miracle fails to occur" ("Crime," 33).

54. Robert Enzer Lewis, "Chaucer's Artistic Use of Pope Innocent II's *De Miseria Humane Conditionis* in the Man of Law's Prologue and Tale," *PMLA* 81 (1966): 485–92; Ann Astell, "Apostrophe, Prayer, and the Structure of Satire in the *Man of Law's Tale,*" *SAC* 13 (1991): 81–97.

55. That the Man of Law performs such a universal complaint is appropriate, given the tradition of legal rhetoric. See Jody Enders, *Rhetoric and the Origins of Medieval Drama* (Ithaca: Cornell University Press, 1992).

56. Lewis, "Chaucer's Artistic Use," 492, citing 1.2841 and 2.1161 from the *Canterbury Tales.*

57. The macaronic verse "On the Times" similarly offers a national juridical jeremiad. See T. Wright, *Political Poems and Songs* (London, Longman, Green, Longman, and Roberts, 1859–61), 1:270–71. On Gower, see *The Complete Works of John Gower,* vol. 4, ed. G. C. Macaulay (Oxford: Clarendon, 1902), esp.

I.1963–82, VI.1–4, and VII.1325–30. Of course, due largely to the derogatory allusion in the Man of Law's prologue to Gower's stories of incest, the question of the relationship between the lawyer's performance and Gower has become a literary critical cottage industry. While the scope of this chapter precludes extensive reflection on the import of the geographic and juridical correspondences between the *Man of Law's Tale* and the *Vox*, we can note how such links may support what John Fisher describes as "the temptation to identify the Man of Law with Gower himself" ( *John Gower: Moral Philosopher and Friend of Chaucer* [New York: New York University Press, 1964], 287); see also Alfred David, "The Man of Law versus Chaucer"). We can also speculate that if, as so many critics have suggested, the lawyer's reference to Gower's depiction of incest serves to undercut the latter's "moral" reputation, the status of the lawyer's tale as a geographic jeremiad suggests Chaucer's own capacity to write moral literature.

58. Justinian, *Institutes* I.i, cited and discussed in Grennen, "Chaucer's Man of Law," 511–12.

59. *Rot. Parl.* vol 3, 50. Cf. Grennen, "Chaucer's Man of Law," 511–12. On the law in England as an object of both utopian desire and social criticism, see J. R. Maddicott, *Law and Lordship: Royal Justices as Retainers in Thirteenth- and Fourteenth-Century England,* Past and Present Supp. 4 (Oxford: Past and Present Society, 1978), 65–67.

60. See Harding, *Law Courts,* 119; W. M. Ormrod, *The Reign of Edward III: Crown and Political Society in England, 1327–1377* (New Haven: Yale University Press, 1990), 154; and Michael J. Bennett, *Community, Class, and Careerism: Cheshire and Lancashire Society in the Age of* Sir Gawain and the Green Knight (Cambridge: Cambridge University Press, 1983).

61. Mann, *Chaucer,* 89. See also Muriel Bowden, *A Commentary on the General Prologue to the* Canterbury Tales (New York: Macmillan, 1967), 171.

62. Henry Knighton, *Knighton's Chronicle, 1337–1396,* ed. and trans. G. H. Martin (Oxford: Clarendon, 1995), 372; Maddicott, *Law,* 65–67.

63. As Mann points out, the Man of Law's portrait is so superficial as to resist clear identification of the justice as corrupt (*Chaucer,* 86–91).

64. By viewing Chaucer's lawyer as intent on criticizing and celebrating the law in England, we may be able to reconcile some of the contradictory claims made by literary critics about the Man of Law's relationship to justice. While, for example, Eberle ("Crime") finds the lawyer to be a credible narrator who queries the notion of eternal law that he has inherited, Grennen ("Chaucer's Man of Law") claims the lawyer is devoted laudably to a juridical ideal, and Scheps ("Chaucer's Man of Law") claims the lawyer unsuccessfully celebrates his profession.

65. Lauren Berlant, *The Anatomy of National Fantasy: Hawthorne, Utopia, and Everyday Life* (Chicago: University of Chicago Press, 1991), 21.

66. Elsbeth Probyn, "Bloody Metaphors and Other Allegories of the Ordinary," in *Between Woman and Nation: Nationalisms, Transnational Feminisms, and the State,* ed. Norma Alarcon, Caren Kaplan, and Minoo Moallem (Durham: Duke University Press, 1999), 52. See also Marina Warner, *Monuments and Maidens: The Allegory of the Female Form* (London: Weidenfeld and Nicolson, 1985); Nira Yuval-Davis and Floya Anthias, *Women-Nation-State* (London: St. Martin's, 1989); Anne McClintock, *Imperial Leather: Race, Gender, and Sexuality in the Colonial Conquest* (New York: Routledge, 1995); and Nuala Johnson, "Monuments, Geography, and Nationalism," *Environment and Planning D: Society and Space* 1995 (13): 51–66.

67. Pollock and Maitland, *History,* 485; Dinshaw, *Chaucer's Sexual Poetics,* 91; Elizabeth Fowler, "Civil Death and the Maiden: Agency and the Conditions of Contract in *Piers Plowman,*" *Speculum* 70 (1995): 760–93; Shulamith Shahar, *The Fourth Estate: A History of Women in the Middle Ages,* trans. Chaya Galai (London: Methuen, 1984). Of course, this is not to say that women did not have any agency in the Middle Ages. Custance's claim that "Wommen are born to thraldom and penance, / And to been under mannes governance" certainly offers an oversimplified assessment of an extremely complex situation (2.286–87). Most notably, work over the last few decades has revealed the powers enjoyed by widows and queens. Indeed, scholars have shown how even ordinary Englishwomen of the lower and middling "classes" could take advantage of certain legal opportunities during the late Middle Ages. Judith M. Bennett, for example, has demonstrated how, while medieval women brewers lacked the contractual authority of their male counterparts in England, they could serve as compurgators, a role generally denied women. See her *Ale, Beer, and Brewsters in England: Women's Work in a Changing World, 1300–1600* (New York: Oxford University Press, 1996), 90–91, 35–36. In her work on medieval prostitution, Ruth Mazo Karras has shown how the law aimed at keeping the profession "accessible," even as it sought to keep "its practitioners in its place" (*Common Women: Prostitution and Sexuality in Medieval England* [New York: Oxford University Press, 1996], 14). Mar-

jorie Keniston McIntosh and other scholars have noted the active role played by women in social regulation, including "deciding when a case should be brought to the attention of male officials for formal prosecution" (*Controlling Misbehavior in England, 1370–1600* [Cambridge: Cambridge University Press, 1998], 24 n. 1). The presence of such opportunities for women, however, by no means suggests any sort of spirit of equality under the law in England. In the case of female social regulators, for example, while such women did enjoy a certain agency under the law, that power all too often was aimed at limiting the behavior of other, "dangerous" women. If the law at times made a space for certain women as public actors, its overall impulse was patriarchal.

68. Jonathan Goldberg, qtd. in *Nationalisms and Sexualities,* ed. Andrew Parker, Mary Russo, Doris Sommer, and Patricia Yaeger (New York: Routledge, 1992), 6.

69. Clarissa W. Atkinson, *The Oldest Vocation: Christian Motherhood in the Middle Ages* (Ithaca: Cornell University Press, 1991).

70. *Liber Decem Capitulorum,* IV, trans. C. W. Marx, cited in *Woman Defamed and Woman Defended: An Anthology of Medieval Texts,* ed. Alcuin Blamires with Karen Pratt and C. W. Marx (Oxford: Clarendon Press, 1992), 229–30.

71. The return of Custance's body especially shores up the authority of canon law over issues of marriage and sexuality. See James A. Brundage, *Law, Sex, and Christian Society in Medieval Europe* (Chicago: University of Chicago Press, 1987), and *Sex, Law, and Marriage in the Middle Ages* (Aldershot: Variorum, 1993).

72. Samuel Ball Platner, *A Topographical Dictionary of Ancient Rome,* rev. Thomas Ashby (Rome: "L'Erma" di Bretschneider, 1965), s.v. "umbilicus romae." *The Oxford Classical Dictionary* (Oxford: Oxford University Press, 1996), s.v. "omphalos." Henry George Liddel and Robert Scott, eds., *A Greek-English Lexicon* (Oxford: Clarendon, 1968), s.v. "ομφαλος." Iain Macleod Higgins, "Defining the Earth's Center in a Medieval 'Multi-Text': Jerusalem in *The Book of John Mandeville,*" in *Text and Territory: Geographical Information in the European Middle Ages,* ed. Sylvia Tomasch and Sealy Gilles (Philadelphia: University of Pennsylvania Press, 1998), 34–35; Bruno Kauhsen, *Omphalos. Zum Mittelpunktsgedanken in Architektur und Städtebau dargestellt an ausgewählten Beispielen* (Munich: Scaneg, 1990).

73. Ranulf Higden, *Polychronicon Ranulphi Higden Monachi Cestrensis,* ed. Churchill Babington and J. R. Lumby, 9 vols., RS 41 (London: Longman, 1865–86), 2:177.

74. Bartholomaeus Anglicus, *On the Properties of Things: John Trevisa's Translation of Bartholomaeus Anglicus De proprietatibus rerum: A Critical Text,* ed. M. C. Seymour et al. (Oxford: Clarendon Press, 1975–88), 1:260. This notion goes back to Vitrivius. See Samuel Y. Edgerton Jr., "From Mental Matrix to *Mappamundi* to Christian Empire: The Heritage of Ptolemaic Cartography in the Renaissance," in *Art and Cartography: Six Historical Essays,* ed. David Woodward (Chicago: University of Chicago Press, 1987), 12.

75. Edgerton, "From Mental Matrix," 29.

76. Elizabeth Bronfen, *The Knotted Subject: Hysteria and Its Discontents* (Princeton: Princeton University Press, 1998), 3. See also Tom Conley, *The Self-made Map: Cartographic Writing in Early Modern France* (Minneapolis: University of Minnesota Press, 1996), 7–11.

77. Anglicus *On the Properties,* I.260.

78. Johnson, "Monuments"; Sarah Radcliffe, "Gendered Nations: Nostalgia, Development, and Territory in Ecuador," *Gender, Place and Culture* 3 (1996): 5–21; McClintock, *Imperial Leather.* On the medieval woman's spatial enclosure see Joanne McNamara, "City Air Makes Men Free and Women Bound," in *Text and Territory,* ed. Tomasch and Gilles, 143–58; and Margaret Hallissey, *Clean Maids, True Wives, Steadfast Widows: Chaucer's Women and Medieval Codes of Conduct* (Westport, CT: Greenwood Press, 1993).

79. Cf. the miscegenational rhetoric of the prose *Brut,* which blames civil strife during Edward II's reign on the paucity of English blood circulating in the veins of the aristocracy (*The Brut, or the Chronicles of England,* Part I, 1906, ed. Friedrich W. D. Brie, EETS OS 131 [London: Oxford University Press, 1960], 220; discussed in *EN,* 6, 17).

80. Roland Smith, "Chaucer's *Man of Law's Tale* and Constance of Castille," *Journal of English and Germanic Philology* 47 (1948): 348. Donegild's aggression toward Custance as foreign queen of England recalls the ill repute of the respective Isabellas of France married to Edward II and Richard II. See Nigel Saul, *Richard II* (New Haven: Yale University Press, 1997), 457.

81. The lawyer's consignment of Donegild to the devil has been loosely related to a like moment in *Inferno* V (cf. Howard H. Schless, *Chaucer and Dante: A Reevaluation* [Norman, OK: Pilgrim Books, 1984]), though the Man of Law's linkage of that lack with the vernacular does not appear in Dante. As Vincent J.

DiMarco writes in his explanatory notes to the *Knight's Tale* in the *Riverside Chaucer,* other references in the *Canterbury Tales* to the inadequacies of the vernacular may reflect a certain "concern about the state of literary English" (832). In contrast, the Man of Law seems to elevate the vernacular as a language that is laudably bereft of descriptors for a base and devilish woman such as Donegild.

82. *IC,* 7. See Schibanoff, "Worlds Apart," on the Man of Law's interest in producing a patriarchal bond between his male fellow pilgrims.

83. While in the slave-boy story, Gregory's attraction to some Angle slaves leads to a Roman Christian mission to England, Trevet's *Chronique* fantastically reverses this plot. Thus instead of narrating how Christian Rome came to the pagan land of Alle, the *Chronique* represents a converted Alle coming to Rome. And rather than describe how England became a holy Roman imperial subject, Trevet represents the fantasy of a Roman empire subject to an English man, as Maurice succeeds Tyberius as Roman emperor.

84. Homi K. Bhabha, "DissemiNation: Time, Narrative, and the Margins of the Modern Nation," in his *The Location of Culture* (London: Routledge, 1990), 139–70.

85. Dinshaw, *Chaucer's Sexual Poetics,* 101–2.


## 5. "From the very ends of the earth"

1. Leah S. Marcus, "Renaissance/Early Modern Studies," in *Redrawing the Boundaries: The Transformation of English and American Studies,* ed. Stephen Greenblatt and Giles Gunn (New York: Modern Language Association, 1992), 43.

2. Sebastian Giustinian, *Four Years at the Court of Henry VIII,* trans. Rawdon Brown (New York: AMS, 1970), 2:314. Page references to this edition and volume appear in the text. On Renaissance theatricality, see: Jacob Burckhardt, *Die Kultur der Renaissance in Italien* (Frankfurt: Deutscher Klassiker Verlag, 1989); Sydney Anglo, *Spectacle, Pageantry, and Early Tudor Policy* (Oxford: Clarendon, 1969); David Bergeron, *English Civic Pageantry 1558–1642* (London: Edward Arnold, 1971); Stephen Greenblatt, *Renaissance Self-Fashioning: From More to Shakespeare* (Chicago: University of Chicago Press, 1980); Louis Adrian Montrose, "'Eliza, Queene of Shepheardes' and the Pastoral of Power," *English Literary Renaissance* 10 (1980): 153–82; idem, "Shaping Fantasies: Figurations of Gender and Power in Elizabethan Culture," *Representations* 2 (1983): 61–94; and Edward Muir, *Civic Ritual in Renaissance Venice* (Princeton: Princeton University Press, 1981). Whereas for Burkhardt, such performances bore witness to a given and essential identity, later poststructuralist critics such as Greenblatt and Montrose stress the contingent and constructed aspects of identity.

3. Jonathan Crewe, *Trials of Authorship: Anterior Forms and Poetic Reconstruction from Wyatt to Shakespeare* (Berkeley: University of California Press, 1990), 108.

4. Stephen J. Greenblatt, *Learning to Curse: Essays in Early Modern Culture* (New York: Routledge, 1990), 161–63.

5. Crewe, *Trials,* 113.

6. According to Ann Barton, Greenblatt grossly misrepresents the cultural history of Wolsey's hat (Ann Barton, "Perils of Historicism," review of *Learning to Curse: Essays in Early Modern Culture* by Stephen J. Greenblatt, in *The New York Review of Books,* March 28, 1991, 53–56). Thanks belong to Alvin Snider for this reference.

7. Crewe, *Trials,* 108, 117.

8. Greenblatt, *Learning,* 162.

9. Ibid., 161.

10. Harley MS 1419, fol. 246r and fol. 247r, transcribed in David Starkey, ed., *The Inventory of King Henry VIII: Society of Antiquaries MS 129 and British Library MS Harley 1419* (London: Harvey Miller, 1998), 287–88. The inventory officially is of Henry's holdings, but the location of the maps in the cardinal's palatial home—like other entries for Hampton Court such as its famous tapestries—makes it clear that they were earlier possessed by Wolsey.

11. On the complex nature of the history of European cartographic practice, whether in print or manuscript form, see Elizabeth L. Eisenstein, *The Printing Press as an Agent of Change: Communication and Cultural Transformations in Early-Modern Europe,* 2 vols. (Cambridge: Cambridge University Press, 1979).

12. On the impact of Jacobus Angelus's Latin translation of Ptolemy on European cartography, see Leo Bagrow, *History of Cartography,* revised and enlarged by R. A. Skelton (Cambridge: Harvard University Press, 1964), 70–73.

13. On the impact of European exploration on world cartography, see Tony Campbell, *Earliest Printed Maps, 1472–1500* (London: British Library, 1987); and Rodney Shirley, *The Mapping of the World: Early Printed World Maps, 1472–1700* (London: Holland Press, 1983).

14. *Albion* appears in the upper left-hand corner of the world maps that illustrate the manuscript and printed translations of the *Geographia* produced up to 1534. The British Isles also initiated the series of local maps in editions of Ptolemy. England's primacy of place in the atlases results partly from its geographic marginality (Ptolemy's table of coordinates works its way from one insular corner of the world to another), and partly from Ptolemy's claim that it is one of the "most noteworthy islands or peninsulas" in the world (Ptolemy, *Geography,* chapter 7, section 5, trans. J. Lennart Berggren and Alexander Jones in *Ptolemy's Geography: An Annotated Translation of the Theoretical Chapters* [Princeton: Princeton University Press, 2000], 110). On still other ways in which Ptolemy did not overturn older beliefs and perspectives, see Samuel Y. Edgerton Jr., "From Mental Matrix to *Mappamundi* to Christian Empire: The Heritage of Ptolemaic Cartography in the Renaissance," in *Art and Cartography: Six Historical Essays,* ed. David Woodward (Chicago: University of Chicago Press, 1987), 11.

15. Jeffrey Knapp, *An Empire Nowhere: England, America, and Literature from* Utopia *to* The Tempest (Berkeley: University of California Press, 1992); Lesley B. Cormack, *Charting an Empire: Geography at the English Universities* (Chicago: University of Chicago Press, 1997); Bernhard Klein, *Maps and the Writing of Space in Early Modern England and Ireland* (London: Palgrave, 2001).

16. A. E. Nordenskiöld, *Facsimile-atlas to the History of Cartography* (New York: Dover, 1973), 20. Claudius Ptolemaeus, *Geographia Strassburg 1513,* intro. R. A. Skelton (Amsterdam: Theatrum Orbis Terrarum, 1966).

17. J. J. Scarisbrick, *Henry VIII* (Berkeley: University of California Press, 1968), 123. See also D. B. Quinn and A. M. Quinn, eds., *New American World: A Documentary History of North America to 1612* (New York: Arno, 1979), 1:171–79.

18. *Calendar of State Papers and Manuscripts, Relating to English Affairs Existing in the Archives and Collection of Venice, and in Other Libraries of Northern Italy,* ed. Rawdon Brown et al., 9 vols. (London: Longman, Green, 1864–98), 3:607.

19. This despite the insistence of Wolsey who "would have no nay therein, but spake sharply to the mayor to see it put in execution to the best of his power" (James A. Williamson, *The Voyages of the Cabots and the English Discovery of North America under Henry VII and Henry VIII* [London: Argonaut, 1929], 100).

20. Scarisbrick, *Henry VIII,* 123.

21. As Scarisbrick puts it, Wolsey's plan, if carried out "would have been perhaps the largest English maritime venture of the sixteenth century" (ibid., 123–24). Another early advocate of English geographic exploration is John Rastell. Brother-in-law to Thomas More, an investor in overseas expansion, and the author of the ca. 1518 play, a *New Interlude and a Merry of the Nature of the Four Elements,* Rastell laments the failure of the English to assume a leading role the exploration and conquest of the "new lands" (Williamson, *Voyages of the Cabots,* 90).

22. Catherine Delano-Smith and Roger J. P. Kain, *English Maps: A History* (London: British Library, 1999), 54–55.

23. E. G. R. Taylor, *Tudor Geography, 1485–1583* (London: Methuen, 1930), 14.

24. Shirley, *Mapping,* xxxviii.

25. William Caxton, *The discripcion of Britayne* (Westminster: William Caxton, 1480) (STC 13440a). Wynkyn de Worde published the *Description* in 1498, 1520, and 1528 (STC 13440b, 9997, 10001–2); Julian Notary published it in 1504 and 1515 (STC 9998, 10000).

26. David Wallace, *Premodern Places: Calais to Surinam, Chaucer to Aphra Behn* (Malden, MA: Blackwell, 2004), 61–62. On the peculiarly charged place of Calais during the time of its English governance, see ibid., 22–90.

27. That meeting took place outside of Calais, two weeks into the conference. Explaining to the French that he needed to convince Charles not to withdraw from the conference, Wolsey traveled to Bruges for a meeting with the German leader that resulted in a treaty aligning the Empire and England against France.

28. *State Papers of the Reign of Henry the Eighth,* 11 vols. (London: Public Record Office, 1830–52), 6:85–86. J. S. Brewer, J. Gairdner, and R. H. Brodie, eds., *Letters and Papers, Foreign and Domestic, of the Reign of Henry VIII, 1509–47,* 21 vols. (London: Royal Stationer's Office, 1862–1910), vol. 3, entry number 1515. All references to this source are by volume and entry number.

29. On Henry's imperial ambitions in 1519, see G. R. Elton, *Reform and Reformation: England, 1509–1558* (London: Arnold, 1977), 83.

30. Wolsey elsewhere in the letter reveals his own ambitions. When, for example, he reminds Henry how the king has placed "your synguler affyance in me, puttyng the burdeyn of your afferys on my shuldres," and when he informs Henry that Charles has "bowndyn Hym sylf to me," we witness the chancellor's own will to power.

31. B.M. Cotton MS. Titus B i. 98, cited in A. F. Pollard, *Wolsey* (London: Longmans, Green, 1929), 16.

32. Scholars are divided on the question of just how serious Wolsey's papal ambitions were (Elton, *Reform*, 85–86). Both scholarly camps may be right, insofar as Wolsey emblemizes the ambivalent England/Rome dynamic we have been tracing.

33. Peter Gwyn, *The King's Cardinal: The Rise and Fall of Thomas Wolsey* (London: Barrie and Jenkins, 1990), 68.

34. Taking full advantage of the sovereignty to which his legateship entitled him, Wolsey summoned churchmen from throughout the realm to his legatine councils and courts. Through that centralization of diocesan government, he both enabled the crown to override the authority of local ecclesiastical officials and effectively paved the way for the crown's supreme governance of an English church after 1534.

35. As Helgerson has made clear, even for the Elizabethan cultural producers working "from the 1570s on . . . barbarity reigned at home" (Richard Helgerson, *Forms of Nationhood: The Elizabethan Writing of England* [Chicago: University of Chicago Press, 1992], 242–43).

36. *State Papers, Henry the Eighth*, 6:182; *Letters and Papers, Henry VIII*, vol. 3, 3464.

37. On Leo, see Ludwig Pastor, *The History of the Popes, vols. VII and VIII*, trans. Ralph Francis Kerr (St. Louis: Herder, 1914). On Roman culture in the early sixteenth century, see also Peter Pardner, *Renaissance Rome, 1500–1559: A Portrait of a Society* (Berkeley: University of California Press, 1976); and Charles Stinger, *The Renaissance in Rome* (Bloomington: Indiana University Press, 1985).

38. Pardner, *Renaissance Rome*, 4.

39. John Foxe, *Acts and Monuments*, ed. Rev. Stephen Cattley, 8 vols. (London: Seely and Burnside, 1837–41), 4:589.

40. Frederick J. Furnivall, ed., *Ballads from Manuscripts*, 2 vols. (London: Taylor, 1868–72), 1:333.

41. V. R. Redstone, "The Parents of Cardinal Wolsey," *The Athenaeum*, vol. 1 (London, 1900): 400; V. R. Redstone, "Wulcy of Suffolk," *Suffolk Institute of Archaeology and Natural History* 16 (1917): 72–89; T. W. Cameron, "The Early Life of Thomas Wolsey," *English Historical Review* 3 (1888): 458–77.

42. Cameron, "Early Life," 460.

43. Giustinian, *Four Years*, 314; George Cavendish, *The Life and Death of Cardinal Wolsey*, ed. Richard S. Sylvester, EETS OS 243 (Oxford: Oxford University Press, 1959), 4, with most abbreviations expanded. Page references to this edition of Cavendish appear in the text.

44. Furnivall, *Ballads*, 1:333.

45. Muir, *Civic Ritual*, 211.

46. Stinger, *Renaissance*, 48.

47. Steven Mullaney, *The Place of the Stage* (Chicago: University of Chicago Press, 1988); Clifford Geertz, "Centers, Kings, and Charisma: Reflections on the Symbolics of Power," in *Culture and Its Creators: Essays in Honor of Edward Shils*, ed. Joseph Ben-David and Terry Nichols Clark (Chicago: University of Chicago Press, 1977), 150–71; Lawrence Manley, *Literature and Culture in Early Modern London* (Cambridge: Cambridge University Press, 1995).

48. Furnivall, *Ballads*, 1:360.

49. Gilles Deleuze, *Cinema 1: The Movement Image* (London: Athlone Press, 1986); see also Nigel Thrift and John-David Dewsbury, "Guest Editorial: Dead Geographies—and How to Make Them Live," *Environment and Planning D: Society and Space* 18 (2000): 411–33.

50. Michel de Certeau, *The Practice of Everyday Life*, trans. Steven Rendall (Berkeley: University of California Press, 1984), 117–18.

51. Wolsey's pole-axes would receive special attention from his critics. See William Tyndale, *Doctrinal Treatises and Introductions to Different Portions of the Holy Scriptures*, ed. Henry Walter (Cambridge: Cambridge University Press, 1848), 251; Jerome Barlowe and William Roye, *Rede Me and Be Nott Wrothe*, ed. Douglas H. Parker (Toronto: University of Toronto Press, 1992), 87. Ironically, while Wolsey used the pole-axe to elevate himself, the term "pole-axe" would later signify the tool of a butcher, the supposed modest occupation of the cardinal's father. See OED, s.v. "butcher."

52. Georg Simmel, "Adornment," 1905, in *The Sociology of Georg Simmel,* ed. Kurt H. Wolff (Glencoe, Ill.: Free Press, 1950).

53. Barlowe and Roye, *Rede Me,* 1118, 1099.

54. Ibid., 1095–96.

55. Polydore Vergil, *The 'Anglica Historia' A.D. 1485–1537,* ed. and trans. Denys Hay, Camden Series 3, vol. 74 (London: Royal Historical Society, 1950), 255.

56. *Letters and Papers, Henry VIII,* vol. 2, 894.

57. Norbert Elias, *The History of Manners,* trans. Edmund Jephcott (New York: Pantheon, 1978), 79–80.

58. Erasmus, *De civilitate morum puerilium,* cited in Elias, *History,* 74.

59. Richard Helgerson, *The Elizabethan Prodigals* (Berkeley: University of California Press, 1976); Frank Whigham, *Ambition and Privilege: The Social Tropes of Elizabethan Courtesy Theory* (Berkeley: University of California Press, 1984); John Huntington, *Ambition, Rank, and Poetry in 1590s England* (Urbana: University of Illinois Press, 2001).

60. Derek Wilson, *In the Lion's Court: Power, Ambition, and Sudden Death in the Court of Henry VIII* (London: Hutchinson, 2001), 135. See also Helen Miller, *Henry VIII and the English Nobility* (Oxford: Oxford University Press, 1986), 107–8.

61. Richard Halpern, *The Poetics of Primitive Accumulation: English Renaissance Culture and the Genealogy of Capital* (Ithaca: Cornell University Press, 1991), 111.

62. John Skelton, *Speke Parott,* in *John Skelton: The Complete English Poems,* ed. John Scattergood (New Haven: Yale University Press, 1983), line 496. All line quotations of Skelton's poetry are taken from this edition.

63. Stanley Fish comments that the seeming superabundance of difficult elements in *Speke Parott* "would seem to render any reading provisional" (Stanley Eugene Fish, *John Skelton's Poetry* [New Haven: Yale University Press, 1965], 140).

64. Skelton would register his outrage at Wolsey's processional excess in other poems as well, such as lines 301–20 of "Collyn Clout" (Scattergood, ed., *John Skelton,* 254).

65. A. R. Heiserman, *Skelton and Satire* (Chicago: University of Chicago Press, 1961), 166–68; *Speke Parott,* 190–203. On Skelton's use of the disorderly aspects of his poem as a vehicle for political satire, see Greg Walker: "'Ordered Confusion?': The Crisis of Authority in Skelton's *Speke, Parott,*" *Spenser Studies* 10 (1992): 213–28.

66. That, for Skelton, Wolsey's motives at Bruges indeed did boil down to his papal ambitions, emerges in line 70 of *Speke Parott,* "In Popering grew peres, whan Parrot was an eg." While the line overtly points to Poperinghe, a Flemish town famous for its fruit, it also suggests the Flemish site of Wolsey's "popering," i.e., where the cardinal obtained Charles's pledge. That reading of "popering" is confirmed when we look to Galathea's penultimate speech, in which she derides Pace's journey "Over Skarpary" (Mt. Scarperio) to Rome "to cache a molle" (the papal mule) and Parrot's reply, in which he claims that "Hyt ys to fere leste" Wolsey wear the papal "garland on hys pate" (413; 435). On the manner in which "Popering grew peres" suggests Wolsey's sexual affairs, see F. W. Brownlow, "The Boke Compiled by Maister Skelton, Poet Laureate, Called Speake Parrot," *English Literary Renaissance* 1 (1971): 21.

67. John Skelton, *Poems,* ed. Robert S. Kinsman (Oxford: Clarendon Press, 1969), 174.

68. Wallace, *Premodern Places,* 22.

69. *State Papers, Henry the Eighth,* 6:85; *Letters and Papers, Henry VIII,* vol. 3, 1515.

70. Covering a little more than the first three books of Diodorus's twenty-volume universal history, Skelton's text generously mixes topography into its mythical account of eastern peoples and overview of Greek mythology.

71. F. M. Salter and H. L. R. Edwards, eds., *The Bibliotheca Historica of Diodorus Siculus,* trans. John Skelton, vol. 2, EETS OS 233 (London: Oxford University Press, 1956), 263. Page references to this edition appear in the text.

72. *Ibid.*

73. Fish, *Skelton's Poetry,* 138.

74. Bruce Thomas Boehrer, *Parrot Culture: Our 2,500-Year-Long Fascination with the World's Most Talkative Bird* (Philadelphia: University of Pennsylvania Press, 2004), 31; *Diodorus,* 213.

75. Wilma George, *Animals and Maps* (Berkeley: University of California Press, 1969), 30, 35.

76. Book, poem, and line references to Ovid come from *The Second Book of Amores,* ed. and trans. Joan Booth (Warminster: Aris and Phillips, 1991).

77. John Sparks with Tony Soper, *Parrots: A Natural History* (New York: Facts on File, 1990) 8, 104–5.

78. George, *Animals*, 57–60.

79. Other medieval works such as John Mirk's sermon on Matthew and Lydgate's "Ballade at the Reverence of Our Lady" associate the bird with what Mirk calls "þe ioye of paradise." See *Mirk's Festial: A Collection of Homilies by Johannes Mirkus (John Mirk)*, ed. Theodor Erbe, EETS ES 96 (London: Kegan Paul, Trench, Trübner, 1905), 256; and *John Lydgate: Poems*, ed. John Norton-Smith (Oxford: Clarendon Press, 1966), 27.

80. On the human, miraculous, and divine qualities of the parrot, see Boehrer, *Parrot Culture*, especially 32–34.

81. Ibid., 28. That particularly papal interest in parrots (along with parrots' association with luxury and "social eminence") also informs Skelton's decision to feature the bird in a poem attacking Wolsey's designs on the papacy (ibid., 47).

82. Sparks and Soper, *Parrots*, 102; Boehrer, *Parrot Culture*, 55.

83. Greg Walker, *John Skelton and the Politics of the 1520s* (Cambridge: Cambridge University Press, 1988).

84. Ibid., 190–217.

85. Ibid., 190.

86. Cf. Halpern's analysis of how Parrot's "flying apart to avoid capture" represents a kind of bursting of boundaries, as does Skelton's own "flying apart" at the level of the signifier in his notoriously hard-to-pin-down poem (*Poetics*, 130).

87. On the national and international ambitions at work in the Garland, see David A. Loewenstein, "Skelton's Triumph: The Garland of Laurel and Literary Fame," *Neophilologus* 68 (1984): 611–22; and Andrew Hadfield, *Literature, Politics, and National Identity: Reformation to Renaissance* (Cambridge: Cambridge University Press, 1994), 23–50.

88. Pollard, *Wolsey*, 166.

89. Franz Wasner, "Fifteenth-Century Texts on the Ceremonial of the Papal '*legatus a latere*,'" *Traditio* 14 (1958): 296.

90. Ibid., 298.

91. Edward Hall, *The Union of the Two Noble and Illustre Famelies of Lancastre & Yorke*, ed. Henry Ellis (London: Johnson et al., 1809), 593. On Campeggio, see William E. Wilkie, *The Cardinal Protectors of England* (Cambridge: Cambridge University Press, 1974).

92. There was a French precedent for Wolsey in his role as a permanently resident legate *a latere*, Cardinal Georges d'Amboise. See *Dictionnaire de biographie française* (Paris: Letouzey et Ané, 1933–) 2:497–98.

93. *Letters and Papers, Henry VIII*, vol. 4, 5750.

94. In part, we can understand the fact that Wolsey never took the trouble to go to Rome as yet another instance of the cardinal's apparent tendency to dispense with conventional methods to attain his ends. "According to tradition, Magdalen" College fired Wolsey "when he employed college funds for building purposes without bothering to get the necessary authority: he was always to love building and to believe in ignoring the rules" (Elton, *Reform*, 47–48).

95. Scarisbrick, *Henry VIII*, 47; D. S. Chambers, "Cardinal Wolsey and the Papal Tiara," *Bulletin of the Institute of Historical Research* 28 (1965): 20–30; Gwyn, *King's Cardinal*, 85 n. 2. See also Elton, *Reform*, 85–87.

96. I refer to the years 1515–18. See D. S. Chambers, "English Representation at the Court of Rome in the Early Tudor Period" (D.Phil., Oxford University, 1962).

97. Edmund Martène and Ursin Durand, eds., *Veterum scriptorum et monumentorum historicorum . . . amplissima collectio*, 9 vols. (Paris: Apud Montalant, 1724–33), 3:1270; *Letters and Papers, Henry VIII*, vol. 2, 1928.

98. Joycelyne G. Russell, *The Field of Cloth of Gold: Men and Manners in 1520* (New York: Barnes and Noble, 1969), 83.

99. Elton, *Reform*, 71.

100. Marga Cottino Jones, "Rome and the Theatre in the Renaissance," in *Rome in the Renaissance: The City and the Myth*, ed. P. A. Ramsey (Binghamton: Center for Medieval and Early Renaissance Studies, 1979), 238.

101. Stinger, *Renaissance*, 299.

102. *Letters and Papers, Henry VIII*, vol. 2, 4073.

103. Gwyn, *King's Cardinal*, 98–99.

104. Scarisbrick, *Henry VIII*, 73.

105. Anglo, *Spectacle*, 136.

106. Ibid.

107. See also Castiglione's comment that Wolsey "wishes the whole world to be dependent upon him" (*Calendar of State Papers and Manuscripts, Relating to English Affairs Existing in the Archives and Collection of Venice, and in Other Libraries of Northern Italy,* 38 vols. [London: H. M. Stationery Office, 1864–1947], 3:1450).

108. The events also celebrated the proposed Turkish crusade and the marriage Wolsey arranged between the Dauphin and Henry's daughter Princess Mary.

109. Hall, *Union,* 595.

110. *Calendar Venetian State Papers,* 2:1088.

111. Anglo, *Spectacle,* 134.

112. Ibid., 136.

113. Pollard, *Wolsey,* 114; *Letters and Papers, Henry VIII,* vol. 2, 4540.

114. On Christian allegorical uses of the cornerstone and other elements of the temple, see Christiania Whitehead, *Castles of the Mind: A Study of Medieval Architectural Allegory* (Cardiff: University of Wales Press, 2003), 7–27.

115. André Chastel, *The Sack of Rome, 1527* (Princeton: Princeton University Press, 1983), 9.

116. Anglo, *Spectacle,* 210.

117. *Lantree Du legat Dedans la Ville Damyans avecqz la triumphe De La Ville. . . . . IIIl. Jour. Daoust,* modernized ed. by V. Jourdain, *Les spectacles populaires à l'entrée du Legat d'Angleterre à Amiens (4 Aout 1527)* (Cayeux-sur Mer, 1910). Cited and discussed in Anglo, *Spectacle,* 227–30.

118. Scarisbrick, *Henry VIII,* 195.

119. My much abridged account of Wolsey's fall draws from Pollard, *Wolsey,* 264–302; Scarisbrick, *Henry VIII,* 228–34; Elton, *Reform,* 103–15; Gwyn, *King's Cardinal,* 501–639; E. W. Ives, "The Fall of Wolsey," in *Cardinal Wolsey: Church, State, and Art,* ed. S. J. Gunn and P. G. Lindley (Cambridge: Cambridge University Press, 1991), 286–315; Christopher Haigh, *English Reformations: Religion, Politics, and Society under the Tudors* (Oxford: Clarendon, 1993), 88–100; and G. W. Bernard, "The Fall of Wolsey Reconsidered," *Journal of British Studies* 35 (1996): 277–310. Much scholarship on Wolsey's fall has centered on its precise cause, with scholars including Haigh and Ives pointing to an aristocratic faction of which Anne Boleyn was a part, and with other critics such as Bernard pinning the blame on Henry. The scope of my analysis prevents full engagement with this thorny issue; what I do aim to stress, however, is that Wolsey's ability to manipulate Rome for England figures prominently among the bundle of reasons for the cardinal's demise.

120. The theological defense of the king was flimsy indeed: citing passages from Leviticus on marriage prohibitions, it claimed that Henry's marriage to Catherine was invalid as she was his deceased brother Arthur's wife. Hardly strong enough to withstand papal scrutiny, the king's case, it soon became clear, needed to be heard in the one place where it was assured a sympathetic audience, England (Scarisbrick, *Henry VIII,* 163–97).

121. *Letters and Papers, Henry VIII,* vol. 4, 5297.

122. Ibid.

123. Haigh, *English Reformations,* 93–94. See also Gwyn, *King's Cardinal,* 51–53; and Elton, *Reform,* 65–66, 112. Upon his death, Wolsey had retained still his York archdiocese.

124. Elton, *Reform,* 86, 115; Gwyn, *King's Cardinal,* 266.

125. Peter Marshall and Alec Ryrie, eds., *The Beginnings of English Protestantism* (Cambridge: Cambridge University Press, 2002), 8.

126. Taylor, *Tudor Geography,* 13.

127. British Library, Royal Manuscript 13 E 7 fol. 187; cf. *Polychronicon,* 2:20–21. The manuscript is illustrated by a T-O map (see Taylor, *Tudor Geography,* fig. 1).

128. The first citation appears in a 1532 letter describing how the king's excusator at Rome claimed that the king deserved to be excused by the pope from appearing in Rome for his divorce case, due to the more than one thousand miles separating Rome and England (*Quod regnum Angliae distat ab Urbe per mille miliaria et ultra; Letters & Papers, Henry VIII,* vol. 5, 801). The second quote appears in the 1532 Thomas Berthelet publication, *A Glasse of the Truthe,* a book possibly penned partly by Henry himself (STC, 2nd ed. 11918). In a lengthy speech in which he marshals evidence from the Councils of Nicene and Constantinople on behalf of his claim that "all matters what so ever they were, oughte to be finisshed and ended, where they were begonne" (42), the character of a canon lawyer concludes by implying how England of all places mer-

its such jurisdiction, given Pope Eginus's claim "That if for ouermoche farrenes . . . it be grevous and payne-full to bringe a cause to the See of Rome: that it be had to the primate" (44). The third quote appears in a letter describing how English ambassadors at Rome asserted that Henry "could not go *ad loca tam remota* as Rome" to have his case heard (*Letters and Papers, Henry VIII,* vol. 5, 892).

129. The quote appears in a letter to Clement VII in which Henry VIII claims that "It was never heard that a king of England was cited to Rome. Had it been to Avignon the matter would have been different" (*Letters and Papers, Henry VIII,* vol. 5, 610); see also Nicholas Pocock, ed., *Records of the Reformation: The Divorce, 1527–1533,* 2 vols. (Oxford: Clarendon, 1870), 2:148.

130. *Statutes of the Realm,* ed. A. D. Luders et al., 11 vols. (London: Record Commission, 1810–28), 3:428.

131. *State Papers, Henry the Eighth,* 1/232, fol. 219v, printed in Furnivall, *Ballads,* 1:317; and Sharon L. Jansen, *Political Protest and Prophecy under Henry VIII* (Woodbridge: Boydell, 1991), 141.

132. If read as an intransitive verb, "remeueth" technically suggests that Rome is the subject of the phrase. But the notion that Rome would willingly travel to England does not jibe with the politics of this poem, which, as I point out later, is pro-Catholic. Henry, in other words, is the implicit agent of the line, which Furnivall thus translates as "When Henry VIII is Pope of England (*Ballads,* 1:317). See OED, s.v. "remove."

133. Scarisbrick, *Henry VIII,* 324.

134. Eamon Duffy, *The Stripping of the Altars: Traditional Religion in England, c.1400–c.1580* (New Haven: Yale University Press, 1992), 421.

135. Muriel St. Clare Byrne, ed., *The Lisle Letters* (Chicago: University of Chicago Press, 1981), 5:478.

136. Duffy, *Stripping,* 423.

137. Byrne, ed., *Lisle Letters,* 5:478.

138. Burckhardt, *Die Kultur der Renaissance,* 353, 137. Greenblatt and Gunn, *Redrawing the Boundaries.*

# INDEX

race, 35, 37–42, 110, 176n79
Ranulf III (earl of Cheshire), 75
Raybin, David, 94, 102
*Rede Me and Be Nott Wrothe* (Jerome Barlow and William Roye), 127
Reformation (English), 25–22, 121, 141–44
*Regularis concordia,* 33, 38
Reynolds, Susan, 52
*Richard II* (Shakespeare), 147n27
Robert the Englishman, 52
Rome, 22–26
  centrality of, 2–3, 28–30, 60, 108–9, 121–22
  Christianity and, 24, 31, 88, 99–100, 152n90, 165n133
  civility and, 24, 60, 65
  empire, 24, 87–90
  England and, 23–26, 54, 65, 69–70, 87–90, 93–102, 111–13, 116, 121–24, 128, 134–44
  Gerald de Barri map and, 66–70
  historiography and, 8
  Ireland and, 55, 68
  in mappae mundi, 2–3, 28–30, 69, 97, 152n87
  as mother church, 97–98, 107–13
  as navel of the world, 108–9
  processions in, 125
  renaissance, 121–23
  as Whore of Babylon, 113
  *See also* law (canon); law (Roman)
Russell, Joycelyne G., 136
Ryrie, Alec, 141

Salter, Elizabeth, 50, 52
Sassen, Saskia, 91
Sawley map, *47,* 52, 53, 69
Scarisbrick, J. J., 137, 143, 178n21
Schibanoff, Susan, 94, 173n24
Schism (Great), 24, 99–100, 152n90
Shahar, Shulamith, 105
Simmel, Georg, 126
Skelton, John
  careerism of, 133–34
  *Collyn Clout,* 180n64
  *Garlande or Chapelet of Laurell,* 131
  *Phyllyp Sparowe,* 129
  translation of the *Diodorus,* 131–32, 180n70
  *Ware the Hauke,* 129
  Wolsey and, 129–34, 180n64
  See also *Speke Parott*
Smalley, Beryl, 82
Smith, Roland, 110
Soja, Edward, 80–81
Solinus C. Julius, *Collections of Memorable Matters,* 3, 50, 52, 85
*Speke Parott* (John Skelton)
  Calais and, 130–31
  insularity and, 130–31, 133
  isolation (English) and, 131–34
  obscurity and, 129–30, 180n63

parrots and, 131–33, 138, 140
  Wolsey in, 129–34
Sponsler, Claire, 165n130
Statue of Liberty, 103
Statutes
  of Praemunire, 99, 141
  of Provisors, 99
Stein, Robert, 52
stereotype, 58–59, 62
Stinger, Charles, 137
St. Sever map, *4*
St. Werburgh's Abbey, 167n31
  book writing at, 77
  Richard of Seynesbury (abbot), 75
  William de Bebington (abbot), 75
  unrest at, 75

Taylor, E. G. R, 118, 142
Taylor, John, 72–73, 91, 170n89
theatricality, 114–16. *See also* Wolsey, Thomas
þeod, 28, 153n4
Thomas Aquinas, Saint, *Summa Theologiae,* 98
Todorov, Tzvetan, 88
T-O maps, 2, *3*
Tomasch, Sylvia, 95
*Topography of Ireland* (Gerald de Barri), 53, 58–70
  Bede and, 54
  East in, 59–62
  Henry II in, 70
  Irish barbarity in, 58, 61–63
  Irish climate in, 59–62
  Irish isolation in, 53, 59–60, 62, 64
  Irish monasticism in, 62 -65, 163n89
  Rome in, 66
towns, rise of, 63, 65, 163n99
*translatio imperii,* 24–25, 69, 88–89, 143
Trevet, Nicholas, *Chronique,* 95, 105, 112, 173n40, 177n83
Turville-Petre, Thorlac, 9–10, 32
typology, 98, 102

universal peace, 137–39, 182n108

Vercelli map, 132
Vergil, Polydore, 128
Vikings
  invasion of England, 33, 36
  slave trade, 36–37
Vincent of Beauvais, *Mirror of History,* 80–81
Virgil, *Eclogues,* 3, 30, 93–94, 111, 123–24

Walker-Boutall map, 1–2, plate 1
Wallace, David, 96, 120, 178n26
Warren, Michelle, 10
Wetherbee, Winthrop, 103
"When Rome remeueth Into England," 143, 183n132
Whitby writer, 41

White, Hayden, 88
whiteness, 38–40
   Anglo-Saxon, 38–40, 42
   of angels, 42
Wigham, Frank, 128
Wilcox, Jonathan, 154n28
wilderness, 15–20, 151nn78–79
William of Malmesbury, 51–52, 74
Wolsey, Thomas (Cardinal)
   Amiens pageants and, 139–40
   arbitrator of Europe, 120–22, 136–40
   Calais and, 131
   careerism, 114–16, 121–22, 130, 133, 179n30
   chancellor of England, 122
   class origins, 124–25
   elevation of England, 115–16, 121–22, 136–40,
     142–44
   English criticism of, 124–33
   fall from power, 140–41, 182n119
   isolation of England and, 115–24, 130–44
   maps owned by, 116–20, 177n10
   New World exploration, 117–18, 178n19, 178n21
   papal ambitions of, 116, 121–23, 130, 140–41,
     179n32
   papal legate *a latere,* 134–36

   processions of, 125–30, *127,* 135–37, 179n51
   Renaissance prototype, 114–16, 140–44
   Rome and, 115–16, 121–24, 134–44, 181n94
   secret meeting with Charles V, 120–22, 178n27
   Skelton and, 129–34
   theatricality of, 114–16, 125–29, 135–40, 144
   Universal Peace and, 136–39
woman
   alterity of, 94, 97–98, 102–3, 106–7, 110–13
   East and, 94
   maternal function, 97, 107–11, 172n23
   nation and, 95–98, 101–13
   navel and, 108–9
   Rome and, 97
   social powers in Middle Ages, 106–7, 175n67
   as symbol, 102–7
"wonderful" parliament, 105
Woodward, David, 67
world maps. *See* mappae mundi
Wormald, Patrick, 157n78
Wyclif, John, 99–100

Yaeger, Patricia, 12

Žižek, Slavoj, 13, 87, 170n87